"In the Same Light as Slavery":
  Building a Global Antiterrorist Consensus

D1457983

"In the Same Light as Slavery": Building a Global Antiterrorist Consensus

Edited by Joseph McMillan

Institute for National Strategic Studies
National Defense University Press
Washington, D.C.
2006

Opinions, conclusions, and recommendations expressed or implied within are solely those of the contributors and do not necessarily represent the views of the Defense Department or any other agency of the Federal Government. Cleared for public release; distribution unlimited.

Portions of this work may be quoted or reprinted without permission, provided that a standard source credit line is included. NDU Press would appreciate a courtesy copy of reprints or reviews.

Library of Congress Cataloging-in-Publication Data

"In the same light as slavery" : building a global antiterrorist
consensus / edited by Joseph McMillan.
   p. cm.
  ISBN 1-57906-075-7
  1. Terrorism—Prevention. 2. Terrorism—Prevention—International
cooperation. I. McMillan, Joseph.
  HV6431.I586 2006
  363.325'17—dc22
                 2006038602

First printing, December 2006

NDU Press publications are sold by the U.S. Government Printing Office. For ordering information, call (202) 512–1800 or write to the Superintendent of Documents, U.S. Government Printing Office, Washington, D.C. 20402. For GPO publications on-line, access their Web site at: http://www.access.gpo.gov/su_docs/sale.html.

For current publications of the Institute for National Strategic Studies, consult the National Defense University Web site at: http://www.ndu.edu.

Contents

Illustrations

Tables

Figures

"In the Same Light as Slavery":
Building a Global Antiterrorist Consensus

Chapter One

Introduction

Joseph McMillan

> *. . . to make clear that all acts of terrorism are illegitimate so that ter-*
> *rorism will be viewed in the same light as slavery, piracy, or genocide:*
> *behavior that no respectable government can condone or support and*
> *all must oppose.*

—National Security Strategy of the United States, 2002[1]

It did not take long after 9/11 for the American government and public to realize that a critical obstacle to combating terrorism effectively was the surprising willingness of people in many parts of the world to excuse or, worse yet, applaud terrorist acts, depending on the cause in whose name they were committed. Notwithstanding the enormity of the attacks on New York and Washington and the wave of sympathy for the United States expressed in most quarters in the immediate aftermath, simply reaching international agreement on the meaning of terrorism proved impossible once someone intoned the mantra that "one man's terrorist is another man's freedom fighter."

To overcome the attitudes that generated support for terrorism among key elements of the world's population, the Bush administration concluded that it would be necessary to build a global antiterrorism consensus. Working from the grassroots up, the United States would persuade people that the intentional use of violence against noncombatants for political ends was evil in itself regardless of the merits of the cause to which terrorism was used. The administration's recognition of the need to undertake such an effort found its most memorable public expression in the words quoted in the epigraph above.

In the 4 years since that strategy was unveiled, progress in achieving the objective of a strong, effective global antiterrorist environment remains uneven. In the West, revulsion at further outrages in Bali, Madrid, London, and elsewhere seems to have strengthened antiterrorist attitudes. In selected Muslim countries, similar attacks have also generated a backlash, but in most instances opprobrium attaches only to attacks by Muslims against Muslims. Attacks carried out by Muslims against non-Muslims continue to be condoned by a large share of the population, with many in the Islamic world still expressing the opinion that the intentional use of violence against noncombatants—terrorism—can be justified under some circumstances.

1

The question that cannot be evaded is why, if this is such a high national priority as to be singled out in the President's National Security Strategy, so little headway seems to have been made in attaining the stated goal.

No shortage of explanations has been offered for this lack of progress. Probably the most widely expressed blames the ineffectiveness of U.S. public diplomacy (or strategic communications, depending on the term preferred) for the failure to solidify a global antiterrorist consensus. The usual implication is that if the United States could just get its communications act together, the problem would readily be solved.[2] A plethora of studies by institutions ranging from the Council on Foreign Relations to the Defense Science Board have addressed the challenge of altering foreign audiences' perceptions of the United States and the issues of concern to it, and while many of these studies include valuable recommendations, most focus primarily if not entirely on questions of bureaucratic roles and missions, processes, and organizations within the U.S. Government.[3]

Yet a number of other hypotheses purport to explain the persistence of support for terrorism within many Muslim societies, hypotheses that have nothing to do with the ineffectiveness of American strategic communications. Some, influenced by Samuel P. Huntington's "clash of civilizations" thesis,[4] argue that Muslim support for terrorism is one manifestation of the inevitable conflict between two fundamentally opposed value systems that are being pushed into closer contact through the process of globalization, and each of which claims exclusive universal validity.[5] While Huntington himself did not assert that the clash of civilizations would necessarily be a violent one, his memorable phrase that "Islam has bloody borders"[6] has been widely interpreted as supporting such a view.

A second approach looks to explain terrorism as a function of factors internal to Islam as a religion. Terrorism and support for terrorism are seen as the byproducts of an ongoing struggle over the "soul of Islam," although how the contending factions should be understood remains unclear—is it modernizers versus reactionaries, traditionalists versus revolutionaries, moderates versus extremists, or the peaceful versus the violent? Others, who also see the root of the problem as internal to Islam, reject all of these dichotomies. They essentially accept the analysis offered by al Qaeda that true Islam really is a religion of violence and intolerance, in which there are no moderates—those who appear to be moderates simply do not understand their own religion.

Yet a third broad approach asserts that support for terrorism within the Muslim community has nothing in particular to do with Islam as a religion but is driven primarily by non-religious factors. Some contend that support for terrorism is a function of pervasive unhappiness with one or more aspects of U.S. policy, whether it be support for Israel vis-à-vis the Palestinians, the perceived propping up of authoritarian Muslim regimes, the invasion of Iraq, or some other grievance. Alternatively, support for terrorism is explained as the result of one or a combination of the various social, political, and economic ills afflicting the Muslim world.[7] In either case, no amount of improved public diplomacy will alter Muslim attitudes toward terrorism until the offensive policies or underlying conditions change. The strategic implication is that building a grassroots consensus against terrorism is not to be achieved directly through a "war of ideas" but through actions on other fronts.

Each of these views has been widely articulated and vigorously promoted since 9/11. Unfortunately, while each of the explanations offered may seem plausible, the public debate has been largely based on speculation and opinion. When the results of empirical research have been adduced in support of one approach or another, it has usually been based on selective culling of data to bolster one position against another, and often to preserve other equities from criticism. Assertions that poverty in the Muslim world is a primary cause of terrorism often are grounded not on research into the relationship between Muslims' attitudes toward terrorism and their socioeconomic status but on the commentators' previously held opinions about the value of foreign assistance. Conversely, when someone denies that there is a linkage between terrorism and U.S. policy toward Israel, it usually says more about that person's commitment to the U.S.-Israeli relationship than about any factual knowledge of how the two may be connected in the minds of people in the Muslim world.

As a result, we still have an unclear understanding of the extent to which support for terrorism is a function of rejection of Western values versus disagreement with U.S. policy, of how the quality and type of education provided in various countries affects support for terrorism, and of the causal links among poverty, poor governance, lack of democracy, and support for terrorism. To set off on a project to change people's attitudes without first knowing in considerable detail what those people really think and believe—and why they think and believe it—would seem doomed to failure, no matter how well organized and funded or skillfully executed the project might be.

This volume is an effort to begin overcoming this knowledge deficit. It opens with an essay laying down the baseline from which to begin tackling the problem of continued public sympathy and support for terrorism in predominantly Muslim regions. In "Public Opinion in the Arab and Muslim World: Informing U.S. Public Diplomacy," Mark Tessler reviews the results of extensive survey research in a number of majority Muslim countries, examining not only what Muslims think about terrorism but also how those attitudes correlate with a range of possible factors that might be connected with support for terrorism. He finds that polling data do not bear out many of the widely asserted associations between support for terrorism on the one hand and economic status, education, or personal Islamic religiosity on the other. Instead, the factors that correlate most strongly with support for terrorism are how a person views U.S. policy and how he views the legitimacy of his own country's government.

Steven N. Simon examines the issue of Muslim public opinion from a different perspective in "Muslim Perceptions of America: The Sources of Hostility," an in-depth look at the intellectual roots of anti-Americanism in the Muslim world and the way Islamist radicals manipulate public attitudes toward the United States. He finds that most of the key themes enunciated by both Islamist and non-Islamist critics of the United States are not uniquely Islamic but rather reflect a long history of European anti-American commentary predating the American Revolution. Comparing these themes with the results of surveys conducted in the Muslim world over the past decade reveals the strong resonance that they evoke among the target audience, raising serious questions about the potential for strategic communications programs to shift public attitudes toward the United States in any fundamental way.

Even assuming that strategic communications can make a difference, Christine Fair observes in "Accessing Information in the Muslim World" that nearly 5 years after the 9/11 attacks, confusion still exists within the U.S. Government about how such initiatives should be targeted. This confusion arises in part from the fact that the Muslim world is enormously diverse, embracing significant populations in more than 30 countries as well as a large number of smaller communities scattered around the globe. Members of these communities differ widely in culture, national identities and interests, language, political affiliations, education, social organization, and many other ways, including the ways in which they access and consume information. They also have very different degrees of access to various forms of media. As Fair points out, understanding how Muslims in these disparate communities obtain information is a prerequisite to understanding how they form opinions, which in turn is essential when undertaking to change how they think about terrorism, Islamic extremism, and the United States. Her chapter takes an important step toward filling the void in our understanding of this process.

In "Perceived Oppression and Relative Deprivation: Social Factors Contributing to Terrorism," Caroline F. Ziemke examines the complex of forces that affects public support for terrorism in the Muslim world. She observes that many of the factors that are assumed in public discourse to contribute to terrorism—such as poverty, lack of education, social pathologies, and repressive authoritarian government—turn out on closer examination to have little explanatory power. Instead of grasping at these easy monocausal explanations of terrorism, it is necessary to analyze the Muslim community in all its complexity, since the elements that make the jihadist agenda attractive and its methods acceptable to Muslims vary widely from one segment of the Islamic world to another. At the same time, a number of cross-cutting social issues, albeit ones playing out in different ways in different places, are essential to this analysis, including relative deprivation, identity crises and alienation resulting from mass migrations, and the inability of governments to keep up with rising economic and political expectations. In particular, it is important to recognize the modernistic trends by which Islam is increasingly being interpreted and articulated in isolation from the cultural and intellectual setting in which it has historically existed.

Since 9/11, there has been considerable discussion of the role of education, or the lack thereof, in the development of terrorists and of popular attitudes supportive of terrorism in the Islamic world. In "*Madrassas, Pesantrens*, and the Impact of Education on Support for Radicalism and Terrorism," Kumar Ramakrishna investigates the ways in which educational systems in much of the Muslim world create the cognitive basis for the stark binary worldviews that tend to foster support for extremism. He argues that in many traditional societies undergoing rapid sociocultural change, widespread cognitive dissonance arises from the collision of modernity and traditional value systems. Some people are temperamentally well suited to cope with this dissonance, while others find themselves psychologically disoriented by the ambiguities inherent in this internal clash of cultures. However, the educational systems prevalent in most Muslim societies, with their emphasis on rote memorization and discouragement of independent analysis and reasoning, do not equip their students to deal effectively with these ambiguities. Instead, they lead those who are not inherently able to deal with the conflict between modernity and tradition to gravitate to a black-or-white, right-or-wrong, all-or-nothing moral worldview. Ramakrishna illustrates the case through an extensive discussion of Islamic educational institutions in Indonesia and concludes that American efforts to address support for extremism through educational reform can only succeed if they enable young Muslims to think more for themselves rather than automatically deferring to religious or other authorities to solve the problem of meshing tradition with modernity.

In "Sacred Values and the Limits of Rational Choice: Conflicting Cultural Frameworks in the Struggle against Terrorism," Scott Atran explains how Western analysts habitually underestimate the importance of what he calls "sacred values" in constraining and shaping individual behavior in social conflicts. Drawing on recent psychological and anthropological research, he illuminates the dangers of undertaking military and political operations in foreign societies without a full understanding and appreciation of the value frameworks within which members of those societies operate. Specifically, he shows that decisions made on the basis of sacred values cannot be constructively influenced by the kind of instrumental calculations of risk and reward we are accustomed to applying in political conflicts that take place within a single cultural milieu. Indeed, attempts to manipulate an opponent through cost-benefit tradeoffs when the opponent considers sacred values to be at stake actually generate rage rather than accommodation and exacerbate rather than ameliorate the conflict. Atran also explores the role of small-group dynamics in reinforcing the blowback that can be provoked by initiatives calling sacred values into question. The insights offered by Atran's work have serious implications for the U.S. campaign to propagate democratic norms as a way of countering the appeal of radicalism and terrorism, as well as underlining the importance of keeping U.S. words and actions toward the Islamic world closely synchronized.

"Restoring America's Good Name: Improving Strategic Communications with the Islamic World," by Peter W. Singer and Hady Amr, addresses the continuing problems within the U.S. Government in establishing effective programs of strategic communications to offset the precipitous decline in America's image and reputation among the population from which radical Islamist terrorists draw their sustenance and whose political support they seek to gain. Amr and Singer argue that, while the administration has paid lip service to the need for effective public diplomacy, it has failed to give sufficient attention, resources, and priority to the effort. In 2004, for example, barely a quarter of the State Department's budget for public diplomacy was directed toward the Muslim world, even though that audience is the principal battlefield in what is supposed to be the defining conflict of our time, the war on terror. Furthermore, the efforts that have been made have been hamstrung by a lack of nuance in addressing specific subregional concerns, a failure to focus on critical swing audiences, and an insistence on treating the new Middle Eastern media, such as al Jazeerah and al Arabiyah, as the primary causes of America's image problems rather than as potential vehicles for addressing those problems. Amr and Singer offer a series of broad recommendations to put U.S. strategic communications on the right track, as well as a number of specific information initiatives for consideration.

The concluding chapter, "Influencing Attitudes, Shaping Behaviors: Implications for U.S. Strategy," summarizes the factors that make it so difficult to solidify a broad-based consensus against terrorism among members of the Islamic community, or *umma*. Considering the deep-rooted nature of negative Muslim attitudes toward the United States, do we need to find a different strategic communications approach—one that focuses on delegitimizing terrorism (the objective actually set forth in the President's strategy) rather than on altering the way Muslims see the United States? In other words, is there a way to get people to stop trying to kill us without making them love us? If so, how could the United States go about attaining this more modest objective, and what elements of its other policies would have to be adjusted to that end?

There is a growing recognition in the United States that the violent Islamist movement, of which al Qaeda is the best-known component, is conducting what amounts to a transnational insurgency, one shaped by the forces of globalization and calling into question the political foundations of the predominantly Muslim states as well as of the wider international system. As the Department of Defense's 2006 *National Military Strategic Plan for the War on Terrorism* recognizes, winning the "long war" against this movement depends in large measure on depriving the extremist movement of its support base within the worldwide Islamic *umma*.[8] Indeed, only by splitting the people from the insurgents can we resolve the dilemma so astutely pointed out by Secretary of Defense Donald Rumsfeld in 2002: how do we prevent a new generation of terrorists from arising faster than we can deal with the current one?[9]

The question is not whether there must be an ideological component of the war on terror but rather how the campaign of ideas can be most effectively structured and prosecuted. The studies in this volume contend that the strategic approach must be complex and nuanced; we cannot prevail with arguments at the level of bumper-sticker slogans and slick advertising campaigns designed to make Muslims feel good about America. Indeed, we must understand that countering ideological support and sympathy for Islamist terrorism requires more than merely rhetorical action. It requires us to learn the lesson taught by the anarchists of the 19th century, the lesson that clearly has been mastered by the likes of Osama bin Laden and Ayman al-Zawahiri: that "propaganda by words" must be inextricably bound to and reinforced by "propaganda by deeds." If this book does nothing more than to heighten awareness of the complexity of this task, it will have served its purpose.

Notes

[1] *National Security Strategy of the United States of America* (Washington, DC: The White House, 2002), 6.

[2] Typical of this genre is Steven Johnson and Helle Dale, "Iraqi Prisoner Crisis: Correcting America's Communications Failure," Heritage Foundation Executive Memorandum no. 935, June 2, 2004. Johnson and Dale, for instance, admit that the actual abuses at Abu Ghraib prison caused "skepticism" about U.S. policy, but assert that it was "weak U.S. public diplomacy" that allowed this skepticism "to balloon into condemnation."

[3] These include the U.S. Advisory Commission on Public Diplomacy, *Building America's Public Diplomacy through a Reformed Structure and Additional Resources* (Washington, DC: Department of State, September 2002); Council on Foreign Relations, *Finding America's Voice: A Strategy for Reinvigorating U.S. Public Diplomacy* (New York: Council on Foreign Relations, June 2003); Advisory Group on Public Diplomacy for the Arab and Muslim World, *Changing Minds, Winning Peace* (Washington, DC: Department of State, October 2003); and Defense Science Board, *Report of the Defense Science Board Task Force on Strategic Communication* (Washington, DC: Department of Defense, September 2004); as well as at least three Government Accountability Office reports in 2003, 2005, and 2006.

[4] First set forth in Samuel P. Huntington, "The Clash of Civilizations?" *Foreign Affairs* 72, no. 3 (Summer 1993), 22–49.

[5] See, for example, Benjamin R. Barber, *Jihad vs. McWorld* (New York: Ballantine Books, 2001).

[6] Huntington, 35.

[7] All the above arguments are made in Bernard Lewis, *The Crisis of Islam: Holy War and Unholy Terror* (New York: Modern Library, 2003).

[8] *National Military Strategic Plan for the War on Terrorism* (Washington, DC: Department of Defense, 2006), 7.

[9] "Rumsfeld's War-on-Terror Memo," *USA Today*, October 22, 2003.

Chapter Two

Public Opinion in the Arab and Muslim World: Informing U.S. Public Diplomacy

Mark Tessler

American public diplomacy seeks to foster throughout the world, and particularly in Arab and Muslim countries, a better understanding and appreciation of the United States. This has been a priority of the U.S. Government since September 11, 2001, by which time it had become clear not only that the United States faced a threat from small terrorist organizations claiming inspiration from Islam but also that a large number of ordinary citizens in the Arab and Muslim world had a negative view of the United States. In many cases, these ordinary men and women were also sympathetic to the terrorists. U.S. public diplomacy has sought to change this situation and improve America's image among Arabs and Muslims. Thus far, however, success has been limited. Anti-Americanism remains widespread, and although support for terrorism has declined in some countries during the last year or so, for the most part it remains at disturbingly high levels.

Against this background, the present study seeks to shed light on both the character and the determinants of Arab and Muslim attitudes toward the United States, the West, and international terrorism. It draws upon public opinion data collected through surveys in a number of Arab and non-Arab Muslim countries, some by international polling organizations and some by the author in collaboration with local scholars and institutions. The presentation and analysis of these data proceed from the assumption that public diplomacy, and efforts to achieve better relations with the Arab and Muslim world more generally, will succeed only if guided by a proper understanding of the attitudes and orientations of Arab and Muslim publics. Such an understanding requires attention not only to what people think but also to why they hold particular views. It also requires that insights about the nature and determinants of public attitudes be the result of systematic and rigorous empirical investigation, rather than, as is sometimes the case, stereotypes about the character of Arab culture and Islam. The present study seeks to make such a contribution.

Do They Really Hate Us?

Ever since the deadly terrorist attacks of September 11, 2001, and to some extent even before, Americans have been looking at Arabs and other

9

Muslims and asking, "Why do they hate us?" Terrorist attacks against the United States and other Western powers are the actions of a handful of Arabs and Muslims. But while few Arabs and Muslims condone terrorism—defined as acts of violence against noncombatants for political purposes—and fewer still actually carry out terrorist acts, there is little doubt that anger at the United States is intense and widespread in many Arab and Muslim countries.

Polls carried out by Zogby International in five Arab countries and three non-Arab Muslim countries in spring 2002 and in seven Arab countries in fall 2002 document antipathy toward the United States. While the samples are somewhat skewed in favor of urban and more affluent respondents, the findings are clear and consistent enough to leave little doubt about the views of most ordinary men and women in these countries. Figure 2–1 presents responses to a question from the fall 2002 survey that asks respondents for their overall impression of the United States. The available responses are very favorable, somewhat favorable, somewhat unfavorable, and very unfavorable. The figure shows the proportion in each country with a very unfavorable and a somewhat unfavorable opinion. In no case do fewer than 60 percent of the respondents have either a somewhat unfavorable or a very unfavorable opinion of the United States, and in all cases but one, that of Morocco, those with a very unfavorable opinion greatly outnumber those whose opinion is merely somewhat unfavorable. In four of the seven countries—including Egypt and Saudi Arabia, America's most important strategic allies in the Arab world—more than 75 percent of those interviewed have a negative view of the United States. Respondents who expressed no opinion or "don't know" have not been included when calculating percentages.

Figure 2–1. **Attitudes Toward the United States in Seven Arab Countries**

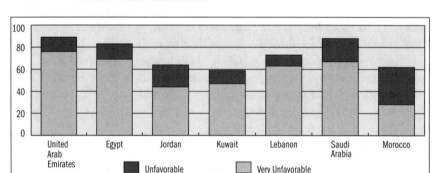

Source: Zogby Surveys, Fall 2002.

Subsequent surveys by the Pew Global Attitudes Project show that America's image is up slightly in several Arab and Muslim countries but overall is still negative, and in some cases very negative. Figure 2–2 presents findings from the representative national surveys carried out by the Pew project in spring 2004 in two Arab and two non-Arab Muslim countries and in spring 2005 in three Arab and three non-Arab Muslim countries. Comparisons between the Zogby and Pew surveys should be made with caution since the former are less representative of some segments of the population. The basic conclusion to which all of the data point is nonetheless clear and beyond dispute: most ordinary men and women in the Arab and Muslim world have an unfavorable view of the United States. Figure 2–2 combines the proportion with a very unfavorable and a somewhat unfavorable view of the United States; respondents who expressed no opinion or "don't know" have not been included when calculating percentages. In only one case, that of Morocco in 2005, does less than a majority have a negative view of the United States. The proportion of those with an unfavorable image of the United States otherwise ranges from 68 percent in Turkey to 95 percent in Jordan in the 2004 survey, and from 58 percent in Lebanon to 80 percent in Jordan in the 2005 survey.

There are two common and somewhat interrelated assumptions about the reasons for this antipathy toward the United States. One has to do with an alleged dislike of American and Western civilization and values. Whether presumed to be rooted in sincere distaste for Western norms and lifestyles or in some combination of ignorance and jealousy, this view supposes that Arab and Muslim antipathy reflects a profound misunderstanding of American society and, beyond that, a failure to appreciate all that the United

Figure 2–2. **Percent of Respondents with Unfavorable Views of the United States**

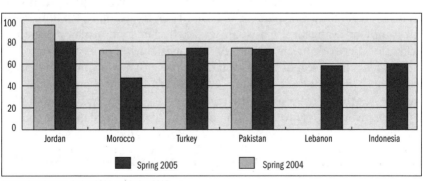

Source: Pew Surveys, Spring 2004 and Spring 2005.

States has done to assist Arab and Muslim peoples. This is the assumption that gave rise to the State Department's public diplomacy campaign devoted to "shared values." Videos produced as part of the effort were designed to combat stereotypes about the United States and show that America is an open and tolerant society that provides opportunities for all, including Muslims. The videos were well done, and one might wish that more Americans could see them in order to gain a better understanding of Arab-American and Muslim-American life. But the campaign was a failure in the Arab and Muslim world, as its architects themselves acknowledge, and this suggests that it did not address what was really at the heart of attitudes toward the United States.

The second assumption, which is related, asserts that the origins of antipathy toward the West are to be found in Islam. According to this line of reasoning, Muslims possess and are attached to a civilization that is rich but whose core values are antithetical to the progressive and enlightened norms of the West—hence the antipathy. The best-known articulation of this view probably is Samuel Huntington's "clash of civilizations" thesis.[1] Bernard Lewis earlier used the same phrase when describing tensions between Islam and the West[2] in his influential 1990 article, "The Roots of Muslim Rage: Why So Many Muslims Deeply Resent the West and Why Their Bitterness Will Not Be Easily Mollified." Huntington wrote about "Islam's bloody borders" in this connection and stated, more specifically, that "some Westerners have argued that the West does not have problems with Islam but only with violent Islamic extremists . . . But evidence to support [this assertion] is lacking. . . . The underlying problem for the West is not Islamic fundamentalism. It is Islam."[3] This thesis has gained wide currency during the last decade, to the extent that even the late Pope John Paul II spoke of a "clash of civilizations that at times seems inevitable."[4]

Regrettably, no shortage of prominent voices has taken up this theme and asserted that Islam is indeed the reason why "they hate us." Anti-Americanism and anti-Western sentiment more generally are said to flow naturally from the basic character of Islam. Thus, for example, Pat Robertson, a prominent evangelical Christian leader, declared on a major American television network in December 2002 that Islam is "violent at its core."[5] Franklin Graham, son of Billy Graham and a well-known Christian evangelist in his own right, said of Islam, "I believe it's a very evil and wicked religion."[6] Another illustration is the reaction of some conservatives to a plan by the University of North Carolina to assign a book on Islam to incoming freshmen. The Family Policy Network, a conservative Christian organization, filed suit against the university. Fox News Network talk-show host Bill O'Reilly denounced the teaching of "our enemy's religion" and compared the assignment to teaching *Mein Kampf* in 1941.[7] And most recently, a French scholar writing in the *New York Times* about whether conflict in the Middle East fuels hatred of the United States argued that the "true cause" of Muslim terrorists is not the crises in Palestine, Iraq, or Afghanistan, but rather, "global Islamic dominion."[8]

This is not the place to take up questions about the true character of Islam. Muslims themselves, including knowledgeable and devout Muslims, do not agree about who is qualified to speak for Islam or about which of the competing interpretations advanced in the name of religion are legitimate and authoritative. Nor is it necessary to ask about the motivations and reasoning of those who describe Islam as wicked or evil or inherently violent. But it is essential to assess the degree to which Islam, either as a religion or as a civilization, is at the root of the widespread anti-Americanism in the Arab and Muslim world. In part, this is to avoid myths and stereotypes out of a sense of fairness, and also because we are demanding, quite properly, that Arabs and Muslims strive to avoid stereotypes in their thinking about the United States. As expressed by columnist Nicholas Kristof, if we expect Muslim leaders to confront the stereotypes and prejudices that are common in their societies, we must confront the equivalent stereotypes and prejudices here in the United States.[9]

In the context of the present chapter and the volume of which it is a part, however, another reason is even more important. If we are to establish meaningful relations with Arab and Muslim societies, and particularly if we are to fashion public diplomacy and other policies that succeed in reducing the undeniable antipathy in these societies toward the United States, it is essential to have an accurate view of what is fueling this antipathy. Alternatively, if our policies and outreach programs are influenced by assessments that are wide of the mark or, worse yet, by stereotypes and myths, there is little chance of making things better and a risk that our actions will make things even worse.

Additional analyses of the Zogby data and other survey data provide an opportunity to explore some of these propositions about the reasons for anti-Americanism. The data are not definitive, and the findings they yield may not convince those who are wedded to civilizational analyses or convinced of a particular position regarding the character and influence of Islam. But the in-depth information about what ordinary men and women think about the United States and why they think that way that the data provide offers little or no support for the explanations of anti-Americanism summarized above.

The Zogby survey from fall 2002 asked respondents for their impressions not only of the United States but also of several other countries, including France and Canada. Figure 2–3 presents respondent views of the United States

Figure 2–3. **Negative Impressions of the United States, France, and Canada in Seven Arab Countries**

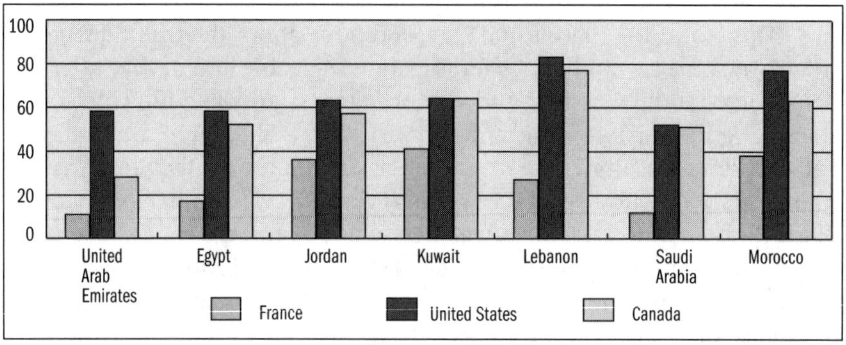

Source: Zogby Surveys, Fall 2002.

and two other Western countries. If negative views of Western civilization are at the heart of the anti-Americanism reported in figure 2–1, impressions of France and Canada should be negative to approximately the same degree as those of the United States. This is not the case, however. Figure 2–3 shows that in every case, views of France and Canada are less negative than those of the United States, and in most cases much less negative. It thus seems clear that respondents are bringing to their judgments of the United States something other than, or more than, a dislike of Western values and lifestyles.

Data from the spring 2002 Zogby surveys offer insights about what, if not a dislike of the West in general, might be at the root of anti-Americanism. The interview schedule asked respondents for their impressions of various aspects of American society and policy. Figure 2–4 presents the impressions of men and women in five Arab countries about American science and technology, education, democracy, television and movies, and policies regarding the Arab world in general and the Palestinian problem in particular. Figure 2–5 presents responses to the same questions of men and women in three non-Arab countries. The figures show, not surprisingly, that there is consistent dislike of American policy toward the Palestinian issue. The figures also show that dislike of American policy is broader, however, extending to U.S. policy toward the Arab nations as a whole. It is notable that these views characterize citizens in non-Arab Muslim countries as well as those in Arab countries.

Perhaps less widely appreciated and most relevant to the present analysis is the fact that negative impressions of the United States do not extend to American society and culture or to American democracy. In all eight countries

Figure 2–4. **Impressions of American Society and Policies in Five Arab Countries**

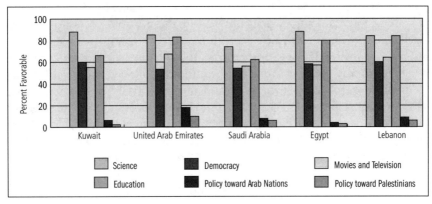

Source: Zogby Surveys, Spring 2002.

Figure 2–5. **Impressions of American Society and Policies in Three Non-Arab Muslim Countries**

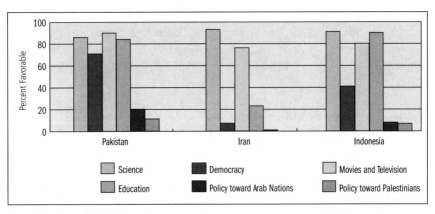

Source: Zogby Surveys, Spring 2002.

represented in figures 2–4 and 2–5, with the partial exception of non-Arab Iran, well over half of the respondents, and in many cases three-quarters or more, have a favorable impression of American science, democracy, television and movies, and education. Perhaps attitudes relating to science and technology are not relevant for drawing conclusions about whether a clash of civilizations is at the heart of Arab and Muslim anti-Americanism, but positive views of American democracy, media, and education would seem to make clear that explanations of antipathy toward the United States that emphasize cultural issues and civilizational conflict are at variance with the views that ordinary citizens in the Arab and Muslim world actually hold.

The 2005 Pew survey does not explore these attitudes toward Western society and politics, with one exception: attitudes toward democracy. The survey asks respondents: "Some people in our country feel that democracy is a Western way of doing things that would not work here; others think that democracy is not just for the West and can work well here. Which comes closer to your opinion?" Figure 2–6 presents responses to this question for the three Arab and three non-Arab Muslim countries in the survey. Those who expressed no opinion or "don't know" are excluded from the calculations. As with the Zogby surveys, there is some variation but, overall, assessments of the concept of democracy are usually high in absolute terms and always high relative to the views about U.S. policy noted earlier. The proportion believing that democracy can work well in their country ranges between 83 percent and 90 percent in the 3 Arab countries, a level of support that is even higher than that recorded in the Zogby surveys. Again, if anti-Americanism really did reflect a clash of civilizations, one would expect a very different pattern of responses.

Available survey data can also be used to examine the assertion that Islam itself is the source of much of the anti-Americanism in the Arab and Muslim world. Attitudes toward democracy are one indicator of views about Western norms related to societal organization, and in the Arab world, support for democracy is broad and deep. Not everyone supports democracy,

Figure 2–6. **Views About Whether Democracy Can Work Well in Several Countries**

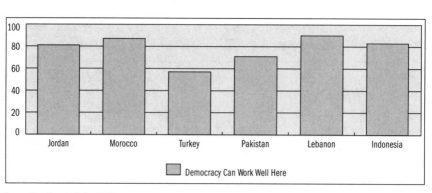

Source: Pew Surveys, Spring 2005.

however, and perhaps those who are less favorably disposed toward democracy are more religious or otherwise attached more strongly to Islam. Should this be true, it would support those who argue that Islam is an important source of antipathy toward the West. But the data suggest that this is not the case. A number of recent studies, based on 10 data sets collected over the last 15 years in Egypt, Jordan, Palestine, Morocco, Algeria, and Turkey, consistently show that there is no relationship between Islamic involvement and attitudes toward democracy.[10] The analyses are based on different samples collected at different points in time and in countries whose character and circumstances vary considerably. The survey items used to measure attitudes toward democracy and involvement with Islam also vary significantly. Even given the possibility that aspects of research design or measurement may unintentionally bias findings and obscure existing relationships, it is significant that in not one case was there a statistically significant relationship between attitudes toward democracy and the personal involvement of Muslim respondents with their religion. An example of these findings, based on regression models from Algeria and Jordan, is shown in table 2–1. The data are from the World Values Survey, conducted in Jordan in 2000 and Algeria in 2002.[11]

Not many representative sets of survey data from the Arab world, other than those focusing on democracy and governance, include items on both personal religiosity and attitudes toward Western culture and society. But with support from the National Science Foundation and the American Institute for Maghrib Studies, the author conducted a survey in Algeria in 2004 that provides such data. Algeria, one of the largest countries in the Arab world, has been subject to strong Western influences, primarily from France, longer than any other Arab country. It is also a country with a deep attachment to Islam, in which Islamic political movements have found fertile ground in recent years. Algeria is thus an instructive case with which to explore the influence (or absence thereof) of Islamic attachments on views about Western culture.

The data again show that personal religiosity has no explanatory power. Those with a deeper attachment to Islam who are more likely to rely on the religion for guidance in personal affairs are no more or less likely than others to have either a positive or a negative view of Western culture. Two questions are dependent variables in the analysis: "Do you agree or disagree that the culture of the United States and other Western countries has many positive attributes?" and "Do you agree or disagree that while U.S. policies toward other countries are sometimes bad, most Americans are good people?" Figure 2–7 presents the distribution of responses to these questions. Sixty-two percent of the respondents agree with the first proposition, and 56 percent

Table 2–1. **Multiple Regression Showing the Influence of Islamic Orientations on Attitudes Toward Democracy in Jordan (2000) and Algeria (2002)**

	Favorable attitude toward democracy	
	Jordan	Algeria
Greater mosque involvement	.039	-.058
	(.692)	(-1.158)
Persons holding public office should be religious	.062	.063
	(1.684)	(1.551)
Religious leaders should not influence how people vote	.016	.070
	(.440)	(1.794)
Positive evaluation of government leaders	.102	.137
	(2.716)*	(3.500)*
Higher education	.073	.018
	(1.800)	(.385)
Older age	-.009	.039
	(-.227)	(.817)
Male	.108	-.003
	(1.923)	(-.062)
Higher income	.057	-.058
	(1.510)	(-1.455)
Resides in larger town	-.078	.161
	(-2.106)**	(4.085)*

The table shows standardized coefficients (betas) and gives t statistics in parentheses.
*p < .01, ** p < .05

agree with the second. These percentages are not as high as Americans and Europeans might wish, but they are nothing like the very low numbers that result when respondents are asked about American foreign policy. Responses to two additional questions, also shown in figure 2–7, make this clear and echo the Zogby and Pew findings noted earlier. Respondents are asked, "In general, do you agree or disagree that the United States is following good policies with respect to other countries?" and "Do you agree or disagree that the American administration is pursuing the right policy in Iraq?"

Table 2–2 presents the results of regression analyses that show the relationship between personal religiosity and the two items from figure 2–7 pertaining to Western culture and American society. Religiosity is measured by

Table 2–2. **Logistic Regression Showing the Influence of Islamic Orientations on Attitudes Toward Western Culture and Society in Algeria (2004)**

	Agree that cultures of the United States and other Western countries have many positive attributes		Agree that while U.S. policies toward other countries are sometimes bad, most Americans are good people	
Lesser Islamic involvement	.100 (.067)	.123 (.064)	.038 (.066)	.114 (.084)
Lesser satisfaction with political and economic situation		-.199 (.088)*		-.262 (.087)***
Higher education	.222 (.060)***	.283 (.283)***	-.076 (.061)	-.043 (.080)
Older age	-.056 (.032)	-.013 (.041)	-.083 (.033)**	-.068 (.041)
Female sex	.099 (.135)	.205 (.176)	-.100 (.137)	-.026 (-.176)

Note: Dependent variable is coded 0 = less positive attitude; 1 = more positive attitude.
Table presents logit coefficients (B) with standard errors in parentheses.
* p < .05, **p < .02, ***p < .01

an index composed of two correlated items. One asks whether, and to what extent, the respondent finds comfort in religion. The other asks respondents how often they would consult various persons for guidance if they had a personal problem; the extent to which they would consult "an imam" is the second item in the religious involvement index. The regression models presented in table 2–2 include sex, education, and age as control variables. The religiosity index is not significantly related to either dependent variable, indicating that the data do not support assertions that posit Islam as a major source of anti-Western sentiment. An interesting point, to be explored more fully in the next section, is that a lack of confidence in the domestic political and economic situation does promote antipathy toward the West. To show this, a second model has been run for each dependent variable. These models, which are also included in table 2–2, include a domestic satisfaction index constructed by combining four interrelated items from the interview schedule:

■ "People have different views about the system for governing this country. In your opinion, how good a job is the government doing?"

■ "How much respect is there for democracy and human rights nowadays?"

Figure 2–7. **Algerian Attitudes Toward Western Culture and U.S. Foreign Policy**

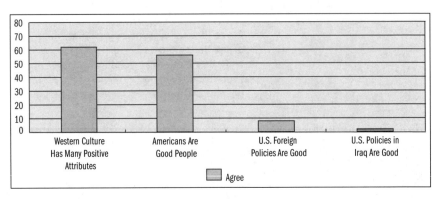

■ "Do you think the circumstances of the country will improve or get worse during the next 5 years?"

■ "I am going to name a number of public and civic institutions. For each one, could you tell me how much confidence you have in it: a great deal of confidence, quite a lot of confidence, a little, too little, or none at all?"

The implications of these analyses for U.S. efforts to reduce anti-Americanism in the Arab and Muslim world are both clear and challenging. They are clear, first, in that they demonstrate the limited utility of civilizational analyses that see anti-Americanism as flowing from a dislike of Western norms and values and, equally, of assessments that posit Islam as the source of hostility toward the West. Such analyses also are based on flawed reasoning that directs attention away from the heart of America's strained relations with Arabs and other Muslims. The second way in which the findings are clear is in demonstrating that a judgment that U.S. policies and actions are detrimental to the interests of the people in these regions is the single strongest factor in producing anti-Americanism. The findings are challenging as well as instructive, however, in that changes in fundamental U.S. policy toward the region, even if desirable, are beyond what can be addressed through public diplomacy. Perhaps public diplomacy can be used to persuade Arabs and Muslims that they misjudge U.S. policy toward their part of the world, but it certainly will not be easy, in part because it is not self-evident that U.S. policy is in fact radically different than what people in the Arab and Muslim world believe it to be. In any event, at a minimum, public diplomacy needs to find a way to talk about perceptions of policy, and perhaps about policy itself, if it hopes to engage Arabs and Muslims on concerns that are the most important sources of anti-Americanism.

Why Some Support Terrorism

Of course, having anti-American attitudes does not automatically lead to support for terrorism conducted against the United States and its allies. What is it that prepares so many people in the Arab and Muslim world to tolerate, or even support, terrorist attacks against America?

Efforts to understand what makes terrorism possible, and thereby to develop productive approaches to combating it, require attention to the attitudes of ordinary men and women. Popular support for terrorist acts directed at Western targets, or at least a willingness to "understand" and to that extent tolerate such acts, is not uncommon in the Arab and Muslim world. Such support varies from country to country and also rises and falls in accordance with events. But many of the polls discussed above report a significant level of approval for events like 9/11, for the principle of "armed jihad" against the West, and for al Qaeda and Osama bin Laden. Figures 2–8 and 2–9 summarize a few of the findings from the Pew surveys conducted in 2005 and earlier. The figures present responses to questions about whether violence against civilians is justified in defense of Islam and whether or not respondents have confidence in Osama bin Laden as a world leader. Support for terrorism measured by either item varies substantially from country to country and also from year to year, suggesting that context and circumstances are probably more important than enduring factors like religion and culture in shaping these attitudes. Nevertheless, support for terrorism has been and remains substantial. With the exception of Turkey, over 45 percent of the respondents in every country expressed a positive attitude toward terrorism in response to at least one item in one survey.

Ordinary citizens' attitudes toward terrorism are, or should be, a central concern of the war on terrorism for two reasons. First, like other rebel or

Figure 2–8. **Percent of Respondents Agreeing that Violence Against Civilians is Often or Sometimes Justified in the Defense of Islam**

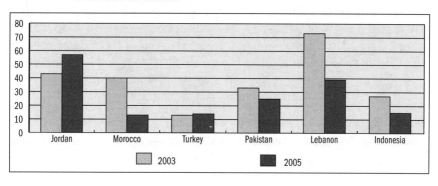

Figure 2–9. **Percent of Respondents with Much or Some Confidence in Osama bin Laden as a World Leader**

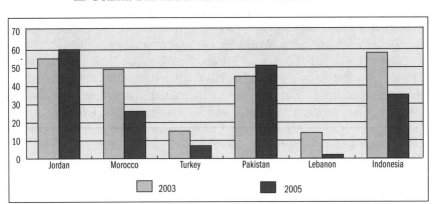

insurgent movements seeking to challenge those in power and upset the existing political order, terrorist organizations require at least a passively supportive society in which to hide and from which to obtain the resources necessary for survival.[12] In many instances, as in the case of insurgents in Iraq, they also depend on the information and intelligence they derive from broad popular support.[13] Thus, as succinctly expressed by Mao Tse-Tung, a guerrilla movement can "neither survive nor flourish if it separates itself from [the people's] sympathies and cooperation."[14]

Second, if terrorist organizations are to become strong enough to challenge established power structures, they, like other rebel movements, need to recruit people to provide infrastructure support and to become combatants. Quite naturally, recruits are most frequently drawn from those with a favorable attitude toward the organization and its actions.[15] For example, a Singapore government study reports that the first stage of an 18-month recruitment process into Jemaah Islamiya involves identifying highly sympathetic individuals from large religious classes.[16] Research in Egypt, Jordan, and several other Arab countries points to a similar process.[17] It is possible in this connection to think of the contest between terrorist organizations and legal authorities as a competition over popular support.[18]

Popular support not only is vital for terrorist organizations; it is often a strategic objective as well. This reflects a realization on the part of the insurgent movement's leaders that their opponents cannot be defeated by conventional means. As expressed by Osama bin Laden, "Due to the imbalance of power between our forces and the enemy forces, a suitable means of fighting must be adopted. . . . In other words, [it is necessary] to initiate a guerrilla war."[19] Moreover, terrorism is frequently a means of generating popular support and attracting recruits.[20] Writing about the anticolonial struggle in Algeria, for example, Frantz Fanon pointed out that fighting back was itself a goal of terrorism; it served to free an oppressed people symbolically and thereby demonstrated the possibility of resistance.[21] This is a common theme among organizations that use terrorism, including those that operate in the name of militant political Islam.[22] Al Qaeda documents emphasize that terrorism is a means of overcoming "the degradation and disbelief which have spread into Muslim lands."[23]

Counterterrorism experts also recognize the importance of popular support for terrorist organizations.[24] In a review of homeland security policies, Scott Atran argues that the most important line of defense against terrorism may be finding ways to reduce popular support for terrorist organizations and activities.[25] Direct military responses, by themselves, appear to be relatively ineffective, particularly in combating groups with a global network. The experience of Israel in forecasting and combating terrorism by Palestinian groups lends support to this assessment. According to Reuven Paz, organizations like Hamas are highly responsive to the will of the Palestinian people.[26] Similarly, according to Ami Ayalon, former head of Israel's security services, reductions in Palestinian terrorism between 1995 and 2000 were not a consequence of Israeli security policies but were rather a response to Palestinian public opinion. Because of the correlation between popular support and militant actions, Israel has been able to use public opinion surveys to forecast decreases and increases in Palestinian terrorism with substantial accuracy.[27]

The preceding makes clear that it is important to understand what leads some ordinary citizens in the Arab and Muslim world to approve of terrorism against the West, or against members of their own society for that matter. There are obvious security and intelligence dimensions to the struggle against terrorism, and these are of primary importance in the short run. In the long run, however, nothing may be more important than the front of public opinion, than finding ways to reduce the extent to which terrorism finds tacit support among significant segments of the population in the Arab and Muslim world. Thus, identifying the factors that give rise to such attitudes among Arab and Muslim publics is essential. Civilizational analyses and assertions about the role of Islam are again common in this connection. Although some are diatribes rather than scholarly analyses, they echo the clash of civilizations arguments summarized earlier and assert that hatred of the West is inherent in Islam.[28] Some also point out that terrorist organizations often seek to demonize and foster antipathy toward Western culture in order to build support among the broader public.[29]

Although many recent surveys have investigated support for terrorism in Arab and non-Arab Muslim countries, only a few of these surveys ask enough questions to permit an examination of the determinants of this support. Two data sets that may be used for this purpose are from large and representative national surveys conducted in Algeria and Jordan in 2002. These two countries present an instructive contrast with respect to both their experience with terrorism and their political and economic circumstances. Since they differ in many important ways, a comparison of findings from the two countries approximates a "most different systems" research design. Similarities between them, if any, will suggest that the observed relationships are probably at least reasonably generalizable since they will have been found to obtain under widely differing conditions. The timing of the surveys is probably advantageous as well. Both surveys were conducted after September 11, but not so soon as to reflect the shock of the day's events. Rather, given that the research in both countries was carried out in the late spring and summer of 2002, the immediate emotional impact of the attacks had presumably dissipated to a significant extent, to be replaced by more typical attitudes and opinions. Similarly, given that the surveys preceded the U.S. invasion of Iraq, responses were not influenced by the heightened anger at the United States and the heightened sympathy for the Iraqi resistance that were widespread in the Arab world in 2003 and 2004.

Attitude toward terrorism is the dependent variable in this analysis. A single item asking directly about September 11 was used to measure this attitude in the Algerian survey. Two highly interrelated items were combined to form an index measuring attitudes toward terrorism in the Jordanian case. These items are given below. Response distributions are presented in figure 2–10.

Algeria: As you know, a group of religious fundamentalists hijacked four civilian airliners in September and crashed them into buildings in New York and Washington, DC, killing several thousand people. What is your opinion of this action: strongly approve, approve, disapprove, strongly disapprove?

Figure 2–10. **Attitudes Toward Terrorism in Algeria and Jordan**

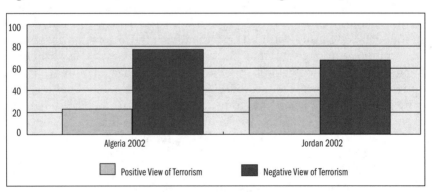

Jordan: I would now like to read you the names of some international figures. As I read each one, please tell me whether you believe he is very trustworthy, fairly trustworthy, not very trustworthy, or not at all trustworthy, or haven't you heard or read enough about them to say.

(The questions called for evaluations of 10 different individuals. Among these, in addition to Osama bin Laden, were United Nations Secretary General Kofi Annan, U.S. President George W. Bush, Saudi Arabian Crown Prince Abdullah, and Egyptian President Hosni Mubarak.)

As you may know, after the military campaign in Afghanistan began, some people called on all Muslims to join in armed jihad against the United States. Do you strongly support, somewhat support, somewhat oppose, or strongly oppose this call to armed jihad?

The Algerian data permit inclusion of a large number of independent variables. These are grouped into nine conceptual categories:

■ personal demographic attributes, including gender, age, education, and whether family is able to save or has to either draw upon savings or borrow money

■ personality and psychological orientation, measured by three interrelated questions that ask whether the respondent (1) is happy, (2) believes that most people are basically good, and (3) feels at ease in expressing self and interacting with others

■ religious involvement, measured by two interrelated questions that ask about (1) frequency of mosque attendance and (2) frequency of spending time with friends at mosque

■ attitude toward the relationship between Islam and politics, measured by three interrelated questions that ask whether the respondent believes that (1) it would be better if more men of religious learning held public office, (2) the shari'a should be the only basis of law, and (3) religion limits democracy

■ conservatism-liberalism in the interpretation of Islam, measured by a scale based on three interrelated questions that ask whether respondent believes that (1) Islam prohibits coeducation at universities, (2) Islam gives the same political rights to Muslims and non-Muslims, and (3) a country that is truly Islamic should not have a parliament with the right to pass laws

■ attitude toward democracy, measured by three interrelated questions that ask whether the respondent believes (1) a democratic political system is a very good way of governing, (2) Western democracy is the best political system for Algeria, (3) despite problems, democracy is the best political system

■ evaluation of Western culture, measured by a question asking whether respondent believes exposure to the culture of the United States and other Western countries has a harmful effect on Algeria

■ evaluation of Algerian political system, measured by scale based on six interrelated questions asking about degree of confidence in Algeria's parliament, political parties, police, military, civil service, and large corporations

■ evaluation of U.S. foreign policy, measured by whether respondent believes some or most U.S. policies toward other countries are good or whether almost all U.S. policies toward other countries are bad.

The Jordanian interview schedule contained items pertaining to most of the same independent variables. The two exceptions are personality and psychological orientation and attitudes toward democracy. The Jordanian data set does contain measures of all of the religious and cultural orientations present in the Algerian survey.

Regression analyses showing the relationship between each independent variable and the dependent variable are presented in tables 2–3 (Algeria) and 2–4 (Jordan). In both analyses, responses to the dependent variable have been dichotomized and binary logistical regression has been employed. In the Algerian case, the dependent variable has been divided into the categories of "approve" and "disapprove" of the attacks of September 11, 2001, with, as shown in figure 2–10, 23 percent approving and 77 percent disapproving. The dependent variable has also been dichotomized in the Jordanian case. The division is between the 33 percent of respondents who express very strong support for both Osama bin Laden and armed jihad against the United States and the 67 percent who express less support for one or both. The findings shown in tables 2–3 and 2–4 are strikingly similar, which is all the more notable given the two countries' different experiences with terrorism and the two differing interview schedules employed.

Table 2–3. **Logistic Regression Showing Influence of Personal Attributes, Personality and Psychological Orientations, Religious and Cultural Values, and Political Assessments on Support for Terrorism in Algeria**

Personal Attributes

Female	-.136
	(.340)
Older	-.228
	(.159)

Better educated	.028
	(.077)
Draws upon savings or borrows	.347
	(.206)

Personality and Psychological Orientation

Is happy	-.169
	(.221)
Believes other people are basically good	-.012
	(.317)
At ease interacting with others	.262
	(.289)

Personal Religious Involvement

Higher mosque interaction	.160
	(.159)
More frequent religious service attendance	.117
	(.086)

Islam and Politics

Not want more people of religion in public office	-.027
	(.134)
Not more important than law from shari'a	-.148
	(.156)
Not believe religion limits democracy	-.098
	(.170)

Interpretation of Islam

Islam does not prohibit coeducation	-.036
	(.110)
Islam does not require inferior political rights for non-Muslims	-.071
	(.112)
Islam does not prohibit having a parliament that can pass laws	-.185
	(.109)

Democracy and Governance

Democracy is a good way to govern	-.245
	(.252)
Democracy is the best political system	.071
	(.198)

Western democratic system is best for Algeria	.114
	(.177)

Western Culture

Western culture is harmful to our country	-.190
	(.167)

U.S. Foreign Policy

Almost all U.S. foreign policies are bad *	.631
	(.292)

Confidence in Algerian Political System and Institutions

Lower confidence *	.327
	(.155)

Note: Dependent variable is coded 0 = less support for terrorism, 1 = greater support for terrorism. Table presents logit coefficients (B) with standard errors in parentheses.
*p<.05

Table 2–4. **Logistic Regression Showing Influence of Personal Attributes, Religious and Cultural Values, and Political Assessments on Support for Terrorism in Jordan**

Personal Attributes

Female	.119
	(.348)
Older*	-.019
	(.009)
Better educated	-.061
	(.080)

Personal Religiosity

Prays more often	.114
	(.203)
Visits mosque more frequently	.044
	(.199)
Relies on religious teachings more often to guide daily decisions	.373
	(.190)

Islam and Politics

Sharı'a should be the only basis of law	.377
	(.329)
Political leaders should be selected by clerics	.003
	(.010)

Interpretation of Islam

Islam prohibits men and women from working together	.117
	(.123)
Non-Muslims should not hold important positions in Muslim states	-.061
	(.100)
Islamic country should not have parliament that passes laws	-.131
	(.107)

American Society and Culture

Negative impression of American values	-.006
	(.006)
Western culture a threat to Jordan's culture	-.008
	(.100)
U.S. practices democracy in its own country	-.126
	(.116)

Confidence in Jordanian Political System and Institutions

Lower confidence**	.554
	(,237)

U.S. Foreign Policy

U.S. violates human rights around the world***	.288
	(.110)
U.S. treats Jordan with respect*	-.252
	(.109)

Note: Dependent variable is coded 0 = less support for terrorism, 1 = greater support for terrorism. Table presents logit coefficients (B) with standard errors in parentheses.
*p<.05, **p<.02, ***p>.01

Turning first to Algeria, a notable finding concerns the large number of relationships that are not statistically significant. None of the four demographic attributes bear an independent and statistically significant relationship to support for terrorism. Nor do any of the three questions pertaining to personality and psychological orientation. And again, none of the three questions pertaining to democracy bear an independent and statistically significant relationship to support for terrorism.

Findings about the independent variables pertaining to religion and culture are of particular interest in light of the civilizational analyses that are often advanced to explain support for terrorism. The finding that not one of these independent variables has significant explanatory power is thus important. As noted above, the analysis includes eight independent variables measuring three different kinds of orientations pertaining to Islam: religious involvement, attitude toward the relationship between Islam and politics, and conservatism-liberalism in the interpretation of Islamic law. In no instance is the relationship between one of these independent variables and support for terrorism statistically significant. This is also the case for the item asking whether exposure to the culture of the United States and other Western countries has a harmful effect on Algeria. Those who answer this question in the affirmative are no more likely than others to express approval of the attacks of September 11.

The last two categories of independent variables are related to support for terrorism to a statistically significant degree. The first of these concerns views about U.S. foreign policy. Not surprisingly, respondents who believe that almost all U.S. policies toward other countries are bad are more likely than other respondents to express approval of the attacks of September 11, 2001. The second category concerns judgments about the Algerian political system. The interview schedule contains a battery of questions asking about confidence in various political and public institutions, including parliament, political parties, police, military, civil service, and large corporations. Responses to these items have been combined to form an index, which is strongly related to support for terrorism. Specifically, respondents with lower levels of confidence in these institutions, and hence a more unfavorable evaluation of the Algerian political system, are much more likely than others to approve of the attacks on the United States. Thus, in contrast to orientations pertaining to religion and culture, discontent with the Algerian political system clearly predicts and helps to explain approval of the attacks on the United States.

The findings from Jordan are strikingly similar. Although the Jordanian analysis has fewer independent variables, the data set does permit the inclusion of measures of the three categories of orientations pertaining to Islam, assessments of Western culture, judgments about U.S. foreign policy, and confidence in the Jordanian political system, as well as personal demographic attributes. None of the demographic variables are related to the dependent variable to a statistically significant degree. Nor is even 1 of the 11 different independent variables pertaining to religion and culture. At least some of these relationships should be statistically significant if support for terrorism is indeed fostered by religious and cultural values in the Arab and Muslim world. As in the Algerian analysis, however, this is not the case.

By contrast, again as in the Algerian case, judgments about American foreign policy and evaluations of the domestic political system are related to support for terrorism to a degree that is statistically significant. Jordanians with a more negative attitude toward U.S. foreign policy, measured by an index composed of items that ask about the American President, U.S. handling of the Israeli-Palestinian crisis, and U.S. policy toward Iraq, are more likely than others to express favorable views about bin Laden and armed jihad. So, too, are Jordanians with lower levels of confidence in the country's government and parliament. Given that Algeria and Jordan are very different societies, it is striking and significant that in both cases, religious and cultural orientation has no ability to account for variance in attitudes toward terrorism but that political judgments, domestic as well as foreign, do have significant explanatory and predictive power.

Conclusion

A remarkably consistent set of conclusions emerges from this diverse array of data and analyses. The data discussed in this study were collected in 12 different countries, in some cases on several different occasions. They were collected by different polling organizations and researchers, and they used different questions when asking about the same topic or theme. And yet, despite this diversity, the same findings emerge in the areas of particular concern to the present analysis.

Consistent findings come through in three interrelated areas, which constitute the principal lessons and contribution of the present investigation. First, anti-Americanism in Arab and Muslim countries is primarily a reflection of antipathy to U.S. foreign policy, as it is or at least as it is perceived, rather than a rejection of Western norms and values. Some Arabs and Muslims do reject Western norms, but this is not the view of most of those who have a negative impression of the United States. Second, religion and culture have little explanatory and predictive power. Explanations and predictions of anti-Americanism and support for terrorism derived from the clash of civilizations hypothesis, the reification of Islam, or other civilizational analyses are not supported by the data. Third, assessments of political and economic circumstances do have explanatory and predictive power. Anti-Americanism and support for terrorism are fostered to a significant degree by unfavorable assessments of those factors, both domestic and international, that Arabs and other Muslims believe to be responsible for the political and economic status quo.

The implications of these findings for U.S. public diplomacy are clear on the one hand but challenging on the other. They are clear in that they suggest that strategic communications policies and programs with a focus on normative considerations, including religion, are unlikely to have a significant impact. They are challenging because the alternative, addressing issues of U.S. foreign policy and political economy, will not be easy and may not be possible at all. At the very least, however, those responsible for American public diplomacy must have a realistic understanding of the nature and dynamics of public opinion in the Arab and Muslim world. To the extent possible, American officials must also struggle to find acceptable and productive ways to engage ordinary Arabs and Muslims on the political and policy concerns that are shaping views on issues important to the United States.

Notes

[1] Samuel P. Huntington, *The Clash of Civilizations and the Remaking of World Order* (New York: Simon and Schuster, 1996); Samuel P. Huntington, "If Not Civilizations, What? Paradigms of the Post–Cold War World," *Foreign Affairs* 72, no. 5 (November/December 1993), 186.

[2] Bernard Lewis, "The Roots of Muslim Rage: Why So Many Muslims Deeply Resent the West and Why Their Bitterness Will Not Be Easily Mollified," *Atlantic Monthly* 266 (September 1990), 47; Bernard Lewis, *What Went Wrong: Western Impact and Middle Eastern Response* (New York: Oxford University Press, 2002).

[3] Huntington, *The Clash of Civilizations*, 209, 217.

[4] Associated Press, November 29, 2002.

[5] Richard W. Stevenson, "As Ramadan Draws to a Close, Bush Praises Muslims for 'Spirit of Tolerance,'" *The New York Times*, December 6, 2002, A18.

[6] Nicholas D. Kristof, "Bigotry in Islam—And Here," *The New York Times*, July 9, 2002.

[7] "A Conservative Christian Group Sues the University of North Carolina for Assigning a Book on Islam," *Democracy Now!* August 8, 2002, available at <webactive.com/pacifica/dem-now/dn20020808.html>.

[8] Olivier Roy, "Why Do They Hate Us? Not Because of Iraq," *The New York Times*, July 22, 2005, A19.

[9] Kristof.

[10] Mark Tessler, "Islam and Democracy in the Middle East: The Impact of Religious Orientations on Attitudes Toward Democracy in Four Arab Countries," *Comparative Politics* 34 (April 2002), 337–354; Mark Tessler, "Arab and Muslim Political Attitudes: Stereotypes and Evidence from Survey Research," *International Studies Perspectives* 4, no. 2 (May 1, 2003), 175–180; Mark Tessler, "Do Islamic Orientations Influence Attitudes Toward Democracy in the Arab World: Evidence From the World Values Survey in Egypt, Jordan, Morocco, and Algeria," *International Journal of Comparative Sociology* 2 (Spring 2003), 229–249; Mark Tessler, "Islam and Democracy in the Arab World: Evidence from Opinion Research in the Maghrib," in Amin Saikal and Albrecht Schnabel, *Democracy and Peace in the Middle East* (Tokyo: United Nations University, 2003); Mark Tessler and Ebru Altinoglu, "Political Culture in Turkey: Connections Among Attitudes Toward Democracy, the Military, and Islam," *Democratization* 11, no. 1 (February 2004), 21–50.

[11] Ronald Inglehart, *Human Beliefs and Values: A Cross-Cultural Sourcebook Based on the 1999–2002 Values Surveys* (Mexico: Siglo XXI Editores, 2004).

[12] Nelson Kasfir, "Dilemmas of Popular Support in Guerrilla War: The National Resistance Army in Uganda, 1981–86," available at <duke.edu/web/licep/6/kasfir/kasfir.pdf>; Paul Collier and Anke Hoeffler, "Greed and Grievance in Civil War," *World Bank Policy Research Paper* 2355 (Washington, DC: The World Bank, 2000); J. Weinstein, *Resources and the Information Problem in Rebel Recruitment*, available at <armedgroups.org/index.php?option=content&task=view&id=28>.

[13] Barry R. Posen, "Fighting Blind in Iraq," *The New York Times*, June 7, 2005, A23.

[14] Mao Tse-Tung, *On Guerrilla Warfare* (Chicago: University of Illinois Press, 1961).

[15] Harvey W. Kushner, "Suicide Bombers: Business as Usual," *Studies in Conflict and Terrorism* 19, no. 4 (October–December 1996), 329.

[16] *White Paper: The Jemaah Islamiyah Arrests and the Threat of Terrorism* (Singapore: Ministry of Home Affairs, 2003), available at <www2.mha.gov.sg/mha/detailed.jsp?artid=667&type=4&root=0&parent=0&cat=0>.

[17] Diane Singerman, "The Networked World of Islamist Social Movements," in *Islamic Activism: A Social Movement Theory Approach*, ed. Quintan Wiktorowicz (Bloomington: Indiana University Press, 2004); Carrie R. Wickham, "Interest, Ideas, and Islamist Outreach in Egypt," in Wiktorowicz; Quintan Wiktorowicz, *The Management of Islamic Activism: Salafis, the Muslim Brotherhood, and State Power in Jordan* (Albany: State University of New York Press, 2001).

[18] Dale F. Eickelman and James Piscatori, *Muslim Politics* (Princeton, NJ: Princeton University Press, 1996), 5; Wiktorowicz, *Islamic Activism: A Social Movement Theory Approach*, 18.

[19] Rohan Gunaratna, *Inside Al Qaeda* (New York: Columbia University Press, 2002).

[20] Robert A. Pape, "The Strategic Logic of Suicide Terrorism," *American Political Science Review* 97, no. 3 (August 2003), 343–361.

[21] Frantz Fanon, *The Wretched of the Earth* (Hammondsworth: Penguin, 1967).

[22] Jeremy Ginges, "Deterring the Terrorist: A Psychological Evaluation of Different Strategies for Deterring Terrorism," *Terrorism and Political Violence* 9, no. 1 (Spring 1997), 170.

[23] Gunaratna.

[24] See Scott Atran, "Genesis of Suicide Terrorism," *Science* 299, no. 5612 (March 7, 2003), 1534; Jerrold M. Post, "Rewarding Fire With Fire: Effects of Retaliation on Terrorist Group-Dynamics," *Terrorism* 10 (1987), 23–25.

[25] Scott Atran, "The Strategic Threat from Suicide Terror," AEI-Brookings Joint Center for Regulatory Studies, December 2003, available at <aei-brookings.org/publications/abstract.php?pid=410>.

[26] Reuven Paz, "Is Hamas Reevaluating the Use of Terrorism?" International Policy Institute for Counter-Terrorism, December 28, 1998, available at <ict.org.il/articles/articledet.cfm?articleid=50>.

[27] Ami Ayalon, "Fighting Terrorism: Lessons from the Front Line," in *The Battle of Ideas in the War on Terror: Essays on U.S. Public Diplomacy in the Middle East*, ed. Robert B. Satloff (Washington, DC: Washington Institute for Near East Policy, 2004).

[28] Robert Spencer, *Islam Unveiled: Disturbing Questions about the World's Fastest Growing Religion* (San Francisco: Encounter Books, 2002); Mark A. Gabriel, *Islam and Terrorism: What the Quran Really Teaches About Christianity, Violence, and the Goals of Islamic Jihad* (New York: Charisma House, 2002).

[29] Albert Bandura, "Mechanisms of Moral Disengagement," and Ehud Sprinzak, "The Psychopolitical Formation of Extreme Left Terrorism in a Democracy: The Case of the Weathermen," in *Origins of Terrorism*, ed. Walter Reich (New York: Cambridge University Press, 1990).

Chapter Three

Muslim Perceptions of America: The Sources of Hostility

Steven N. Simon

Burgeoning anti-Americanism in the Muslim world is widely recognized in the United States, where it is often assumed to be the product of a particular religion and culture. Although these anti-American sentiments certainly reflect language and ideas that are specific to Islam, many key themes actually come from outside the Islamic tradition. In some instances, these criticisms of America align with values embedded in Muslim experience and intellectual life, while in others they seem to be force-fit into an Islamic mold. Understanding and responding to Muslim anti-Americanism requires a grasp of its multiple, exogenous secular sources as well as its specifically religious origins.

Intellectual Sources of Anti-Americanism in the Muslim World

Muslim attitudes toward the United States are rooted in or influenced by non-Muslim perceptions of America predating the intensive U.S. encounter with the Arab world that began in the early post–World War II period.[1] Some of these primarily European attitudes toward North America preceded the establishment of the republic. From the time of the early European settlement of the New World, natural scientists and writers presented an understanding of the continent as essentially uninhabitable by cultured people. The educated, if uninformed, view of the continent was of a vast miasmic forest, hostile climate, and savage indigenous population. The undeveloped state of the native culture was held to be the result of the effluvial and toxic atmosphere. It was presumed that European settlers would fall victim to the noxious environment and swiftly descend to the primitive level of the autochthonous peoples. Indeed, a cultivated French traveler to North America in the late 1700s, Cornelius de Pauw, titled his description of the colonial settlers, "On the American's Moronic Spirit."[2]

Negative images of North Americans persisted even after wide acquaintance with actual conditions on the continent became a fact in Europe. In the late 18th and early 19th centuries, with a few notable exceptions, European

The author is indebted to Amir Stepak and Sara Moller of the Council on Foreign Relations and Jeffrey Martini of Georgetown University for their assistance in preparing this chapter.

commentators derided life in the colonies and then in the independent United States as uncultured, coarse, corrupt, and doomed to political and social failure. American towns and cities were portrayed as squalid, religious practice as hopelessly unexalted, separation of church and state as unsustainable, and politics as geared to the lowest common denominator of a low society. These sharply critical views of Americans and their new republic did not fade with the evident success of the state. They were combined with a new source of fear and disgust, namely a populist, Whiggish set of political values, rejection of the monarchy as a legitimate institution and, more generally, of traditions derived from established European political practice and social organization. The American project was perceived as a threat to European stability and existing political prerogatives. As a result, Americans and their politics were scorned both in the popular European press and in the somewhat more elevated discourse of national elites.

An image of the United States as a dangerous wellspring of radicalism gained greater traction during the revolutions of 1848. Not all Europeans were appalled by American values. Those who manned the barricades had as an inspiration not only the French revolution but also the republicanism of the United States.

Gradually, these views of the United States evolved into two opposing censorious images. Among the European right, America was seen as a radical juggernaut inspiring revolutionary sentiment in Europe and degrading the high culture of the old regime. On the left, America was held to be the avatar of unregulated capitalism, from which emerged robber barons, large corporations, and widespread exploitation of labor. The Russian Revolution of 1917 and its long aftermath reified these negative images, particularly those that reflected a leftist critique of American politics and society. The key characteristics attributed to the United States were derived from Marxist analysis, but they incorporated preexisting prejudices. This is unsurprising, especially given the alluvial way in which negative stereotypes of the United States had accumulated and coalesced since the earliest European settlement of the continent. Thus, America was predatory, instinctively imperial, and aggressive; an oppressor of its own working class as well as the population of countries it sought to devour; racist, self-righteous, and inimical to the human spirit. American capitalism trampled the values of dignity and self-fulfillment, while celebrating self-centeredness and consumption for consumption's sake. Indeed, it was essential that an obsession with consumption be instilled, lest ordinary Americans wake up to the spiritual emptiness of their lives and their exploitation at the hands of their capitalist masters. Moreover, Soviet propaganda embraced prevailing anti-Semitic motifs, specifically those asserting a connection between Jews and capital, which had originated in medieval images of the Jew as usurer. In this narrative, Jewish financiers who were said to congregate in New York City were connected to a larger conspiracy of capitalist states to dominate the world. (A variation of these beliefs was systematized in the "Protocols of the Learned Elders of Zion," a late 19th-century Russian fabrication describing a Jewish conspiracy to subordinate the world's population to Jewish objectives, which drew on an earlier French work along the same lines.)

The right made a contribution as well. The Nazi propaganda effort adopted earlier European elite characterizations of American society as mongrel and its culture debased. The key concepts deployed by the Nazis related to racial and ethnic mixing, the degrading influence of African-American and Jewish artistic expression, and, as in Soviet propaganda, the malign presence of Jews in the American financial industry.

Apart from the way in which Soviet theoreticians reframed older critiques of the United States and linked American rapacity to Jewish greed, the Soviet Union used its vast propaganda network to reinforce anti-Americanism, especially in Western Europe, and, after World War II, throughout the Third World. In Europe, negative images of the United States resonated strongly, especially on the left. This was due in part to the fact that Soviet propaganda encompassed anti-American themes that had been circulating among European elites for over a century. The leftist tinge of much of the European intelligentsia, combined with a strong sense of European cultural superiority, was also a factor. In the Third World, Soviet propaganda was effective because it meshed well with the profound anticolonialism that had begun to emerge in South and Southeast Asia as well as the Middle East during the interwar years. The more closely the United States could be linked to European colonial occupation or informal imperialism, the more persuasive this critique would be.

American support for national self-determination in the wake of World War I, however, combined with Washington's critical stance toward the colonial commitments of its wartime alliance partners after World War II, helped to preserve a positive image of the United States, especially in the Middle East. The Truman administration's decisions to vote in favor of partition of Palestine in 1947 and then to recognize Israel in May 1948 could scarcely have been expected to ingratiate the United States in Arab capitals. Yet Washington's self-imposed distance from the Jewish state, which stemmed partly from a desire to avoid outraging Israel's regional neighbors (especially Saudi Arabia) and partly from its suspicion of Israel's socialist government and connections to the Eastern Bloc, did much at first to contain anti-American sentiment.

The Eisenhower administration's condemnation of the British, French, and Israeli military campaign to reverse Egypt's nationalization of the Suez

Canal also helped stave off a decline in America's image in the region. The U.S. position took the anticolonial high ground and demonstrated that the President had both the will and the power to challenge America's European allies and their Israeli protégé. However, Gamal abd al-Nasr's regime, which was arguably rescued by the U.S. vote in the United Nations Security Council (along with that of the Soviet Union) to condemn the invasion, did not acknowledge the U.S. role, thereby undercutting the positive impact Eisenhower's move might otherwise have had.

Two interrelated cold wars—one between East and West and the other between Egypt and Iraq from the mid-1950s to the early 1960s—would soon begin to erode America's standing in Muslim opinion in the Middle East. The nationalist revolution in Iraq in 1958 and Qarim Qassim's repudiation of the Baghdad Pact, and the U.S. break with Egypt over Eastern Bloc weapons procurement, recognition of Communist China, and financing of the Aswan Dam in 1956 accelerated the corrosive process. Nasr's pan-Arab project and Syrian and Iraqi Baathism were interlaced with a strong socialist impulse, which in turn created a receptive atmosphere for Soviet influence and anti-American propaganda. The continuing confrontation with Israel likewise created opportunities for Soviet military and diplomatic support that translated into influence. Covert Soviet support for regional print media ensured that the anti-American tropes of leftist ideology were widely propagated within the region. These ideas blended with anticolonial sentiment through the linkage of the United States and several of its North Atlantic Treaty Organization (NATO) allies that had, in an earlier era, divided the region between themselves in secret agreements and, in the case of the United Kingdom, still retained a military presence in Yemen and the littoral states of the Persian Gulf.[3]

From the 1960s onward, converging trends would continue to undermine favorable views of the United States: the 1967 Arab-Israeli war; the 1973 war in which the United States resupplied the Israel Defense Force in the midst of the conflict; the subsequent oil embargo; and the Iranian revolution, all of which tended to lend credence to propaganda claims, particularly about American neocolonialism and embrace of Jewish interests.

In the wake of Operation *Desert Storm*, the negative regional image of the United States that had been derived from the Soviet version of European anti-Americanism—the United States portrayed as a soulless, bellicose, imperialistic society in league with international capital—was incorporated into a more specifically Islamic critique. From the Islamic perspective, the faults of the United States lay in its support for Muslim governments that radical Islamists regarded as apostate.

Elite Opinion in the Muslim World

Current anti-American discourse among Muslims draws freely on the eclectic range of unfavorable characterizations found in European anti-American thought and on an explicitly Islamic critique, frequently weaving both strands into a unified argument. Osama bin Laden is an exceptionally skilled practitioner of this syncretistic rhetorical style.

Key Themes

The basic tropes of the anti-American argument appear frequently in print media as text or cartoon, sermons that are either broadcast or distributed in playable formats, in broadcast discussion programs, or, as suggested above, in video or audiotapes of famous jihadists. They may also be found in popular song, cinema, and theatrical productions. These conventional formulations fall into the following categories.

Global Bully. The United States, either alone or in a pact with Israel, is set on a program of world domination, starting with the Arab world. Thus, a columnist for the pan-Islamist Turkish newspaper *Milli Gazete* writes in an op-ed entitled "America's Hitler":

> Hitler said that he would establish a new world order if Germany won. Bush is after similar invasions. First he targeted Afghanistan and Iraq. Later he expanded his invasion map to include 22 more Islamic countries where he wants to change the order and the borders. He says that he wants to bring the likes of Karzai and Allawi [to these countries] to power, and in doing so establish his colonial empire.
>
> When a person goes rabid, there is no stopping him. God forbid, if he succeeds in occupying those 22 countries, his lust will expand to cover the whole world. Why expand? Because the five-thousand-year-old dream of the Zionists is to grasp the valleys of both the Nile and Euphrates and build a Jewish state to rule the rest of the world. What I want to say is that the end game for the "Sharon and Bush duo" is to build a state that would rule the world, just like it was for Hitler.[4]

In this excerpt, the American drive to dominate the Islamic world on the way toward global hegemony aligns with Israel's desire to rule the Middle East. In the author's assessment, America is motivated by an expansionist compulsion, which he likens to "rabid" behavior. The degree to which this component of Muslim anti-American discourse resembles earlier European left-wing complaints about the United States is suggested by Jean-Paul Sartre's famous declaration that America had "rabies."[5]

This theme is lavishly illustrated in newspapers by caricaturists who use unflattering symbols for the United States that might be found as well in Western European and other non-Muslim periodicals. As shown in figures 3–1 through 3–4, these symbols include the grim reaper, distributing dynamite around the globe; the bronco-busting cowboy trampling the earth; a malevolent American eagle sinking its claws into a globe that, having been punctured, is beginning to deflate; and the almighty buck, from which the American President reaches out to strangle a poor *fellah*.[6]

In the domain of popular entertainment, Shabaan abd al-Rahim, an Egyptian tradesman who achieved unexpected stardom in 2000 with his hit song, "I Hate Israel, but I Love Amr Mousa," scored another hit in "Two Faces of the Same Coin," which was released in 2004.

The song can be downloaded from the Internet as a video, in which Shabaan is shown in the foreground singing the lyrics, against a cartoon

Figure 3–1. **Anti-American Political Cartoon**

Source: Sherif Hetata, "World Dominations, Inc." Al-Ahram Weekly, no. 666 (November 27-December 3, 2003), accessed at <weekly.ahram.org.eg/2003/666/focus.htm>.

Figure 3–2. **Anti-American Political Cartoon**

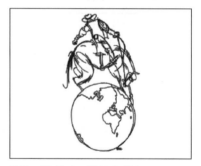

Al-Ahram Weekly, June 26-July 2, 2003.

Figure 3–3. **Anti-American Political Cartoon**

Al-Ahram Weekly, November 22-28, 2001.

Figure 3–4. **Anti-American Political Cartoon**

Al-Ahram Weekly, October 16-22, 2003.

backdrop that shows, among other things, a map suggesting America's imperial ambitions, President Bush in the Oval Office apparently declaring war against Iran and Syria, and a grinning image of an airplane flying into the Twin Towers. The imagery then changes, depicting Ariel Sharon pressing a button festooned with a Star of David, whereby he appears to launch the 9/11 attack.

Two faces of the same coin, America and Israel
They made the world a jungle and ignited the fuse.

America spread its wings,
Doesn't care at all.
No one can stop her,
No one can catch her.

Soon he will say Iran,
And then he will say Syria.
But he is silent about [North] Korea.

About that tower, oh people,
Definitely, his friends were the ones who brought it down.
They were the ones who brought it down.

What terrorism?!
How many years are left,
For America and Israel, acting as bullies.

Day and night Sharon is looking for a fight.
All his life he is a liar and hypocrite,
There are no smuggled weapons or any tunnels.

A person who hates himself.[7]

Shabaan's popular song harnesses the image of a belligerent America with other reinforcing motifs, including America's heedless attitude toward the interests of regional states, Washington's double standard as applied to Muslim and non-Muslim countries, the identity between Israel and the United States, and a conspiratorial Jewish state with which Washington connives on 9/11, presumably to provide a pretext for aggression against Muslim states that will benefit both Israel and the United States.

Intrinsically Violent. A parallel motif, which recalls the image of the United States as a cowboy, holds that Americans are instinctively violent. Popular impressions of American cities as dangerous places, where gunplay and murder are rife, are common in foreign media generally. In this context, the belief is useful in explaining why U.S. foreign policy, in the view of regional observers, is excessively reliant on the use of force. The underlying assumption is that a violent domestic order will inevitably be reflected in a violent approach toward the international order. Such assumptions are not confined to Muslim observers of America. U.S. policymakers, for example, routinely attribute aggressive intentions to North Korea in part because of the atrocious domestic policies of its despotic regime. Thus, a Syrian legislator, Dr. Muhammad Habash, explained American actions to an Iranian television interviewer as follows:

> When the American adventurer arrived [in America], the good Indians carried his luggage and rejoiced while shooing the flies from the face of that American adventurer who came to them. They did not notice the dagger he concealed. . . . I want to talk about the philosophical roots of this condescending culture, a culture that realizes the desire for expansion at the expense of others. . . . Let me tell you. I must clarify this idea. The culture that is exported today, through Hollywood, for example, is a culture of violence, a culture of films ending usually with the policeman bleeding and the robber hugging his lover and smoking a cigar. These images glorify cruelty, glorify force, glorify the man who is victorious because of his might and his weapons. This is the language that still controls these people's culture.[8]

Habash's analysis connects a perception of the United States as a country with overweening self-esteem to an expansionist foreign policy and a culture industry that justifies the use of force to carry out such a policy. The example he uses is meant to show that violence in American culture enjoys a legitimacy that surpasses respect for the rule of law. In an opinion piece from a Turkish newspaper with loose ties to the ruling Justice and Development Party, columnist Dr. Husnu Mahalli posited a variation on this image of Americans, arguing, "Murdering is genetically ingrained in American culture."[9]

This theme has also been showcased in popular entertainment. Khalid Sawi, of the Haraka theater group in Cairo, scored a hit in 2004 with his play "Messing with the Mind."[10] The play begins with actors dressed as U.S. Marines running into the audience shouting, "Stay seated; you have right to die; turn off your cell phones!" and ends with an American general named Fox News yelling, "I hate Arabs!" before being shot in the head. That same year, Youssef Chahine, a prominent Egyptian film director, produced a melodramatic allegory for U.S.-Egyptian relations, in which an aging film director returns to New York to see a lover from his youth and the son he had unknowingly fathered. He and the son soon fall out, however, and the director denounces the son, declaring, "The violence that started at Hiroshima is in you."[11] More recently, this theme was featured in a popular Turkish television series, "Valley of the Wolves—Iraq," in which the villain is Sam William Marshall, an American Special Forces Soldier, who, among other atrocities, slaughters a wedding party.[12]

Satanic. At a rally of Iranian pilgrims in Mecca in January 2006, a speaker denounced the United States against a graphic backdrop depicting the World Trade Center and a flaming American flag. Quoting Ayatollah Ali Khamenei, he declared:

> Today, the fleets of arrogance are, once again, using new methods of deceit, in order to perpetuate and strengthen their control over the Islamic world. Their slogan of spreading democracy and human rights is one of these methods of deceit. The Great Satan, who embodies evil and violence against humanity, raises the banner of defending of human rights, and summons the peoples of the Middle East to democracy.[13]

The characterization of America as Satan or as satanic is common in Islamic clerical discourse. The term *shaytan* is polyvalent and covers a wide semantic range in Koranic Arabic. Shaytan is the one, for example, who can cause people to slip (Koran 2:36, 3:155); lead astray (4:60); instill hatred and envy (5:91); make people forget (6:68, 18:63); tempt (7:27); and provoke strife (17:53). He is the embodiment of guile (4:76) and is associated with abomination (5:90).[14] The homiletic application of this epithet to the United States efficiently articulates many of the key anti-American themes that circulate in other arenas of Muslim political self-expression. The essential qualities are deceit, temptation, and instigation of conflict within the *umma*, the worldwide community of Muslims. By lying, the United States conceals its true motivations and impedes the ability of Muslims to fully grasp the evil import of American policy. Through temptation, America lures Muslims away from the faith that is the source of their strength and ability to resist America's designs. Stirring internecine conflict, either by supporting some Muslim countries against others, or, to cite a common example, turning Muslims within Iraq against each other with the aim of dividing the country and stealing its wealth, is another means by which America gets its way. Hence, Iranian president Mahmoud Ahmedinejad's focus on "the effort by the enemies of Islam to create division in the ranks of the Muslims" and "military and political intervention by the regime of the Arrogance [the United States]" in his December 2006 speech at the summit of the Organization of the Islamic Conference (OIC) in Mecca.[15]

Anti-Islam. The United States is widely seen in the Muslim world as anti-Islamic. Bashar al-Asad, who is generally eager to denounce American policy in the language of anticolonialism and Arab pride in a manner intended to embarrass his regional counterparts, declared at the 2003 OIC summit in Malaysia:

> Those fanatics [the U.S. administration] revealed their brutal vision of human society and started to market the principle of force instead of dialogue, oppression instead of justice and racism instead of tolerance. They even began to create an ugly illusory enemy which they called "Islam," and made it appear as if it is Islam [that was responsible] while Islam is completely innocent of it.

In this passage, al-Asad combines two key motifs, namely an American obsession with violence as the path to dispute resolution and a tendency to demonize Islam, blaming the religion for resistance to American desires, rather than the unjust nature of U.S. policy.

Malaysian prime minister Mahathir Muhammad, speaking at the same summit meeting, concluded that, "We, the whole Muslim *umma*, are treated with contempt and dishonor. Our religion is denigrated. Our holy places desecrated. Our countries are occupied. . . . All Muslims were suffering 'oppression and humiliation' with their religion accused of promoting terrorism."[16]

In a more explicitly Islamist vein, a fatwa issued by Shaykh Hammoud al-'Uqla al-Shu'aybi justified the September 11 attacks by arguing that America is "an enemy of Muslim nations":

> You should know that America is a *kufr* [infidel] state that is totally against Islam and Muslims. In fact it has reached the peak of that arrogance in the form of open attacks on several Muslim nations as it did in Sudan, Iraq, Afghanistan, Philistine [Palestine], Libya, and others, where it—America—allied with the forces of *Kufr* such as Britain, Russia and others. . . . How then can America after all these things not be considered an enemy of the Muslim nations and at war with them?[17]

This view is carried farther by Sheikh Ikrimeh Sabri, Mufti of Jerusalem and the senior religious authority in the Palestinian Authority, who said in late 2004 that:

> This mad Crusade is not merely a war against the Muslims. It is a campaign of hatred currently [being waged] against the great Islamic religion. [This campaign] is growing in intensity with the aim of distorting the character of Islam, and we have already warned about the dangers of this new Crusade 2 years ago.[18]

Here Sheikh Sabri distinguishes between American animosity toward Muslims, which might conceivably originate in America's greed for Muslim wealth or land, and asserts a hatred for Islam itself, or, as an American might phrase it, a clash of civilizations.

Hypocritical. Muslim governments frequently accuse Washington of having "double standards." At the 2004 World Economic Forum in Davos, Switzerland, representatives from the delegations of Saudi Arabia, Egypt, and Iran all criticized Washington's campaign for democracy in the Middle East as hypocritical, saying the Bush administration ignored Israeli weapons of mass destruction and human rights abuses while pressuring Muslim states to disarm and democratize.[19]

Washington's alleged hypocrisy on democracy, human rights, and nonproliferation is a frequent theme in Arab media and politics. Addressing the West's criticism of Hamas' victory in the January 2006 Palestinian elections, Dr. Abd-al-Aziz al-Duwayk, Speaker of the Palestinian Legislative Council, remarked:

> It is odd in general and in the United States and the European Union in particular that they want to promote democracy in this region of the world and we accepted. To their surprise, the Islamic movement in Palestine agreed to the rules of the game and we participated in the elections. They already knew that HAMAS was competing in the elections and our people—who are the most educated in this part of the world—had their say and selected their representatives. To the astonishment of the whole world, these two entities, these two super powers did not accept the final results of democracy. They wanted democracy but they wanted a democracy that is tailored. They did not want a free democracy. They wanted the outcome of this democratic process to be in accordance to their wishes and aspirations.

Of President Bush, al-Duwayk said:

> Instead of congratulating the Palestinians and saying that he is ready to cooperate with the results of the elections and with the representatives of the Palestinian people, he is trying to punish the Palestinians. Why? If he really believes in democracy and not in hypocrisy, he should engage us in a dialogue.[20]

The Abu Ghraib prisoner abuse scandal and the ongoing controversy over Guantanamo Bay have only served to reinforce this image, as a Pakistani journalist noted in late 2005:

> In fact the United States has followed the classic policy of 'might is right' but it has lost moral ground in the process. President

Bush must remember that one has to practice what one preaches and not the other way round. The Americans have always been in the habit of delivering sermons on human rights, freedom, and dignity to the rest of the world. This policy lies tattered, as the whole world has been made aware of the antics they employ when it comes to dealing with difficult situations.[21]

From this perspective, not only does the United States paint itself as a champion of human rights and dignity while itself performing questionable practices on prisoners, it also uses every available opportunity to prevent Islamic countries from benefiting from scientific and technological advancements. The governments of both Pakistan and Iran frequently remind their citizens that while Israel and the West are allowed nuclear technology, the United States prevents Muslim countries from obtaining this technology. In an April 2006 address to a Palestinian conference, Ayatollah Khamenei addressed this theme in a section of his comments titled, "Preventing the Progress and Advancement of Islamic Countries":

The bullying powers use different excuses to prevent transfer of science and technology and progress of the nations of our region. They regard our advancement as a threat to the corrupt Zionist regime. They do not allow the countries of the region to tread on the path to progress and advancement. They even oppose indigenous technologies in the Islamic countries and interpret any scientific advancement as a threat to the security of Qods [Jerusalem] occupier regime.

You can see how they treat our nation that has been able to have access to nuclear technology by relying on the innovations and creative minds of its own scientists. Nuclear technology is one of the primary foundations for progress and serving the people, and in [the] not too distant future, nations without this technology will have no choice but to resort to it in order to meet their growing energy needs and to use it for other scientific and economic purposes.[22]

Dedicated to Israel, Under the Influence of Jews. The belief that the U.S. Government takes orders from Jews/Israelis is well established in Arab and Muslim public opinion. U.S. and Israeli objectives are frequently taken to be identical, prompting American foreign policy initiatives to be viewed through this filter. Thus, the United States is thought to have invaded Iraq and overthrown the Saddam Hussein regime in order to remove a threat to Israel and promote Israel's goal of establishing hegemony over the Middle East from the Nile to the Euphrates. U.S. claims that the overthrow of the regime was motivated by an American desire to liberate Iraqis from a tyrannical ruler, give impetus to regional political liberalization, or preempt future aggression against the United States by a Baathist Iraq are generally given little credence. U.S. concerns regarding Iranian nuclear enrichment efforts are likewise regarded as motivated by fears for Israel's security.

Osama bin Laden's exposition of this view, from his first al Jazeera interview in December 1998, cast the U.S.-Israeli partnership as follows:[23]

> It is now clear that it is Israel that is behind all the attacks on states in the Islamic world. . . . the Jews were able to employ American and British Christians to do the job of attacking Iraq. America claims that it is bringing Iraq to account and to justice, but the fact is that the Israeli authority and Jewish authority, which has become powerful inside the White House as anyone can see—the Defence Minister is Jewish, the Secretary of State is Jewish, the CIA and National Security officials are Jewish, all the biggest officials are Jews—led Christians to clip the wings of the Islamic World. Their real target is not Saddam Hussein but the growing power of the Arab and Islamic world.[24]

The U.S.-Zionist conspiracy is a frequent theme of the Iranian leadership and press. In his comments to a Palestinian conference in April 2006, Ayatollah Khamenei outlined the history of this "nefarious" relationship, stretching back to Israel's creation in 1948: "The connected chain of U.S. plots against Iraq, Syria, and Lebanon with the aim of establishing its dominance over the Middle East under the auspices of the Zionist regime will never succeed and will not earn American leaders anything but fatal ruin."[25]

The following month, an Iranian daily described the "Zionist Lobby" as the U.S. Government's "ruling clique" and declared that "this dirty and unhealthy mutual bond between the two awfully strong networks of U.S. Jews and U.S. statesmen and politicians has created a great and horrendous clique that takes the entire world ransom and practices extortion against most nations around the world."[26]

Similar claims are made regarding Operation *Iraqi Freedom* and the role of influential, highly placed Jews in spurring the United States toward war with Iraq in order to advance Israeli interests. An editorial by Arif al-Agha in *Al-Thawrah*, a Syrian newspaper, titled "The Bush Administration, the Complete Israelization," argued that the war was:

> in the interest of Israel and its plans for expansion and hegemony, as well as Bush's plans to colonize the Arab World, dictate its policy, and divide it on ethnic and racial lines for the sake of U.S. and Israeli interests.

As for the strategy of preemptive wars against the Arab and Islamic world it is a photocopy of the Israeli strategy, which waged more than 5 wars against the Arab states under the same excuses, which Bush reiterates today with or without reason. Even the call for "combating terrorism," which Bush has come up with since 11 September, is a polished copy of an old Israeli policy, which it has exploited recently as an abortive cover to justify its crimes against the Palestinians and continuous occupation of their country.[27]

In Pakistan, a retired lieutenant general told the Islamabad *Khabrain* that the Jews, who "enjoy control [i]n the U.S. administration," were waging war against Iraq for their own existence and "for this, they are using the United States."[28]

Oil-Obsessed. The United States is thought of as determined to seize Middle Eastern oil for itself and as willing to go to any length to do so. Abd al-Bari Atwan, editor of the London-based newspaper *al-Quds al-Arabi*, summarized this viewpoint in a 2003 interview with al Jazeera:

Arab regimes sell oil at prices said to be determined mainly by America, open their countries for U.S. military bases, facilitate American control and domination over the Arab world's economic resources including oil and convert Arab world into a huge consuming market for U.S. products. In addition they are purported to make unnecessary huge arms deals worth billions of dollars which allegedly give them a capacity to suppress the people rather than using the money for socio-economic department.[29]

Many Muslims believe Washington's motive for the 2003 Iraq war was the desire to control the region's oil, rather than the need to eliminate weapons of mass destruction or establish an Islamic democracy in the heart of the Arab world. As preparations for war were under way in January 2003, a Syrian newspaper, *al-Thawrah*, published a scathing portrayal of the United States as oil hungry:

The odor of oil smells from this "declared war," regardless of the attempts by the decisionmakers in the Pentagon and the White House to beautify their statement and coat them in honey to pave the way for their real objectives. The destructive war, being an unjust war by all measurements, will not be to the liking of peoples in any case. This is because Washington is eager to control the natural resources, especially oil, to behave like a great empire against all the peoples of the world, and to blindly support Israel's arrogance and attempts at hegemony, expansion, and aggression.[30]

Similar editorials appeared in the Palestinian daily *Al-Hayah al-Jadidah*, which called oil the "motivator of the present [U.S.] civilization" and lamented that:

> it was for the sake of its [oil's] stability that the region has been split up into states of national minorities and communities headed by the State of Israel; the oil, for which terrorism was created and is being fought!

> It is oil, for whose sake roles are changed, violation of human rights is condoned, and the foe becomes friend, the ally an evil rival, and Sharon a man of peace.[31]

"Arab Attitudes Toward Political and Social Issues, Foreign Policy, and the Media," an October 2005 survey of Arab public opinion conducted in six countries (Jordan, Lebanon, Morocco, Saudi Arabia, Egypt, and the United Arab Emirates) by Zogby International and Shibley Telhami of the University of Maryland, found that three out of every four persons surveyed believed that the main motives behind U.S. foreign policy in the Middle East were "oil, protecting Israel, dominating the region, and weakening the world."[32]

Corrupt and Licentious. U.S. entertainment exports have contributed to a view in the Middle East that the United States is a den of iniquity. Of course, many Americans view their country the same way. The conservative Muslim critique of American society dwells on these supposed ills. The immorality attributed to American behavior at home both explains and contributes to a larger picture of a culture out of control and on the loose in the realm of Islam. A typical online expression of this view follows:

> This is the America that occupies the world with the culture of sex and deviation. This is the pagan civilization in Christian disguise. . . . This is the American civilization whose object is the body and its means is materialism. The spirit has no place in the system of American values. They are dressed with Christian clothes on hearts that know nothing but stealing, robbing, and occupying the possessions of others. Has America left one place in our lives as Muslims without corrupting it?[33]

In his October 2002 "Letter to the Americans," bin Laden assembles the main components of this theme in anti-American discourse. Apart from Americans having rejected God's law in favor of their own, he writes:

You are a nation that permits the production, trading, and usage of intoxicants. You also permit drugs, and only forbid the trade of them, even though your nation is the largest consumer of them;

You are a nation that permits acts of immorality, and you consider these to be pillars of personal freedom. You have continued to sink down this abyss from level to level until incest has spread among you. . . .

You are a nation that permits gambling in all its forms. The companies practice this as well, resulting in investments becoming active and criminals becoming rich.

You are a nation that exploits women like consumer products or advertising tools, calling upon customers to purchase them. . . .

You are nation that practices the trade of sex in all its forms, directly and indirectly;

You have destroyed nature with your industrial waste and gasses, more than any other nation in history. Despite this you refuse to sign the Kyoto agreement so that you can secure the profit of your greedy companies and industries;

Your law is the law of the rich and wealthy, who hold sway in their political parties, and fund their election campaign with gifts. Behind them stand the Jews, who control your policy, media, and economy.

You have claimed to be the vanguard of human rights and your Ministry of Foreign Affairs issue[s] annual reports containing statistics of those countries that have violated any human rights. However all these values vanished when the mujahidin hit you [on 9/11] and you then implemented the methods of the same documented governments that you used to curse. . . . what happens in Guantanamo is a historical embarrassment to America and its values, and it screams in your hypocritical faces: what is the value of your signature on any agreement or treaty?[34]

The striking thing about this indictment of the United States is its largely secular tone. Although the preambular statement condemning the substitution of man's law for the law of God, a core salafi concern, is indisputably religious, much of the substance of bin Laden's critique is typical of both right- and left-wing European rhetoric about the United States. The passages omitted from the summary above, which deal with Washington's refusal to support an international criminal court and to follow through on its rhetorical commitment to democracy by recognizing elected Islamist governments, only reinforce this impression. Interestingly, bin Laden's assessment of the moral qualities of American society strongly resembles the position of conservatives, as well as some liberals, within the United States, particularly regarding exploitation of women, drug trafficking, income disparities, corporate corruption, and threats to civil liberties.

The Islamist Critique

While European anti-American discourse stigmatizes America's public piety, religious language, and a supposedly blurred line between church and state, Islamist critiques often focus on American secularism. Two themes are especially prominent. First, American democracy places man above God and substitutes human legislators for the divine source of law. According to this view, American secularism is an affront to a divinely ordained moral order and a manifestation of extraordinary arrogance. The second theme stresses the spiritual emptiness of secular life compared to the personal and collective sense of fulfillment that flows from belief in God and obedience to his laws. As a corollary to this view, the Islamist critique emphasizes the moral corruption and ethical blindness of American society by pointing out lewd behavior, homosexuality, wealth disparities, crime, and so forth.

This Islamist critique is rooted in the writings of Sayyid Qutb, an Egyptian Islamist ideologue executed by the Nasr regime in 1966 during a purge of the Muslim Brotherhood. In his capacity as an official of the Education Ministry in Cairo, Qutb was sent to the United States in 1948 to study education at Colorado State Teachers College. His experience in the United States was dislocating; he was especially disturbed by what he took to be America's "mad lust for naked flesh, provocative pictures, and sick, suggestive statements in literature, the arts, and mass media. And add to all this," he wrote, "the system of usury which fuels men's voracity for money and engenders vile methods for its accumulation and investment, in addition to fraud, trickery, and blackmail dressed up in the garb of law."[35] Qutb dubbed the United States the new *jahiliyya*, the modern-day equivalent of pre-Islamic Arabia, a society sunk in ignorance and corruption, redeemable only by the advent of Islam.

Resonance Among the Masses: The Quantitative Picture

The best source of quantitative data on Muslim public opinion about these issues is the annual Pew Global Attitudes survey. Unfortunately, Pew primarily surveys Muslim countries that enjoy relatively good relations with the United States or are more easily accessible to and cooperative with U.S.-based polling organizations. Nevertheless, Pew's findings tend to align with the qualitative data regarding public opinion. Thus, Muslim views of the United States are largely unfavorable. According to the Pew June 2006 returns, majorities in every Muslim country surveyed held an unfavorable view: 70 percent each in Indonesia and Egypt, 73 percent in Pakistan, 85 percent in Jordan, and 88 percent in Turkey.[36] In 3 of the countries—Indonesia, Jordan, and Turkey—the figures represented roughly a 10 point increase in anti-Americanism from the previous year's results. The slippage from the 2005 survey, which had showed a slight gain in America's standing in Muslim countries compared to 2004, suggests that, as Pew Global Attitudes project director Andrew Kohut put it, "There will be no quick fix to this. There will not be just one good thing that the United States does that will bring the image of America back to what it was in the 1990s and earlier."[37]

The 2006 findings point to the Iraq war as the overwhelming reason for America's continued poor standing in the Muslim world. When asked if removing Saddam Hussein made the world a safer or more dangerous place, the vast majority answered the latter (see figure 3–5).

Figure 3–5. **Beliefs About Whether War in Iraq Has Made the World Safer**

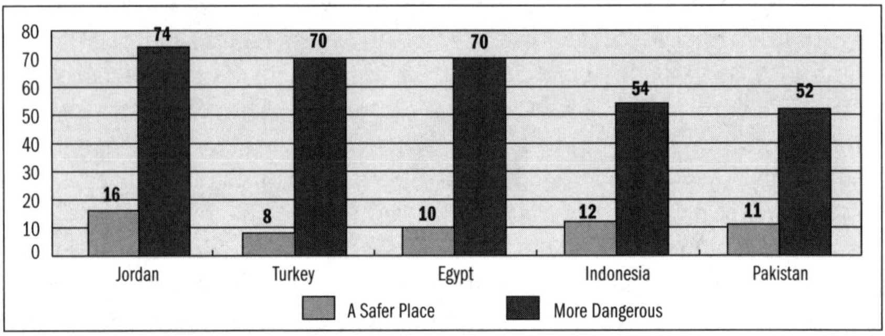

Source: Pew Global Attitudes Project, June 13, 2006.

Prior to the war in Iraq, 61 percent of Indonesians had a favorable opinion of the United States This figure fell to 15 percent in 2003 but grew to 38 percent in 2005, as a result of U.S. aid to the tsunami-ravaged country. But the post-tsunami boost proved to be short-lived, and the figure dropped to 30 percent in 2006.[38]

More than just the Iraq war is to blame for America's poor standing in the Muslim world, however. Other factors, such as America's preponderant power and its policies in the wider Middle East, also contribute to its being viewed unfavorably by majorities in the Muslim and Arab world. Even prior to the Iraq war (as far back as late 2001), Pew began to register "growing dislike" of the United States, driven in large part by concerns about U.S. power and the way the country was conducting the war on terrorism. The changing nature of U.S. power, argues Kohut, is to blame:

> Apart from Iraq, one of the concerns about the world is American power when America is on the defensive. America was the sole superpower even in the 1990s, and there wasn't discomfort with that power because the United States didn't feel itself under attack. [After September 11] the world looks at American power as more threatening when America feels threatened.[39]

Pew also found that in 2005, in all of these countries, apart from post-tsunami Indonesia, large majorities believed that U.S. foreign policy did not consider other countries' interests: Lebanon, 65 percent; Pakistan, 61 percent; Turkey, 86 percent; and Jordan, 83 percent. Indonesian respondents, probably influenced by Washington's humanitarian assistance, differed; 41 percent thought that U.S. foreign policy did take the interests of other countries into account. Except for Jordan, the rather negative results actually represented an upturn in opinion, as compared to 2003. In 2005, the biggest gains were in Indonesia (35 percentage points), Lebanon (17 points), Pakistan (16 points), and Turkey (5 points). In Jordan, the result represented a 2-point decline.[40] As noted above, however, the gains in Indonesia from the post-tsunami boost could not be sustained. In 2006, backsliding in U.S. approval ratings occurred in every Muslim country except Pakistan, where the share expressing a favorable opinion of America actually increased by 4 percentage points in 2006.

A Zogby International poll released in December 2005 confirmed the Pew findings that opinion in the Middle East toward America had deteriorated over the preceding year. In both Egypt and Saudi Arabia, more than 80 percent of respondents said their opinion of the United States had worsened since 2004. In Lebanon, 21 percent reported having a more favorable opinion of the United States, while 49 percent said they had more negative feelings toward America. Majorities in Jordan, Morocco, and the United Arab Emirates (62 percent, 72 percent, and 58 percent, respectively,) said their opinion of the United States had deteriorated since 2004.[41]

Cross-Currents in Mass Opinion

A July 2005 Pew report found significant demographic differences in America's image in the Middle East. Young people and women tended to have the most favorable opinion of the United States (see tables 3–1 and 3–2). These generational and gender gaps were, with two exceptions, visible in all six Muslim countries surveyed. In Turkey, only 17 percent of those 35 and older viewed the United States favorably, compared to 29 percent of those between 18 and 34 years of age. While only 18 percent of Pakistanis age 35 and older had favorable opinions of the United States, the figure was 29 percent for those between the ages of 18 and 34. Women were also more likely to hold a positive opinion of the United States. Of the six countries surveyed, Pakistan had the largest gender gap: only 17 percent of men had a favorable view of America, compared to 28 percent of women.[42]

The first half of the present decade has seen a significant slippage in the degree of confidence that Middle Easterners have in the ability of the United States to deal effectively with regional problems. The deterioration of U.S. credibility is visible even from one year to the next. Pew 2005 survey returns for Indonesia, Pakistan, Turkey, Jordan, and Lebanon found that:

Table 3–1. **Views of the United States by Gender**

	Women (percent favorable)	Men (percent favorable)	Difference
Morocco	52	47	+5
Lebanon	46	39	+7
Indonesia	40	37	+3
Pakistan	28	17	+11
Turkey	25	21	+4
Jordan	20	21	-1

Source: Pew Global Attitudes Project, July 14, 2005.

Table 3–2. **Views of the United States by Age**

	Overall Percent Favorable	Age		Difference
		18–34	35+	
Morocco	49	53	45	+8
Lebanon	42	46	39	+7
Indonesia	38	36	40	-4
Pakistan	23	28	18	+10
Turkey	23	29	17	+12
Jordan	21	22	18	+4

Source: Pew Global Attitudes Project, July 14, 2005.

■ 50 to 66 percent did not agree that the world is safer without Saddam Hussein

■ 70 to 80 percent believed the world would be safer if another country rivaled the United States

■ 60 to 80 percent believed that the United States was a military threat to their country

■ only 12 to 31 percent support the war on terrorism, with post-tsunami Indonesia an outlier at 50 percent.[43]

In 2006, the findings were even starker. In Jordan, Turkey, and Egypt, 7 out of 10 respondents said the U.S. removal of Saddam Hussein had actually made the world more dangerous.[44]

On cultural issues, survey returns tend to support the anecdotal evidence. Thus, an overwhelming majority of respondents in Turkey, Indonesia, Pakistan, Lebanon, Jordan, Kuwait, Morocco, and Palestine think that the spread of American ideas to their country is bad (see figure 3–6).[45]

As an indication of how difficult such results are to interpret—or rather, how complex individual attitudes are to such issues—the same survey showed that, with the exception of Pakistan and Palestine, small majorities or large minorities in Turkey, Indonesia, Lebanon, Jordan, Kuwait, and Morocco agreed with the statement, "I like American music, movies, and television" (see figure 3–7).[46] Similarly, a 2002 Gallup poll of Saudis found that while more than half (54 percent) of all Saudis view the West's values as having had a negative influence on their society, 38 percent said the West produced enjoyable films and music.[47]

Figure 3–6. **Beliefs About Spread of American Ideas and Customs**

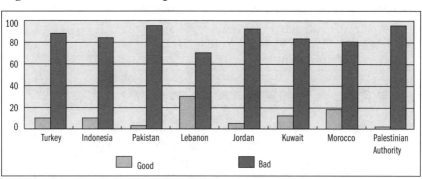

Source: Pew Global Attitudes Project 44-Major Nation Survey (2003) and 2003 21 Population Survey.

Figure 3–7. **Beliefs About American Music, Movies, and Television**

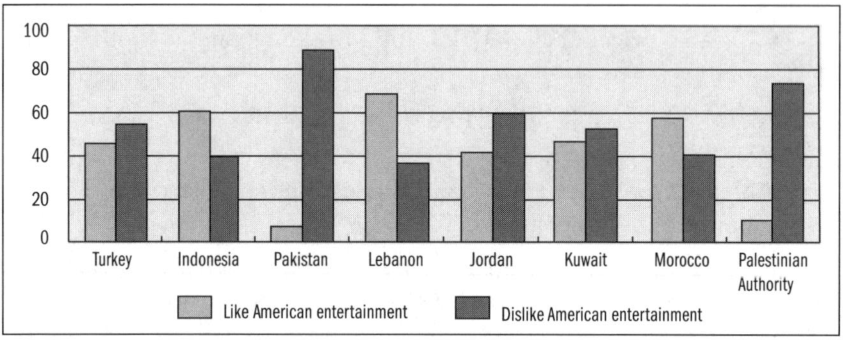

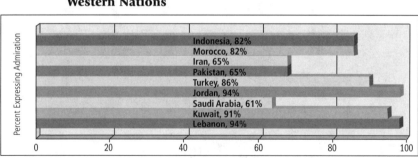

Source: Pew Global Attitudes Project 44-Major Nation Survey (2003) and 2003 21 Population Survey.

Poll results also corroborate the image of the United States as intrinsically violent. A 2002 Gallup poll found that more than 65 percent of Saudis thought America had a high crime rate. Two-thirds described the United States as aggressive, while almost half (43 percent) said the United States was a country easily provoked.[48] The same poll conducted a month later in Pakistan found similar results. A majority of Pakistanis described the United States as "ruthless" (65 percent), "easily provoked" (59 percent), and "aggressive" (54 percent).[49]

The sole positive trait associated with the United States by a majority of respondents in the nine countries surveyed by Gallup (Lebanon, Kuwait, Saudi Arabia, Jordan, Turkey, Pakistan, Iran, Morocco, and Indonesia) was America's level of scientific and technological achievement (see figure 3–8). But a majority of the respondents believed the United States was unwilling to share its technology with less developed or poorer nations.[50] Here too, however, there were demographic differences: those without any formal

Figure 3–8. **Beliefs About Technological Capabilities of Western Nations**

Source: Jeffrey M. Jones, "What Do Islamic World Residents Like About the West?" Gallup Poll Tuesday Briefing, May 28, 2002.

Figure 3-9. **Beliefs About American Ideas of Democracy**

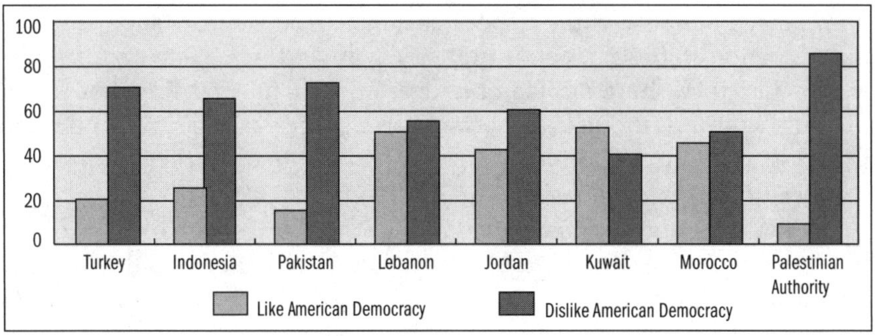

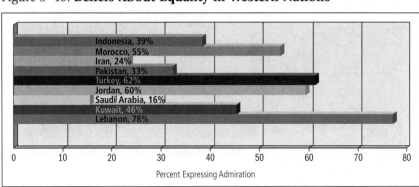

Source: Pew Global Attitudes Project 44-Major Nation Survey, 2002.

education were less likely to say that Western nations were technologically advanced, that they treat minorities in their societies fairly, or that they provide equality for their citizens.[51]

Attitudes toward American-style democracy, as reflected in the 2005 Pew returns, were equally complex. Kuwait was the only country where a majority, albeit a slight one, favored American democracy. In Lebanon and Morocco, respondents were split, with small majorities saying that they disliked American ideas about democracy. The remainder of the countries surveyed showed more widespread dislike: Turkey, 70 percent; Indonesia, 65 percent; Pakistan, 75 percent; Jordan, 60 percent; and Palestine, 85 percent (see figure 3-9).[52]

Similar results were visible in the 2002 Gallup poll, though there was greater variation among countries when it came to how Muslims viewed American democracy. Whereas only 16 percent of Saudis believed citizens in Western nations were guaranteed equality and other rights, the figure was 78 percent among the Lebanese (see figure 3-10).[53]

Figure 3-10. **Beliefs About Equality in Western Nations**

Source: Jeffrey M. Jones, "What Do Islamic World Residents Like About the West?" Gallup Poll Tuesday Briefing, May 28, 2002.

Polls also show that Muslims are skeptical of U.S. democracy efforts in the Middle East. The Zogby International/Telhami poll of October 2005 found that a majority of the respondents in the six countries surveyed (Jordan, Lebanon, Morocco, Saudi Arabia, Egypt, and the United Arab Emirates) believed Washington had objectives other than spreading democracy in Iraq. Two-thirds thought democracy was not the real objective, and more than half (58 percent) thought the war had resulted in a less, not more, democratic Iraq (see figures 3–11 and 3–12).[54]

Similar findings were revealed in the Pew 2006 report. In every country save one, a majority of respondents said they believed U.S. efforts to establish democracy in Iraq would fail: 66 percent in Jordan, 64 percent in

Figure 3–11. **Beliefs About U.S. Objectives in Advocating Democracy in the Middle East**

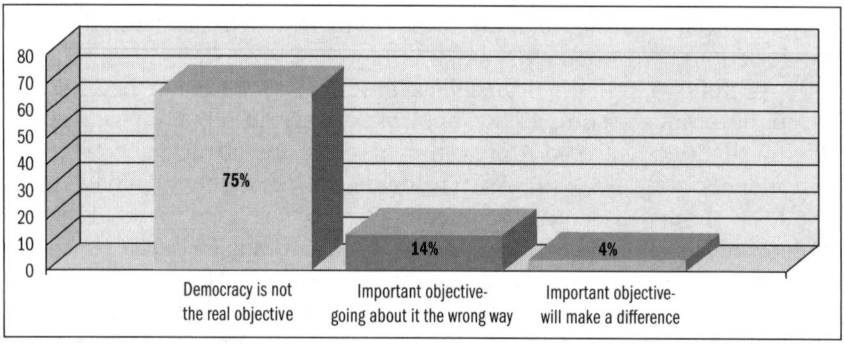

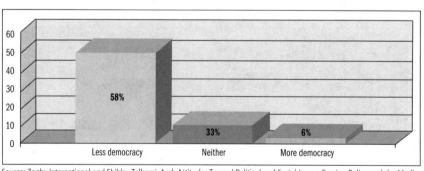

Source: Zogby International and Shibley Telhami, Arab Attitudes Toward Political and Social Issues, Foreign Policy, and the Media, available at <bsos.umd.edu/SADAT/PUB/Arab-attitudes-2005.htm>.

Figure 3–12. **Beliefs About the War in Iraq and the Spread of Democracy**

Source: Zogby International and Shibley Telhami, Arab Attitudes Toward Political and Social Issues, Foreign Policy, and the Media, available at <bsos.umd.edu/SADAT/PUB/Arab-attitudes-2005.htm>.

Figure 3–13. **Beliefs About Prospects for Success of Democracy in Iraq**

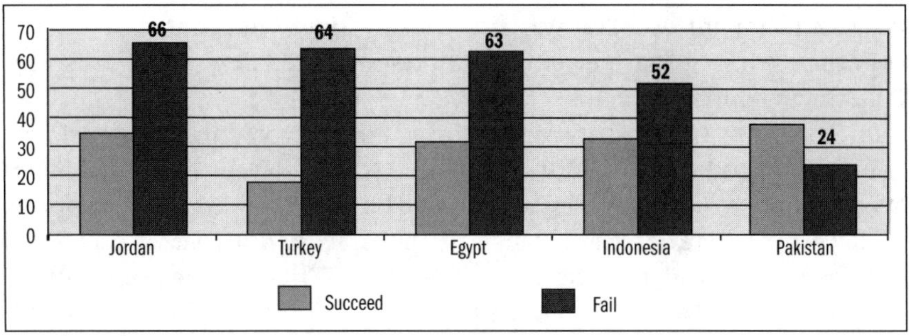

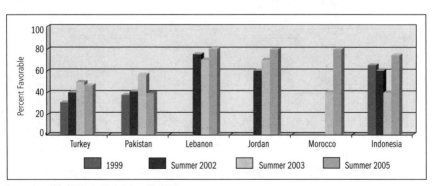

Source: Pew Global Attitudes Project, June 13, 2006.

Turkey, 63 percent in Egypt, and 52 percent in Indonesia. In Pakistan, 38 percent believed democracy would take root in Iraq (see figure 3–13).[55]

Nevertheless, Muslims overwhelmingly maintain positive views toward democracy in general. The 2005 Pew Global Attitudes Project poll found that the percentage of people who believed democracy could work in their countries was on the rise. In Jordan, where only 63 percent said they believed democracy could work at home in 2002, 80 percent thought so in 2005. Yet the Iraq war undoubtedly affected the poll's results. In Indonesia, the percentage of respondents surveyed expressing favorable opinions toward U.S.-style democracy dropped from a 1999 high of more than 60 percent to roughly 40 percent in 2003 (see figure 3–14).[56]

Much of the skepticism surrounding U.S. motives in the Middle East concerns Washington's relationship with Israel. A 2002 Gallup survey found that a majority of Saudis (65 percent) believed the United States adopts biased

Figure 3–14. **Muslim Attitudes Toward U.S.-Style Democracy**

Source: Pew Global Attitudes Project, June 23, 2005.

policies in world affairs. Fewer than 1 in 10 Saudis thought the West displayed "a lot" of concern for better coexistence with the Islamic world. Only 8 percent thought the West was fair in its dealings with Arab and Muslim countries, while just 6 percent felt the West dealt fairly with the Israeli-Palestinian conflict.[57]

The 2002 Gallup survey, conducted in nine predominantly Islamic countries, found only a handful of people who believed the United States acts fairly in its dealings with Palestinians. But the Palestinian issue appears to have much greater significance in the Arab nations surveyed—Saudi Arabia, Kuwait, Jordan, Lebanon, and Morocco—than in the non-Arab nations of Turkey, Pakistan, Iran, and Indonesia. Although an unfair stance toward the Palestinian situation was ranked high among the respondents' grievances, the United States was also perceived as being unfair toward the wider Arab/Islamic world. "Thus," Gallup's editors concluded, "it is not clear whether the Palestinian issue is the sole cause for the perception that Arabs and Muslims are treated unfairly, or whether the Palestinian issue is merely perceived as one example of many cases of unfair treatment."[58]

Many observers believed that in recent years, the war in Iraq had replaced the Arab-Israeli conflict as the prism through which Arabs viewed international events. However, this may once more be changing. In an interview conducted shortly after Hamas' surprise victory, Shibley Telhami told the Beirut *Daily Star*, "The Arabs in the past 2 years had already viewed the U.S. largely through the prism of pain of American policies in Iraq, which are almost all seen in negative terms. . . . Now attention is also shifting back to American policies in Palestine."[59]

Not surprisingly, therefore, on the policy-versus-values question, the Zogby International survey of Arab public opinion in 2002 concluded that

Figure 3–15. **Muslim Attitudes Toward U.S. Freedom and Democracy and U.S. Arab Policy**

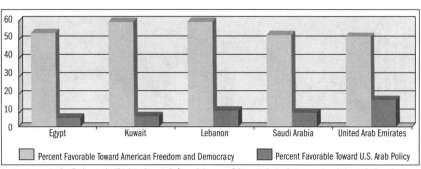

"What drives down Arab attitudes towards 'America' is, quite simply, the U.S. policy in the region" (see figure 3–15).[60]

Many Muslims appear dumbfounded by Washington's attempts to win them over through Arabic language radio and television stations. Writing in 2005 about U.S. public diplomacy efforts and the appointment of Karen Hughes as Undersecretary for Public Diplomacy, former Egyptian Foreign Minister Ahmad Mahir expressed this sentiment, saying:

> I firmly believe that these efforts and attempts will not achieve their purpose, because what is required is not publicity campaigns and the promotion of films that platonically express love and amity, or that promote good but unconvincing ideas—such as the claim, for instance, that the United States has fought for the sake of the Muslims and Arabs in Kosovo, Afghanistan, Bosnia, and Iraq—or that boast about providing aid to Muslim victims of the tsunami.

The problem does not lie in an image that some people are trying—as the Americans imagine—to distort. Nor does it lie in calling for lofty principles over which no two people would disagree. The problem lies in U.S. stands and behavior, which the United States must review, back down on, and amend if it genuinely wants to win the friendship of nations—instead of taking futile measures—until it finds the answer to the question: Why do they hate us? It is a question that has often been asked in Washington but the answers that were given to it were wrong; they came in the form of strange statements we have heard from senior officials who said, "They hate us because we are democratic, because we are progressive, and because we love freedom," and so on.[61]

The Zogby poll also asked respondents the question, "What can the United States do to improve its relations with the Arab world?" Although the responses were open-ended, certain themes consistently appeared, enabling the answers to be grouped into four broad categories: general values (promote freedom, justice, peace, etc.); approach to the Palestinian-Israeli conflict; relations with the Arab countries (respect Islam and Arabs, support Arab countries, withdraw American presence from Arab countries, etc.); and unspecified (other). The results indicate that a majority in every country (with the exception of Jordan) believe the United States can improve its image if it resolves the Israeli-Palestinian conflict and respects Arabs and Islam. A minority in each country wants the United States to take a more active part in promoting general values (see figure 3–16).[62]

The 2002 Gallup poll found that more exposure to the United States and Americans may not necessarily lead to better relations. The poll compared

Figure 3–16. **Beliefs About How the United States Can Improve Relations with the Arab World**

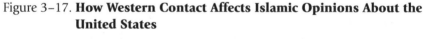

Source: James Zogby, "What Arabs Think: Values, Beliefs, and Concerns" (New York: Zogby International/The Arab Thought Foundation, 2002).

the level of exposure that residents of Islamic countries have to the United States with their opinions about the West. It found that while those exposed to Western culture tend to be more positive about the West than those without such exposure, the effects were modest and the difference often minimal. Gallup found that the effect was strongest in Iran, where those who know an emigrant to the West are four times more likely to rate the United States positively than those who do not. In some cases, exposure to the West negatively affected respondents' attitudes. For example, those with Internet access or those who knew a person who had emigrated to the

Figure 3–17. **How Western Contact Affects Islamic Opinions About the United States**

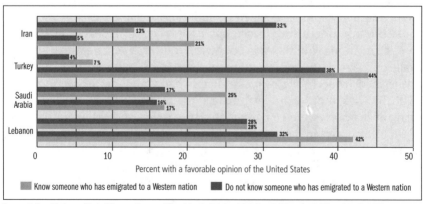

Source: Jeffrey M. Jones, "Does Western Contact Affect Islamic Opinions?" Gallup Poll Tuesday Briefing, May 7, 2002.

Figure 3–18. **Muslim Opinions About Americans as Individuals**

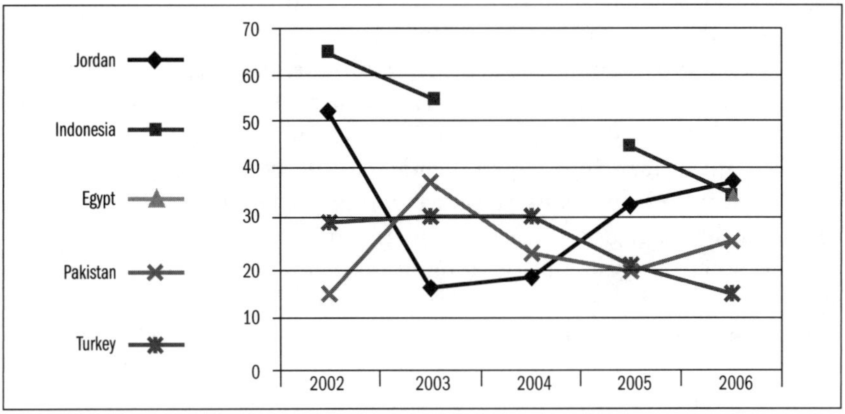

Source: Pew Global Attitudes Project, June 13, 2006.

West were more pessimistic with regard to whether Western nations and the Islamic world will ever understand each other better (see figure 3–17).[63]

Discerning differences in Muslim attitudes toward "America" and "Americans" is often difficult. In the past, however, while "America" may have been disliked, Americans as individuals generally received a higher rate of approval. The Pew 2006 findings, however, suggest this distinction may be disappearing. Favorable opinions of Americans took a hit in 2003 and although in many cases attitudes have since begun to recover, they remain well below pre–Iraq war levels. In Jordan, for example, where 53 percent had a very or somewhat favorable opinion of Americans in 2002, only 38 percent had so in 2006. In Indonesia and Turkey, those expressing positive views of Americans dropped by almost half in the 4-year period (see figure 3–18).

Surprisingly, however, one person whose approval ratings have not declined in the past few years is U.S. President George W. Bush. In Jordan, Egypt, Pakistan, and Indonesia, the percentage of respondents viewing Bush positively is on the rise, though his overall favorability rating is still quite low. Between 2003 and 2006, the number of people expressing much or some confidence in Bush's international leadership grew from 5 percent to 10 percent in Pakistan. Bush's approval rating also doubled in Indonesia from 10 percent to 20 percent over the same period, largely due to U.S. tsunami recovery and aid efforts.[64]

Conclusion

Muslim perceptions of the United States are complex. America is not universally despised within the Muslim world, nor do negative views of the United States necessarily crowd out favorable opinions about specific elements of American society or culture. Individual Muslims, like F. Scott Fitzgerald's intelligent friends, "have the ability to hold two opposing ideas in mind at the same time and still function."[65]

One striking aspect of the Muslim critique, however, is its similarity to negative images of the United States that have circulated within both Europe and the developing world for generations. America's alleged heedlessness, greed, rapacity, solipsism, materialism, coarseness, penchant for violence—indeed, its very size—have stirred the animosity of others for centuries, depending on the precise allegation.

Another intriguing factor is the overlap between the Islamist critique and the terms deployed by other religious traditions, especially evangelical Protestantism, to characterize American popular culture, such as a presumed decline in family values and the elevation of man-made law over the law of God. In this respect, one need only recall the controversy over Alabama's Chief Justice, Judge Roy Moore, who was removed from office in 2003 for refusing to relocate a massive sculpture of the Ten Commandments from the state Supreme Court building.[66] His commitment to this symbolic monument stemmed from a belief that domestic law in the United States was ultimately rooted in and legitimated by divine sanction. This position does not fundamentally differ from the Islamist claim that divine law supercedes human law and that the latter must be grounded in Shari'a if it is to be valid. It is worth noting that the idea that moral behavior is unsustainable in the absence of faith is increasingly common worldwide, with the significant exception of Western Europe. Even this exception is likely to be less stark in the coming years as demographic change increasingly introduces a Muslim perspective into broader European opinion on the role of religion in society and the formation of public policy.

The accusation of hypocrisy that Islamists as well as non-salafi Muslim critics level at the United States does have at least one singularly Islamic dimension that many non-Muslims might not recognize. The term for hypocrite, *munafik*, and other derivatives of the verb stem occur repeatedly in the Koran. It is a freighted word, with a harsher connotation of opprobrium than it carries in English. In the Koranic context, hypocrites are punished by eternal hellfire and are never forgiven by Allah for their hypocrisy.[67] Since the implementation of foreign policy frequently demands the subordination of personal moral principle to strategic interest where these two values conflict, the charge of hypocrisy will remain a feature of the Muslim anti-American repertory and continue to prove difficult to counter convincingly. American reliance on authoritarian regimes for cooperation against al Qaeda at the same time the United States advocates the spread of democracy is certain to reinforce this trend, as will U.S. rejection of democratically elected Islamist governments, such as Hamas in Palestine.

Another salient attribute of Muslim rhetoric about the United States is the way it combines hoary secular canards with Islamic motifs in a seamless web of vilification. The full text of the 2002 essay quoted earlier, "America that We Hate," by Tareq Hilmi, is a good example of the way the full gamut of political, cultural, and religious grievances can be interwoven to form an internally consistent argument that is relatively impervious to attack. The multifaceted nature of the anti-American case presents those attempting to change opinions about the United States with a serious challenge. The bewildering array of media outlets for anti-American rhetoric compounds the problem.

The anecdotal and survey data also confirm that U.S. support for Israel and corresponding disregard for Palestinian concerns, and the Iraq intervention, fuel anti-American sentiment.[68] Grievances stemming from these policies both validate and reinforce the view that the United States is nothing more than an instrument to advance the Jewish objective of controlling the world. Here, too, there would seem to be little scope for improvement given the way events are unfolding.

On a more positive note, the polling data suggest that humanitarian U.S. actions can have a powerful effect on Muslim opinion. The upturn in favorable opinion of the United States in Indonesia and Pakistan after the natural disasters that befell those countries in 2004 and 2005 was almost certainly due to the swift and generous American response. The key to this effect, however, lay not so much in the speed and scale of U.S. action, but in the local perception that the response had no strings attached. This perception undermined, at least briefly, the view of the United States as hypocritical and motivated solely by self-interest, rather than by a sincere regard for Muslims. (Those who regularly interact with Arab Muslims will have encountered the complaint that America has shown itself to be unworthy, even when it carries out actions that would seem to be good for Muslims, because it is ultimately acting not altruistically but merely in its own self-interest. This view can undercut the impact of U.S. policies that worked clearly to the benefit of Muslims, such as support for NATO's intervention in the Balkans.)

Nevertheless, the lesson here is that actions matter. When America's actions align with its professed values, opinions of the United States improve. However, the perceived gap between what the United States says and what it does, particularly in the Middle East, will keep America's standing in Muslim opinion low for the foreseeable future. In the meantime, the debate about whether Muslims oppose American actions or values will continue to cloud the issue. The data show that Muslims infer America's values from its actions. The categories of values and action, therefore, are not separate. Rather, they are connected organically and reciprocally in the eye of the beholder, especially if he or she is also the object of American action. And the current globalization of Muslim identity ensures that a growing number of Muslims take the travail of fellow Muslims in far-flung places to be their own.[69] To the extent that America's professed values and its actions are differentiated, views of America appear to suffer because the United States is seen to be performing in a manner that is inconsistent with—or a betrayal of—those traditional values.

Notes

[1] This essay focuses largely, but not exclusively, on Arab views. The intersection of Arab and non-Arab Muslim opinion has increased owing to the role of mass media, the Internet, and long haul travel in forging a globalized Muslim identity. Within this "imagined community" is a growing sense of shared destiny, purpose, and views of the other, particularly of the United States. On the emergence of imagined communities as "deep, horizontal comradeships," see the classic work of Benedict Anderson, *Imagined Communities: Reflections on the Origin and Spread of Nationalism*, rev. ed. (New York: Verso, 1991); with respect to Muslims, see Olivier Roy, *Globalized Islam: The Search for a New Ummah* (London: Hurst, 2004), 117–147, 197–200, and passim.

[2] Barry Rubin and Judith Colp Rubin, *Hating America* (New York: Oxford University Press, 2004), 10–11. The following précis of non-Muslim anti-Americanism owes much to the Rubins' sophisticated analysis.

[3] Britain withdrew from Aden in 1967 and from the sheikhdoms of Kuwait, Bahrain, Qatar, and the present-day United Arab Emirates in 1971.

[4] "Anti-Americanism in the Turkish Media," MEMRI Special Dispatch Series, no. 870, February 25, 2005, accessed at <memri.org/bin/articles.cgi?Page=subjects&Area=middleeast&ID=SP87005#_edn2>.

[5] "Decidedly there is something rotten in America . . . Meanwhile, don't be surprised if, from one end of Europe to the other, we scream: Watch out, America has rabies! We must cut all ties with it or else we shall be bitten and infected next." Cited in Michel Contat and Michel Rybalka, eds., *Les ecrits de Sartre* (Paris: Gallimard, 1970), 706–708.

[6] Steven Stalinsky, "Anti-American and Antisemitic Cartoons in Leading Egyptian Government Weekly Al-Ahram: 1998–2004," MEMRI Special Report no. 28, April 2, 2004, accessed at <memri.org/sr/sr2804.pdf>.

[7] The video is available at <pmw.org.il/asx/PMW_YaAmAraby.asx>. See also Alaa Shahine, "Singer takes a pop at Bush, Sharon," Al Jazeera, April 5, 2004, accessed at <english.aljazeera.net/NR/exeres/C1E56782-FEC7-40CD-B9EA-F8ADEE5AD3D4.htm>; and Nicole Veash, "Pop crooner hits sour note with Egyptian elite," *Christian Science Monitor*, January 18, 2002, accessed at <csmonitor.com/2002/0118/p01s04-wome.html>.

[8] "Syrian MP Dr. Muhammad Habash Denounces the American Culture of 'Violence' and 'Cruelty'," MEMRI Special Dispatch Series, no. 832, December 22, 2004, accessed at <memri.org/bin/articles.cgi?Page=subjects&Area=middleeast&ID=SP83204>.

[9] "Columnist in Turkish Islamic Daily: 'USA—the God-Damned Country'; 'Murdering is Genetically Ingrained in American Culture'," MEMRI Special Dispatch Series, no. 857, February 2, 2005, accessed at <memri.org/bin/articles.cgi?Page=subjects&Area=middleeast&ID=SP85705>.

[10] Daniel Williams, "Anti-Americanism a Hit with Egyptian Audiences," *The Washington Post*, August 20, 2004.

[11] Mohamed El-Assyouti, "The personal is political," *Al-Ahram Weekly*, no. 713 (October 21–October 27, 2004), accessed at <weekly.ahram.org.eg/2004/713/cu1.htm>.

[12] See <valleyofthewolvesiraq.com/web/indexb.htm>.

[13] "Iranian Pilgrims in Mecca at Anti-American Rally," MEMRI Special Dispatch Series, no. 1067, January 10, 2006, accessed at <memri.org/bin/articles.cgi?Page=archives&Area=sd&ID=SP106706>.

[14] Encyclopedia of Islam, 2^d ed., "Shaytan," 406–409.

[15] "Challenges Facing Islam—Iranian President Ahmadinejad," MEMRI Special Report, no. 39, January 5, 2006, accessed at <memri.org/bin/articles.cgi?Page=archives&Area=sr&ID=SR3906>.

[16] Bashar al-Asad, speech before the 10th Islamic Summit Conference Malaysia, October 15, 2003; Mohamad Mahathir, speech before the Islamic Summit Conference, October 15, 2003.

[17] As cited in Reuven Paz, "Islamists and anti-Americanism," *Middle East Review of International Affairs* 7, no. 4 (December 2003), accessed at <meria.idc.ac.il/journal/2003/issue4/jv7n4a5.html>.

[18] "Recent Anti-American Sermons by Palestinian Authority Preachers," MEMRI Special Dispatch Series, no. 844, January 11, 2005, accessed at <memri.org/bin/articles.cgi?Page=archives&Area=sd&ID=SP84405>.

[19] Saudi Arabia's ambassador to London at the time, Prince Turki al-Faisal, told the assembled diplomats: "Democracy or any semblance of wider participation will have to come from within societies," and he criticized Washington's refusal to recognize one of the region's only democratically elected leaders, Yasir Arafat. Iranian Foreign Minister Kamal Kharrazi told the assembled audience that the United States was not even-handed in pushing democracy. Reuters, "U.S. democracy drive 'hypocritical'," January 24, 2004.

[20] "Interview with Dr Abd-al-Aziz al-Duwayk, Speaker of the Palestinian Legislative Council," *Al-Quds*, April 16, 2006.

[21] Azam Khalil, "American hypocrisy: 'Hypocrisy is the homage which vice renders to virtue'," *The News*, December 14, 2005.

[22] "Iran's Ayatollah Khamene'i Addresses Palestinian Conference, Accuses U.S. of 'Plots'," IRNA, April 14, 2006.

[23] Bin Laden is cited in this article as an articulate expositor of preexisting Arab views of the United States, which he has validated and disseminated in a persuasive and robust manner.

[24] Bruce Lawrence, ed., *Messages to the World: The Statements of Osama bin Laden* (London: Verso, 2005), 67. The attack against Iraq that bin Laden refers to took place in November 1998 (Operation *Desert Fox*).

[25] "Iran's Ayatollah Khamene'i Addresses Palestinian Conference, Accuses U.S. of 'Plots'," IRNA, April 14, 2006.

[26] "Zionism, United States' Ruling Clique," *Jomhuri-ye Eslami*, May 22, 2006.

[27] Arif al-Agha, "The Bush Administration, the Complete Israelization," *Al-Thawrah*, October 19, 2003.

[28] Comments by Lt Gen (Ret.) Faiz Ali Chishti cited in Azam Zaidi, "Iraqis should fight guerrilla war: the U.S. will flee if only 1,000 troops are killed: Chishti," *Khabrain*, March 27, 2003.

[29] Abdel-Bari Atwan interview, Al Jazeera, October 12, 2003, cited in Abdallah, "Causes of Anti-Americanism in the Arab World: A Soci-political Perspective," 69–70.

[30] "Syrian Paper Commentary Says 'Oil' Main Motive for U.S. War on Iraq," *Al-Thawrah*, January 24, 2003.

[31] "Article Comments on Saddam Trial, Sees Oil as Motive Behind U.S. War on Iraq," *Al-Hayah al-Jadidah*, July 3, 2003.

[32] Rami Khouri, "On democracy, Arabs mistrust the American messenger," *Daily Star*, February 3, 2006, accessed at <zogby.com/soundbites/ReadClips.dbm?ID=12625>. For more on the Arab Attitudes Toward Political and Social Issues, Foreign Policy, and the Media Zogby/Telhami poll, see <bsos.umd.edu/sadat/pub/survey-2005.htm>.

[33] Dr. Tareq Hilmi, "Amrika alati nabghad (America That We Hate)," *Al-Sha'b*, October 17, 2003, accessed at <alarabnews.com/alshaab/GIF/17-10-2003/tareq.htm>.

[34] Lawrence, 167–170.

[35] Daniel Benjamin and Steven Simon, *The Age of Sacred Terror* (New York: Random House, 2003), 63–64.

[36] Pew Global Attitudes Project, "No Global Warming Alarm in the U.S., China; America's Image Slips, But Allies Share U.S. Concerns Over Iran, Hamas," June 13, 2006, 11, accessed at <pewglobal.org/reports/display.php?ReportID=252>.

37 "Global Attitudes Toward U.S. Foreign Policy," Brookings-Pew Research Center Briefing Transcript, June 13, 2006, 4.

38 Ibid., 8.

39 Ibid., 11.

40 Pew Global Attitudes Project, "U.S. Image Up Slightly, But Still Negative; American Character Gets Mixed Reviews," June 23, 2005, 4, 12, accessed at <pewglobal.org/reports/display.php?ReportID=247>.

41 "Poll: U.S. image in Arab countries deteriorates," Middle East Online, December 8, 2005, accessed at <zogby.com/soundbites/ReadClips.dbm?ID=12394>.

42 "Islamic Extremism: Common Concern for Muslim and Western Publics, Support for Terror Wanes Among Muslim Publics," Pew Global Attitudes Project, July 14, 2005, 14, accessed at <pewglobal.org/reports/pdf/248.pdf>.

43 Pew Global Attitudes Project, 27–31.

44 Pew Global Attitudes Project, "No Global Warming Alarm in the U.S., China; America's Image Slips, But Allies Share U.S. Concerns Over Iran, Hamas," June 13, 2006, 13.

45 Pew Global Attitudes Project 44-Nation Major Survey (2002), 136–137, accessed at <people-press.org/reports/pdf/185topline.pdf>. Note: Results for Pakistan, Lebanon, and Jordan are from the 2002 44-Nation Major Survey. All others are from the 2003 21 Population Survey.

46 Ibid., 139.

47 Richard Burkholder, "The U.S. and the West—Through Saudi Eyes," Gallup Poll Tuesday Briefing, August 6, 2002, 14.

48 Ibid., 13.

49 Richard Burkholder, "Despite Improved Ties, Pakistanis Cool to U.S.," Gallup Poll Tuesday Briefing, September 10, 2002, 38–39.

50 Jeffrey M. Jones, "What Do Islamic World Residents Like About the West?" Gallup Poll Tuesday Briefing, May 28, 2002, 87.

51 Ibid., 88.

52 Pew Global Attitudes Project 44-Nation Major Survey (2002), 137–138.

53 Jones, "What Do Islamic World Residents Like About the West?" 87.

54 Arab Attitudes Toward Political and Social Issues, Foreign Policy, and the Media, accessed at <bsos.umd.edu/SADAT/PUB/Arab-attitudes-2005.htm>.

55 Pew Global Attitudes Project, "No Global Warming Alarm in the U.S., China; America's Image Slips, But Allies Share U.S. Concerns Over Iran, Hamas," June 13, 2006, 14.

56 Pew Global Attitudes Project, "U.S. Image Up Slightly, But Still Negative; American Character Gets Mixed Reviews," June 23, 2005, 62.

57 Burkholder, "The U.S. and the West—Through Saudi Eyes," 14.

58 Lydia Saad, "Islamic Views of the U.S.: The Palestine Factor," Gallup Poll Tuesday Briefing, April 2, 2002, 10–11.

59 Khouri.

60 James Zogby, "What Arabs Think: Values, Beliefs, and Concerns" (New York: Zogby International/The Arab Thought Foundation, 2002), 64.

61 Ahmad Mahir, "Advice to Bush: Image Improvement Is Achieved by Policies, Not by Propaganda," Al-Sharq al-Awsat, April 3, 2005.

62 Zogby, 83–91.

63 Jeffrey M. Jones, "Does Western Contact Affect Islamic Opinions?" Gallup Poll Tuesday Briefing, May 7, 2002, 10–11.

64 Pew Global Attitudes Project, "No Global Warming Alarm in the U.S., China; America's Image Slips, But Allies Share U.S. Concerns Over Iran, Hamas," 11–12.

65 F. Scott Fitzgerald, The Crack-up, ed. Edmund Wilson (New York: New Directions Publishing, 1945).

66 "Ten Commandments Judge Removed from Office," CNN.Com, November 14, 2003, accessed at <cnn.com/2003/LAW/11/13/moore.tencommandments/>.

⁶⁷ Cf., "Al Munafikun," *The Encyclopedia of Islam*, vol. VII, 2ᵈ ed. (Leiden: E.J. Brill, 1993), 561–562.

⁶⁸ For a well-argued alternative assessment of the significance of the Palestine factor, see Michael Scott Doran, "Palestine Iraq and American Strategy," *Foreign Affairs* (January/February 2003), accessed at <foreignaffairs.org/20030101faessay10219/michael-scott-doran/palestine-iraq-and-american-strategy.html>.

⁶⁹ See Daniel Benjamin and Steven Simon, *The Next Attack* (New York: Henry Holt, 2005), 52–53, and Pew Global Attitudes Project, Final Topline, 2002, accessed at <people-press.org/reports/pdf/185topline.pdf>.

Chapter Four

Accessing Information in the Muslim World

C. Christine Fair

In the aftermath of the September 11 attacks on the World Trade Center and the Pentagon, the U.S. Government's awareness of the significance of public opinion in the Muslim world has been elevated, and courting Muslim publics has been deemed critical to U.S. national security. Efforts to address Muslim public opinion have taken different guises and different names such as *public diplomacy, perception management, information operations,* and *strategic communications.* (Despite the tendency to conflate these concepts, each has a specific intent and means to achieve its own objectives.) One of the earliest efforts following 9/11 was "Initiative 911," a mass-media strategy to influence Muslim opinion sponsored by Senator Joseph Biden (D–DE). In the preface, the authors write that "winning hearts and minds has become a national security imperative. Our foreign policy objectives require that we reach not just leaders but citizens a well. The 'Arab Street' threatens our anti-terrorism effort. . . . Hostility, even hatred, toward the U.S. in many Islamic countries is at an all-time high and growing."[1]

Although over 5 years have passed since the 9/11 attacks, confusion persists about the target of such communication initiatives. Is the target market the Muslim world? That term would refer, perhaps more imprecisely than those who use it intend, to the entirety of the global Muslim population, which is found in large numbers in more than 30 countries and scattered in smaller communities across numerous others. Muslim populations are concentrated in countries of the Middle East, sub-Saharan and North Africa, East Asia, the Caucasus and Eurasia, Central Asia, and South and Southeast Asia, not to mention the concentrations in smaller states that are not shown and the minority diaspora populations scattered around the globe (see table 4–1). While it has become common to equate the Islamic world with the Arab world, Indonesia and India are home to the world's largest and second largest Muslim communities, respectively. Bangladesh and Pakistan, two other non-Arab countries, have the next largest Muslim populations at about 140 million each. Or is the target market truly the "Arab street," rhetorical shorthand for one segment, albeit an important one, within the Muslim world? And does the Muslim world encompass the important diaspora Muslim population in Europe and the Americas?

The purpose of this chapter is to disaggregate what is often referred to as the *Muslim world* and to highlight both the similarities and differences in how the people who comprise it access the news and other information that shape attitudes toward the United States, U.S. policy, radical Islam, and terrorism. Countries that are predominantly Muslim or that have large Muslim minorities tend to have large youth cohorts ranging from 26 percent (for example, the United Arab Emirates, Qatar, and Bahrain) to 49 percent (such as Yemen, Somalia, and Mali), but otherwise they differ vastly in geographic size, in the size of the resident Muslim communities, and in the percentage of Muslims comprising the total population. They also differ in terms of national interests, sectarian beliefs, cultural and ethnic backgrounds, language, political alliances, level and complexity of political and economic development, and social organization. Finally, even within any given country, the Muslim communities are often diverse and heterogeneous.

Understanding how persons in the Muslim world access and consume information is a critical component of any strategic communications campaign. While knowing where people get their information is not tantamount to understanding how they form opinions, it is nevertheless an essential first step that must be taken before setting out to alter those people's views on the United States, Islamic extremism, and terrorism. While many varieties of data could be considered in this effort, we focus on such indicators as literacy and print capital as well as access to Internet, television, and radio, and the types of programming available on electronic mass media. Given the importance of American films in the international market, we also present limited data on access to such films in countries for which such data exist. Where possible, we have presented such available data for the countries noted in table 4–1.

Table 4–1. **Population Breakdown of Selected Muslim Countries, 2002**

Country	Total Population (millions)	Percent of Total Population Muslim	Percent of Population Under Age 15
Afghanistan	22.9	99	43
Algeria	31.3	99	34
Azerbaijan	8.3	93	30
Bahrain	0.7	100	29
Bangladesh	143.8	83	38
China	1,294.9	1–2	24
Djibouti	0.7	94	43
Egypt	70.5	94	35
Eritrea	4	No Data	46

Ethiopia	69	45–50	46
India	1,049.5	12	33
Indonesia	217.1	88	30
Iran	68.1	98	33
Iraq	24.5	97	41
Israel	6.3	14.6	28
Jordan	5.3	92	38
Kazakhstan	15.5	47	26
Kenya	31.5	10	42
Kuwait	2.4	85	26
Kyrgyzstan	5.1	75	33
Lebanon	3.6	56	30
Libya	5.4	97	31
Malaysia	24	No Data	33
Mali	12.6	90	49
Morocco	30.1	99	32
Nepal	24.6	4	40
Nigeria	120.9	50	45
Occupied Palestinian Territories*	3.4	78	46
Oman	2.8	75	37
Pakistan	149.9	97	42
Philippines	78.6	5	37
Qatar	0.6	95	27
Saudi Arabia	23.5	100	39
Somalia**	9.5	100	48
Sri Lanka	18.9	7	25
Sudan	32.9	70	40
Syria	17.4	74	38
Tajikistan	6.2	90	37
Tanzania	36.3	35	45
Thailand	62.2	3.8	26
Tunisia	9.7	98	29
Turkey	70.3	99.8	31
Turkmenistan	4.8	89	35
United Arab Emirates	2.9	96	26
Uzbekistan	25.7	88	34
Yemen**	19.3	100	49

Source: United Nations, *World Population Prospects 1950–2050: The 2002 Revision Population Database* (New York: Department of Economic and Social Affairs, Population Division, 2002).
* Combined percentage is derived from data from Gaza with a population of 1.1 million and 98.7 percent Muslim and the West Bank with 2 million people and 75 percent Muslim. The overall percentage is derived by taking the total Muslim population [1.1 million (98.7 percent) + (2 x 75 percent)] divided by the total population of 3.3 million.
** The United Nations assumes that these populations are 100 percent Muslim.

As will be apparent, the data available for analysis are not free of problems and limitations. In many cases, information simply is not available or is out of date. In other cases, useful information has been collected or made available about key states but is in some way incomplete. There are surprisingly few current open-source repositories for such information. As a result, this chapter cannot claim to provide to the fullest desirable extent the kind of empirical baseline on information access that an effective strategic communication campaign requires. Nevertheless, we have found important (albeit limited) data that go some distance to show how people in different countries access and consume information. Moreover, while what we have is not ideal, it does demonstrate that with adequate resources, such data can be collected. From a programmatic perspective, the analysis argues for a substantially greater U.S. investment in data sources that are more comprehensive, current, and inclusive of countries of strategic importance.

Our effort to detail what we know about the way that people in countries with either Muslim majorities or large Muslim minorities access and consume information will begin by looking at a series of metrics that reflect access to printed materials. This section takes into consideration literacy rates, the estimated "freedom of the press" in countries under analysis, as well as data on the availability of a specific kind of printed materials, daily and non-daily newspapers. We will then turn to estimates of access to the Internet in Muslim countries or those with large Muslim minorities. Next, we look at ownership of radios and televisions and survey the kinds of programming available to those who have access to television, including cable and satellite programming. We will conclude by considering some of the varied implications that arise from this exercise of looking at the data.

Accessing Printed Information

Table 4–2 has pulled together literacy rates for most of the countries identified in table 4–1 for which data are available.[2] According to the United Nations Development Program (UNDP), a literate person is one "who can, with understanding, both read and write a short, simple statement related to their everyday life." Literacy rates—to the extent that they are reliable—are a potential indicator of how many people in a given country can access simply written printed materials by themselves.

One of the first observations to make about these data is that most of the countries shown in table 4–2 (apart from Afghanistan, Iraq, and Somalia, for which no data are available) have adult literacy rates that are over 75 percent. Only 14 countries (Yemen, Bangladesh, Ethiopia, Pakistan, Morocco, Egypt, Eritrea, Sudan, India, Djibouti, Nigeria, Algeria, Tunisia, and Oman) have literacy rates below 75 percent. Another 14 (Iran, Tanzania, United Arab

Table 4–2. **Literacy Rates in Selected Muslim Countries, 2002**

Country	Adult Literacy Rate (percent, over age 15)			Youth Literacy Rate (percent, below age 15)		
		Female	Male		Female	Female rate as percent, of male rate
Algeria	68.9	59.6	78	89.9	85.6	91
Azerbaijan*	98.8	98.2	99.5	99.9	99.9	99.9
Bahrain	88.5	84.2	91.5	98.6	98.9	100
Bangladesh	41.1	31.4	50.3	49.7	41.1	71
Brunei	93.9	91.4	96.3	99.1	99.3	100
Djibouti	65.5	55.5	76.1	N/A	N/A	N/A
Egypt	55.6	43.6	67.2	73.2	66.9	85
Eritrea	56.7	45.6	68.2	N/A	N/A	N/A
Ethiopia	41.5	33.8	49.2	57.4	51.8	82
India	61.3	46.4	69	98	N/A	N/A
Indonesia	87.9	83.4	92.5	98	97.6	98.5
Iran	77.1	70.4	83.5	N/A	N/A	N/A
Iraq	...	N/A	N/A	99.4	N/A	N/A
Jordan	90.9	85.9	95.5	99.8	99.5	100
Kazakhstan	99.4	99.2	99.7	95.8	99.8	100
Kenya	84.3	78.5	90	93.1	95.1	99
Kuwait	82.9	81	84.7	93.1	93.9	102
Kyrgyzstan**	97	N/A	N/A	92.1	N/A	N/A
Lebanon	86.5	81	92.4	97	N/A	N/A
Libya	81.7	70	91.8	97.2	94	94
Malaysia	88.7	85.4	92	69.5	97.3	100
Morocco	50.7	38.3	63.3	88.6	61.3	79
Nigeria	66.8	59.4	74.4	N/A	86.5	95
Occupied Palestinian Territories	90.2	N/A	N/A	98.5	N/A	N/A
Oman	74.4	65.4	82	53.9	97.3	98
Pakistan	41.5	28.5	53.4	95.1	42	64
Philippines	92.6	92.7	92.5	94.8	95.7	101
Qatar	84.2	82.3	84.9	93.5	95.8	102
Saudi Arabia	77.9	69.5	84.1	N/A	91.6	96
Somalia	N/A	N/A	N/A	79.1	N/A	N/A
Sudan	59.9	49.1	70.8	95.2	74.2	88
Syria	82.9	74.2	91	99.8	93	96

Tajikistan	99.5	99.3	99.7	91.6	99.8	100
Tanzania	77.1	69.2	85.2	98	89.4	95
Thailand	92.6	90.5	94.9	94.3	97.8	100
Tunisia	73.2	63.1	83.1	95.5	90.6	93
Turkey	86.5	78.5	94.4	99.8	93.2	95
Turkmenistan	98.8	98.3	99.3	99.7	99.8	100
United Arab Emirates	77.3	80.7	75.6	99.7	95	108
Uzbekistan	99.3	98.9	99.6	67.9	99.6	100
Yemen	40.0	28.5	69.5	N/A	50.9	60

Source: Most data are taken from United Nations Development Program (UNDP). See "Statistics" at <http://hdr.undp.org/statistics/>.
N/A: Not available.
*For some countries for which UNDP does not publish data, we have turned to other sources such as UNESCO. For example, for Azerbaijan, we used data from UNESCO Institute for Statistics, which employs an unspecified definition of literacy.
* *Note that the youth literacy rate for Kyrgyzstan is from 1990. No recent data are available.

Emirates, Saudi Arabia, Libya, Kuwait, Syria, Qatar, Kenya, Lebanon, Turkey, Indonesia, Bahrain, and Malaysia) have literacy rates between 75 and 90 percent. Eleven (Palestinian Territories, Jordan, Philippines, Thailand, Brunei, Azerbaijan, Kyrgyzstan, Turkmenistan, Uzbekistan, Kazakhstan, and Tajikistan) have literacy rates that exceed 90 percent. In most cases, youth literacy rates exceed those of adults. These data suggest that most residents in most countries can understand basic printed materials in their mother tongue or national language. But they also suggest that print media may not be the best way of reaching people in some of the key problem countries, such as Yemen, Pakistan, Egypt, and Sudan.

Print Media: Daily and Non-Daily Newspapers

Data on the accessibility and circulation of print media (daily and non-daily papers) within those Muslim countries for which data exist are available from the United Nations Education, Scientific, and Cultural Organization (UNESCO). While they are the most comprehensive and current publicly available nonproprietary data of this kind, there are serious gaps in their coverage. Table 4–4 depicts both the number of daily paper titles available between 1997 and 2000 and the circulation of such papers per 1,000 persons. Table 4–5 does the same for non-daily papers. For purposes of comparability, we have included data for countries that are both identified in table 4–1 and for which UNESCO has published such information.

Several cautionary notes must be made about these data on newspaper circulation. First, circulation figures certainly underestimate actual levels of readership. This is because in some countries under study, more than one person usually reads the same copy of the paper, especially where newspapers are relatively expensive in the context of the local economy or are difficult to obtain. In addition, in some countries, papers are commonly read aloud in social gatherings, which further expands the effective circulation.

A second point is that, while prima facie these circulation figures may index a diversity of sources of information, simply looking at the number of such titles and their circulation may be misleading. In many of the countries under study here, official or self-imposed censorship may restrict all newspapers to expressing the same basic points of view. Thus, extensive use of data of this kind should probably be preceded both by a review of censorship (official and self-imposed) in the country in question and, if possible, a content analysis of key papers to determine if the wide variety of papers implies an actual diversity of views. While such a comprehensive effort is

Table 4–3. **Freedom House Press Freedom Rankings, 2005**

Country	Ranking	Status
Philippines	35	Partly Free
India	38	Partly Free
Thailand	42	Partly Free
Turkey	48	Partly Free
Nigeria	52	Partly Free
Indonesia	58	Partly Free
Lebanon	60	Partly Free
Kenya	61	Not Free
Pakistan	61	Not Free
Jordan	62	Not Free
Morocco	63	Not Free
Algeria	64	Not Free
Egypt	68	Not Free
Ethiopia	68	Not Free
Malaysia	69	Not Free
Kyrgyzstan	71	Not Free
Oman	72	Not Free
Iran	80	Not Free
Tunisia	80	Not Free
Palestinian Autonomous Territories	84	Not Free
Libya	95	Not Free
Turkmenistan	96	Not Free

Source: *Freedom House, Freedom of the Press 2005* DRAFT Country Reports, "Table of Global Press Freedom Rankings" (New York: Freedom House, 2005), available at <freedomhouse.org/research/pressurvey.htm>.

beyond the scope of this chapter, table 4-3 summarizes Freedom House's assessment of the freedom of the press for those countries detailed herein.[3] Freedom House examined 194 countries and territories and assessed the degree to which their governments permit the free flow of information. Based upon a scoring scheme developed by Freedom House, the media of each country is classified as "Free" (scoring 0 to 30), "Partly Free" (scoring 31 to 60) or "Not Free" (61 to 100).[4] As the data in table 4-3 demonstrate, only 7 of the 22 countries included in these data tables are classified as "Partly Free," while the others are all classified as "Not Free."

With these caveats about the utility of these metrics, we next examine the data for daily papers for 1999 (the year with the most complete data). These data are available in table 4-4. The range on the number of titles is surprising. Turkmenistan, Kyrgyzstan, the Palestinian Territories, Kenya, and Jordan have five or fewer daily titles each, and all of these states have media that are considered "Not Free" by Freedom House. Lebanon, Egypt, and Morocco all have between a dozen and two dozen dailies. Iran has over 105, Indonesia 225, Pakistan 352, and Turkey has 560. Based on 1998 data, India has over 5,000 dailies in circulation. Despite having media that are classed as "Not Free," Iran and Pakistan have some of the highest numbers of daily papers in circulation.

However, the number of titles is not the best measure of penetration of print media. For this, we turn to a notion of circulation that is standardized for the population: total average circulation (or copies printed) per 1,000 inhabitants. Using this measure, Lebanon (classified as "Not Free") had the highest standardized circulation in 1999, with nearly 66 copies per 1,000 persons. Turkmenistan, also classified as "Not Free," had the lowest, with fewer than 6 copies per 1,000 persons.

These data also illuminate a discord between availability of print media and literacy. For instance, Turkmenistan's relative paucity of per capita newspapers is somewhat counterintuitive given that the country has one of the highest reported adult literacy rates of 98.8 percent, well above Lebanon's 86.5 percent. Similarly, "Partly Free" India has one of the highest circulation figures for daily papers (using 1998 data) while having one of the lowest literacy rates.

Turning to the 1999 figures for non-daily newspapers in table 4-5, the Palestinian Territories and Kenya (both considered "Not Free") have the fewest, with 10 non-daily titles each. Jordan and Turkmenistan (also "Not Free") both have fewer than two dozen. Egypt has 45, Kyrgyzstan has 164—both of which are classed as "Not Free." Indonesia, Pakistan, Morocco, Turkey, and Iran all have several hundred. India (using 1998 data) publishes over 38,000 non-daily papers. Only India and Indonesia are deemed "Partly Free," while the rest are considered "Not Free." Turning to standardized circulation, the

Table 4–4. **Daily Newspapers: Number of Titles and Circulation**

Status	Country	Number of Titles				Total Average Circulation (or Copies Printed) per 1,000 Inhabitants			
		1997	1998	1999	2000	1997	1998	1999	2000
Not Free	Algeria	18	24	N/A	N/A	26.38	27.18	N/A	N/A
Not Free	Egypt	14	15	16	N/A	32.8	35.75	31.28	N/A
Not Free	Ethiopia	2	2	N/A	N/A	0.38	0.37	N/A	N/A
Partly Free	India	5,044	5,221	N/A	N/A	48.09	60.04	N/A	N/A
Partly Free	Indonesia	81	172	225**	396**	24.5	22.89	22.91	N/A
Not Free	Iran	N/A	N/A	105	112	N/A	N/A	N/A	N/A
Not Free	Jordan	8	8	5	5	76.24	74.23	N/A	N/A
Not Free	Kenya	4*	4*	4**	N/A	9.2	9.1	8.34	N/A
Not Free	Kyrgyzstan	N/A	N/A	3	3	N/A	N/A	N/A	N/A
Partly Free	Lebanon	N/A	13**	14**	13**	N/A	63.39	65.81	63.25
Not Free	Libya	4*	4*	N/A	N/A	14.39	14.12	N/A	N/A
Not Free	Malaysia	33	33**	N/A	31**	105.31	113.22	N/A	95.26
Not Free	Morocco	21	22	22	23	23.67	25.37	25.42	29.06
Partly Free	Nigeria	25*	25*	N/A	N/A	26.04	25.41	N/A	N/A
Not Free	Oman	5	5	N/A	N/A	N/A	N/A	N/A	N/A
Not Free	Pakistan	359	303**	352	306**	29.71	N/A	39.99	39.26
Not Free	Palestinian Autonomous Territories	N/A	N/A	3	3	N/A	N/A	N/A	N/A
Partly Free	Philippines	42	N/A	N/A	N/A	66.05	N/A	N/A	N/A
Partly Free	Thailand	N/A	34**	N/A	N/A	74.33	196.89	N/A	N/A
Not Free	Tunisia	N/A	N/A	N/A	7	N/A	N/A	N/A	18.91
Partly Free	Turkey	980	960	560	542	N/A	N/A	N/A	N/A
Not Free	Turkmenistan	N/A	N/A	2	2	N/A	N/A	5.81	6.79

Source: UNESCO Institute for Statistics, Culture, and Communications Statistics. These series are the most current available and can be accessed at <uis.unesco.org/ev.php?URL_ID=5208&URL_DO=DO_TOPIC&URL_SECTION=201>.
N/A: Not available.
* National estimation.
**Source: World Association of Newspapers.

"Not Free" Palestinian Territories are notable for having the highest non-daily paper circulation (over 526 copies per 1,000 persons.) "Not Free" Kenya and Pakistan are among the lowest with 3.67 and 12.82 per 1,000 persons respectively. "Not Free" Egypt's circulation is about 21 copies per 1,000, and Indonesia's is 37 per 1,000. "Not Free" Turkmenistan has

Table 4–5. **Non-Daily Newspapers: Number of Titles and Circulation**

Status	Country	Number of Titles				Total Average Circulation (or Copies Printed) per 1,000 Inhabitants			
		1997	1998	1999	2000	1997	1998	1999	2000
Not Free	Algeria	64	82	N/A	N/A	43.9	31.01	N/A	N/A
Not Free	Egypt	46	47	45	N/A	22.96	22.2	20.62	N/A
Not Free	Ethiopia	85	78	N/A	N/A	5.57	6.45	N/A	N/A
Partly Free	India	36,661	38,607	N/A	N/A	61.35	68.99	N/A	N/A
Partly Free	Indonesia	94	433	425*	746*	25.26	38.07	37.17	N/A
Not Free	Iran	N/A	N/A	843	906	N/A	N/A	N/A	N/A
Not Free	Jordan	13	13	17	20	33.55	32.69	N/A	N/A
Not Free	Kenya	N/A	N/A	10*	N/A	N/A	N/A	3.67	N/A
Not Free	Kuwait	N/A	N/A	N/A	N/A	N/A	N/A	N/A	N/A
Partly Free	Kyrgyzstan	N/A	N/A	164	181	N/A	N/A	N/A	N/A
Not Free	Lebanon	N/A	N/A	N/A	7	N/A	N/A	N/A	N/A
Not Free	Malaysia	3	N/A	N/A	N/A	14.56	N/A	N/A	N/A
Not Free	Morocco	807	693	581	507**	122.25	144.22	130.04	141.12
Partly Free	Pakistan	681	N/A	560	N/A	N/A	N/A	12.82	N/A
Not Free	Palestinian Autonomous Territories	N/A	N/A	10	13	N/A	N/A	526.01	644.95
Not Free	Philippines	47	N/A	N/A	N/A	2.79	N/A	N/A	N/A
Not Free	Sudan	11	11	N/A	N/A	192.01	187.76	N/A	N/A
Partly Free	Tunisia	N/A	N/A	N/A	29	N/A	N/A	N/A	98.71
Partly Free	Turkey	400	425	610	688	N/A	N/A	N/A	N/A
Not Free	Turkmenistan	N/A	N/A	23	22	N/A	N/A	64.48	72.86

Source: UNESCO Institute for Statistics, Culture, and Communications Statistics. These series are the most current available and can be accessed at http://www.uis.unesco.org/ev.php?URL_ID=5208&URL_DO=DO_TOPIC&URL_SECTION=201. Last accessed April 26, 2005.
N/A: Not available.
* Source: World Association of Newspapers. Data does not include newspapers published on Sundays only.
**Data does not include non-dailies issued 2 or 3 times a week.

64 copies per 1,000, and "Not Free" Morocco has 130. Many of the contradictory findings of the analysis of daily papers regarding literacy and degrees of media freedom obtain here as well.

We also sought to provide some information about which papers circulate most widely, either in terms of numbers of readers or geographic scope. Nonproprietary and public-use data on these issues are not comprehensive, but data provided to the authors by the World Association of Newspapers, which collects information about the world's highest-circulating newspapers, cast some light. These 100 papers are published in 16 countries and 19 languages, detailed in tables 4–6 and 4–7. There are only two Muslim majority states that publish one of the world's largest 100 papers (Egypt and Pakistan). Arabic is ranked twelfth out of 19 languages in which such papers are published and Urdu (used in Pakistan and in India) nineteenth. Bengali, a language used in both India and in Bangladesh, is ranked 13 of 19. However, it is not possible from these data to know if Indian-origin papers have extensive circulation in Bangladesh or if Pakistan-origin papers in Urdu are readily available in India. India, ranked third of 16 countries in the number of highest-circulating newspapers, has several other languages in the list of 19. Again, from the data available, it is not possible to determine which, if any, of these papers have substantial readership among India's Muslims. The same holds for other countries, such as China and Thailand, with several of the world's top 100 dailies and with small Muslim populations.

These discordant findings between freedom of the media, literacy rates, and availability of newspapers may cast doubt on the reliability of literacy statistics (which are often government-furnished), circulation figures, and

Table 4–6. **Countries Producing the World's 100 Largest Daily Newspapers**

Ranking	Country	Number of Top 100 Dailies
1	China	23
2	Japan	21
3	India	17
4	United States of America	8
5	Taiwan	5
6	Thailand	5
7	United Kingdom	5
8	Germany	3
9	Republic of Korea	3
10	Russia	3
11	Italy	2
12	Austria	1
13	Egypt	1
14	France	1
15	The Netherlands	1
16	Pakistan	1

Source: World Association of Newspapers, *World Press Trends 2005.*

Table 4–7. **Languages in Which the World's 100 Largest Daily Newspapers are Published**

Ranking	Language	Number of Top 100 Dailies
1	Chinese	28
2	Japanese	21
3	English	16
4	Hindi	6
5	Thai	5
6	German	4
7	Korean	3
8	Russian	3
9	Gujarati	2
10	Italian	2
11	Malayalam	2
12	Arabic	1
13	Bengali	1
14	Dutch	1
15	French	1
16	Marathi	1
17	Tamil	1
18	Telugu	1
19	Urdu	1

Source: World Association of Newspapers, *World Press Trends 2005*.

even upon the methodology used by Freedom House to assess media freedom. These data may also suggest that literacy rates should not be used as a simple proxy for the ease with which persons can access printed literature. Nor should published literacy rates be understood to correlate with published indicators of access to established daily and non-daily papers, which is somewhat counterintuitive. Similarly, circulation figures and the numbers of newspapers available should not be seen as a proxy for media freedom.

Internet Usage

Internet usage rates are difficult to determine with any accuracy because of the multitude of methods to access the Internet, including personal computers at home; at schools, workplaces, and research organizations; and via public computing facilities such as Internet cafes. Moreover, definitions of an Internet user per se may differ. Nua.com has compiled data on the penetration of the Internet across the world, despite these challenges. Nua.com data are reproduced in table 4–8 for countries identified in table 4–1. As these data suggest, access to the Internet varies dramatically across the selection of Muslim countries and ones with sizeable numbers of Muslims, such as India. In terms of sheer market size, Israel and the countries of South and Southeast Asia tend to dominate, with millions of Internet users each. Among the states in the Middle East other than Israel, Egypt and Saudi Arabia dominate with nearly 2.5 million users each. The United Arab Emirates, Turkey, and Iran also have large numbers of users, with 900,000, 728,000, and 420,000, respectively.

If we look at usage as a percentage of the overall population, a different ranking of Internet penetration appears: in half of the 46 countries detailed in table 4–8, Internet users are less than 1 percent of the overall population. In another 7 countries, Internet users comprise between 1 and 5 percent of the total population. In 7 countries, Internet users make up between 5 and 10 percent of the population. In 3 countries, they comprise between 10 and 20 percent of the population. Only in 4 countries (Bahrain, United Arab Emirates, Malaysia, and Israel) do users comprise more than 20 percent of the overall population.

Internet cafés are a growing means of accessing the Internet. For example, in Indonesia, warnets (Indonesia's version of the Internet café) have become a popular means of using the Internet among those who cannot afford the hardware or service provider charges. According to the U.S. Embassy in Jakarta, there are over 2,000 warnets covering both urban and rural areas.[5] Moreover, a recent A.C. Nielsen poll found that some 52 percent of all of Indonesia's Internet users access it at warnets. (Thirty-two percent access it at work, 28 percent at school, and 9 percent at a friend's home. Only 6 percent accessed the net at their own homes.) The success of the warnet has spurred the owners of telephone kiosks to add Internet access to their suite of operations.[6] As a perusal of travel guides for countries in the Muslim world demonstrates, Internet cafés are readily available even in remote places. However, while very inexpensive for expatriates, Internet café charges remain quite high by the local economic standards of the countries in question.[7]

Television and Radio Ownership

UNESCO publishes data on the number of television and radio receivers in selected Muslim countries per 1,000 persons from 1970 to 1997. In many countries in our survey, households include multiple nuclear families, so the number of potential viewers per household is considerably larger than would be the case in many Western countries. In addition, in many countries, there are kiosks or small storefronts where people

Table 4–8. **Internet Usage for Selected Muslim and Middle Eastern Countries**

Nation	Population (millions)	Internet Users (millions)	Percent of Population	Internet Service Providers
Afghanistan	29.93	N/A	N/A	1
Algeria	32.53	0.18	0.55	2
Azerbaijan	7.91	0.03	0.32	2
Bahrain	0.69	0.14	20.37	1
Bangladesh	144.32	0.15	0.10	10
Brunei	0.37	0.04	9.40	2
China	1,310	99.80	7.62	3
Djibouti	0.48	0.00	0.69	1
Egypt	77.51	2.42	3.12	50
Eritrea	4.56	0.01	0.22	5
Ethiopia	73.05	0.02	0.03	1
India	1,080	36.97	3.42	43
Indonesia	241.97	12.86	5.31	24
Iran	68.02	0.42	0.62	8
Iraq	26.07	0.01	0.05	1
Israel	6.28	3.13	49.84	21
Jordan	5.76	0.21	3.68	5
Kazakhstan	15.19	0.10	0.66	10
Kenya	33.83	0.50	1.48	65
Kuwait	2.34	0.20	8.55	3
Kyrgyzstan	5.15	0.52	10.02	N/A
Lebanon	3.83	0.30	7.83	22
Libya	5.77	0.02	0.35	1
Malaysia	24.00	10.04	41.83	7
Mali	12.29	0.03	0.24	13
Malta	0.40	0.06	14.80	6
Morocco	32.72	0.40	1.22	8
Nigeria	128.77	0.10	0.08	11
Oman	3.00	0.12	4.00	1
Pakistan	162.42	1.20	0.74	30
Philippines	87.86	5.96	6.78	33
Qatar	0.86	0.08	8.69	1
Saudi Arabia	26.42	2.54	9.61	42
Somalia	8.59	0.00	0.00	3
Sri Lanka	20.06	0.12	0.61	5
Sudan	40.19	0.06	0.14	2

Syria	18.45	0.06	0.33	1
Tajikistan	7.16	0.01	0.07	4
Tanzania	36.77	0.30	0.82	6
Thailand	65.44	7.57	11.57	15
Tunisia	10.07	0.40	3.97	1
Turkey	69.66	7.27	10.44	50
Turkmenistan	4.95	0.00	0.04	N/A
United Arab Emirates	2.56	0.90	35.16	1
Uzbekistan	26.85	0.10	0.37	42
Yemen	20.73	0.02	0.08	1

Source: Central Intelligence Agency *World Fact Book 2005*, available at <cia.gov/cia/publications/factbook/>.
N/A: Not available.

collectively watch television.[8] These data are presented in tables 4–9 and 4–10. What is obvious from these tables is that there is a wide spread in terms of the television and radio ownership in the surveyed countries.

In 1997, the most recent year for which UNESCO reported data, Afghanistan, Pakistan, and Yemen had the lowest availability of televisions (13, 22, and 29 per 1,000 respectively). At the other extreme were Oman, Kuwait, and Bahrain with 694, 505, and 472 television receivers per 1,000 respectively.

Looking at trends in television penetration between 1970 and 1997, vast differences are once again observed among the countries. Growth in this time period was lowest among the states of Southwest Asia, which averaged an 85 percent increase in per capita ownership of sets.[9] Growth was highest in the countries of South Asia (where it almost doubled)[10] and Southeast Asia (a 92 percent increase). In the North African states (Algeria, Egypt, Libya, Morocco, and Sudan), television ownership grew by 89 percent on average over the course of the decade. Despite these past growth rates, however, penetration rates appear to be leveling off in nearly every country.

As shown in table 4–10, the countries with the highest density of radios per 1,000 population in 1997 were Lebanon (907), Oman (607), and Bahrain (580). The countries with the lowest figures were Yemen (64), Pakistan (94), India (120), and Afghanistan (132). Again, the contrast from one part of the Muslim world to another is striking. Moreover, the countries with the lowest availability of television sets also rank among the lowest in the availability of radio receivers. Nevertheless, in some of these countries, such as Afghanistan, radio may still be the most effective way to reach audiences given both the limited availability of television broadcast service and the low literacy rates.

Table 4–9. **Television Receivers per 1,000 People for Selected Countries, 1970–1997**

	1970	1975	1980	1985	1990	1995	1996	1997
Yemen	N/A	N/A	N/A	N/A	26	28	29	29
United Arab Emirates	N/A	50	88	84	90	104	133	134
Turkey	11	26	79	182	232	309	330	330
Syria	19	30	44	57	60	67	69	70
Saudi Arabia	87	110	219	244	246	257	260	262
Pakistan	1.5	5.1	11	13	17	20	21	22
Oman	N/A	2.8	31	632	633	673	682	694
Malaysia	12	37	87	115	148	164	170	172
Lebanon	105	148	281	300	344	366	373	375
Kuwait	134	149	257	372	383	503	510	505
Jordan	20	46	59	58	68	75	81	82
Iraq	37	38	50	59	72	80	82	83
Iran	19	45	51	55	64	69	71	71
Indonesia	0.7	2.2	20	38	57	66	67	68
India	0.1	0.8	4.4	13	32	50	61	65
Brunei	39	87	135	202	233	238	249	250
Bahrain	59	110	259	411	425	466	470	472
Afghanistan	N/A	N/A	2.8	6.9	9.3	10	12	13
Sudan	3.2	6.2	43	51	75	84	85	86
Morocco	13	31	46	63	77	96	114	115
Libya	0.5	35	61	62	99	111	134	140
Egypt	15	16	32	78	101	110	118	119
Algeria	29	31	52	69	74	89	104	105

Source: *1999 UNESCO Statistical Yearbook* (UNESCO Publishing and Berman Press, 1999).

Looking at the trend line between 1970 and 1997 in these countries, growth in radio penetration in the North African states was the lowest (47 percent) and highest in South Asia (62 percent)[11] and Southeast Asia (59 percent). Growth in radio penetration in Southwest Asia was 55 percent.[12] As is the case with television penetration, growth rates appear to have leveled off by the end of this time series.

These data may suggest that different mixes of radio and television are necessary to reach target audiences in these varied countries. One critical piece of data needed to develop an appropriate mix of programming is how users of television and radio trade off time across these technologies. Detailed knowledge of how different household members use television and

Table 4–10. **Radio Receivers per 1,000 People for Selected Countries, 1970–1997**

	1970	1975	1980	1985	1990	1995	1996	1997
Yemen	N/A	N/A	N/A	N/A	27	43	64	64
United Arab Emirates	135	198	236	245	268	272	354	355
Turkey	101	105	113	139	160	163	176	178
Syria	187	188	195	212	254	264	275	278
Saudi Arabia	122	131	260	280	290	301	319	321
Pakistan	46	54	64	84	89	92	92	94
Oman	277	341	487	561	566	594	601	607
Malaysia	138	163	411	421	430	433	433	434
Lebanon	243	477	749	768	882	891	892	907
Kuwait	202	202	284	465	513	681	688	678
Jordan	161	173	188	192	220	235	269	271
Iraq	110	114	161	196	215	224	228	229
Iran	102	120	163	210	238	257	262	263
Indonesia	83	103	119	128	145	149	155	155
India	31	34	38	65	79	119	119	120
Brunei	116	149	212	247	265	272	299	302
Bahrain	296	313	360	508	549	574	579	580
Afghanistan	51	53	75	100	117	122	125	132
Sudan	159	200	225	250	261	271	271	272
Morocco	118	133	155	178	219	231	246	247
Libya	111	139	158	211	231	252	256	259
Egypt	125	126	137	241	302	311	315	317
Algeria	182	187	197	219	233	239	239	242

Source: *1999 UNESCO Statistical Yearbook* (New York: UNESCO Publishing and Berman Press, 1999).

radio would also allow us to craft a tailored message to the particular demographics using the appropriate media. However, household-level consumer data alone will not be sufficient for this task. In many countries, individuals access radio or television programming through public and quasi-public equipment. For example, one may find listeners clustered around a radio at a small kiosk in the bazaar. Throughout South and Southeast Asia, television (and video) parlors are available for public use, often on a nominal fee basis. The audiences at these facilities are usually young men. Consequently, the penetration rates shown in these tables likely underestimate the degree to which young people (particularly men) can actually access radio and television programming.

Satellite and Cable Availability and Programming

Data current as of 1999 on households with access to cable and satellite television in the Middle East and South and Southeast Asia (see table 4–11) suggest that in some countries, such as the United Arab Emirates, Saudi Arabia, and Qatar, nearly every household with a television set has either cable or, more typically, satellite service. In most other countries, few television-owning households have access to either cable or satellite. Because these data are often collected by visual inspection or through surveys of families with satellite or cable access, actual access may be underestimated. In many countries with poor regulation and law enforcement, several buildings will often share satellite services through illegal wiring. In some cases, one person in a building with such access will market pirated content to other tenants in the same or other buildings. The fact that the practice is illegal means that individual surveys of families will not uncover the actual number of households involved. Unfortunately, there is no reliable way at present to correct for this certain bias.[13]

Given that Muslims in many countries have considerable access to cable or satellite television, it is worthwhile in assessing how these people access information to consider briefly the cable and satellite services available to them.

Middle East Broadcasting Center (MBC): MBC is owned and operated by the Saudi ARA Group International. It is a commercial Arabic-language single-channel service initiated in 1991 from London. It provides a middle-of-the-road assortment of news, information, and entertainment. It was rated in early 1997 as the most watched television service in the Middle East, particularly for its news and current affairs programming.[14] We have no data from which to determine whether this is still the case 8 years later, since the rise of the next two services.

Al Jazeera Satellite Channel: Al Jazeera was launched from Qatar in 1996. Prior to 2001, Arab media analysts attributed its rise in popularity to its unique and unprecedented handling of social and political issues in the Arab world, ranging from corruption to polygamy, in an open and forthright manner.[15] However, its reporting of U.S. military operations following the 9/11 terrorist attacks propelled it into preeminence. Analysts at the U.S.-based al Hurra television service compare al Jazeera's rise since 2001 to that of CNN with its 24-hour coverage of Operation *Desert Storm* in 1991.

Al Arabiya: Al Arabiya, based in Dubai's Media City, was launched in March 2003 by a consortium of the Saudi-controlled MBC, Lebanon's Hariri Group, and other investors from Saudi Arabia, Kuwait, and the other Gulf States, for the express purpose of competing with al Jazeera. In contradistinction to its rival, al Arabiya's bosses pledged at its inception that "we are

Table 4–11. **Africa and the Middle East: Cable and Satellite Television Households**

Country	Total TV Households (Thousands)	Total Cable and Satellite Households (Thousands)	Cable Households (Thousands)	Satellite Households* (Thousands)
Afghanistan	5**	N/A	N/A	N/A
Algeria	2,045–3,200**	600–1,200**	N/A	600–1,200**
Bahrain	94	4	4	N/A
Bangladesh	873	100	100	N/A
Bhutan	3–10	3–10	N/A	3–10
Brunei Darussalam	0.133–0.204	0.007	N/A	N/A
Egypt	8,313–11,550	150–650**	N/A	150–650**
India	54,000b –58,541b	16,080–29,958	15,180b–25,758	900–1,200
Indonesia	26.3**– 30	0.041**–3.513	0.013**	0.028**–3.5
Iran	7,000–10,790	N/A	N/A	N/A
Iraq	1,600–1,800	N/A	N/A	N/A
Israel	1,144**–1,500	980–1,120	960–1,100	20
Jordan	256–740**	5.6–111	0.6–1	5–110**
Kuwait	230–675	126	N/A	126
Lebanon	630**–644**	103–265	5	98–260
Libya	800	7	N/A	7
Morocco	3,670–3,720**	901–960**	N/A	901–960**
Malaysia	3.1**–3.682	0.229–0.32**	0.013**	0.028**–3.5
Oman	1,395	199	N/A	199
Pakistan	7,289b–9,248	1,003–1,364	8–364b	995–1,000
Philippines	8.6**–10.86	0.63–1.411	0.6**–1.086	0.03–0.325
Qatar	89	77	52	25
Saudi	2,967–2,970	2,070**–2,233	330**	1,740–1,893
Sudan	2,240–3,200	15	N/A	15
Syria	1,042–2,210**	300–440**	N/A	300–440**
Tunisia	1,540**–2,380	110**–131	N/A	110**–131
Turkey	10,550**–14,967	1,583–2,288	883**–1,360	700**–928
United Arab Emirates	377	282	N/A	282
Yemen	N/A	N/A	N/A	N/A

Source: *Satellites, Communications, and Broadcasting Markets Survey,* 2000 Edition, Worldwide Prospects to 2009, Euroconsult Research Report by Stephane Chenard, May 2000, 254–255.
* Includes individual direct to home and collective SMATV antennas.
**Data from 1998.

not going to make problems for Arab countries. . . . We'll stick with the truth, but there's no sensationalism."[16] Al Arabiya claims to cater to Arab audience interests in politics, business, current affairs, sports, science, finance, lifestyle, talk-show programs, documentaries, and social and educational programs. Its programming can be seen in all the Middle East countries, the Far East, Southeast Asia, North Africa, Europe, the Americas, and Australia.[17]

Future Television: This service was launched in 1993 from Lebanon and claims to be Lebanon's fastest-growing station. It has wide reach in the Middle East and broadcasts around the clock.[18]

Lebanese Broadcasting Corporation (LBC). LBC was launched in 1985 as a private organization, the first in the Arab world. This station claims to take 60 percent of the Arabic-language market share, a claim that is difficult to reconcile with reports that MBC had the highest viewership in 1997 and the growth of the newer satellite services since then. In 2000, LBC began transmitting to Europe, the United States, Africa, and Asia.[19]

Orbit Satellite Television and Radio Network: This service was launched in 1994 from Rome via the ARABSAT transponder and is owned by the Mawared Group of Riyadh, Saudi Arabia. In 2000, Orbit elected to move its operations over time to Bahrain. Its digital technology can support 24 television and 24 radio channels covering the entire range of news, sports, and entertainment. The Orbit digital television network reaches 23 countries in the Middle East and North Africa and can be received by dishes as small as 18 inches. It also broadcasts a number of Arabic-language channels to Europe and has plans to expand to Asia.[20]

Arab Radio and Television Network (ART): ART is headquartered in Jeddah, Saudi Arabia, and Amman, Jordan. It was launched in 1993 with five channels beamed to the Arab world from transmitters in Italy. By January 2000, ART offered a wide array of channels: Variety, Sports, Music, Children, Movies, *Iqraa* (a religious channel, from the title of a chapter of the Koran, meaning *read* or *proclaim*), Knowledge, Cartoon Network/TNT, *Ala Keyfak* (*as you like it*), and ART Promo. It has also launched customized services to Europe, North Africa, Latin America, and Asia. ART produces more than 6,000 live and recorded shows annually including family dramas, series, plays, documentaries, music videos, and sports programs. This network also has the largest Arabic movie library in the Middle East.[21]

Showtime: This is a joint venture of Viacom and the Kuwait Investment Projects Company. It claims to be the leading digital satellite pay-TV network in the Middle East and North Africa and offers more than 51 premium channels of predominantly Western television programming including the Movie Channel, MTV, TV Land, Nickelodeon, Sony TV, and guest channels like

Discovery and Bloomberg. By August 2000, viewers could access dozens of digital channels. In addition, Showtime offers more than 10 CD audio channels. It claims to offer more channels than any other network in the Middle East. [22]

Arab News Network (ANN): While this London-based service is owned by Algeria-based businessman Rafik Khalifa, it is connected to Rifaat Assad, the dissident brother of Syrian President Hafez Al Assad, and is chaired by Rifaat Assad's son, Sumar. Since its inception in 1997, ANN has been relentless in broadcasting polemics against the Syrian regime.[23] ANN's satellite transmissions reach countries in the Middle East and North Africa as well as Europe. It is funded by commercials from both Arab and major international brands. It broadcasts 24-hour news coverage and analysis in Arabic. ANN claims to have "a firm commitment to democracy and freedom of speech."[24]

In addition, consumers in the Middle East who do not have the use of a satellite dish can also watch satellite television programming through a wide array of cable service providers, such as Dubai Cablevision, Cable Network of Egypt, Qatar Cablevision, Global Direct Television, and Emirates Cable TV and Multimedia (E-Vision).

Despite the proliferation of satellite and cable television services, the production of content to fill the air time persists as a major barrier to the development of Arabic programming. In part, high production costs have apparently prompted ambivalence on the part of government and private broadcasters with respect to financing new projects. As a compromise, the content-hungry service providers gravitate to dubbed versions and reruns of old serials. Western programming is also imported for Arab television. For example, dubbed novelas (high-end soap operas) from Venezuela and Mexico are shown with apparently wide appeal on LBC. Western musical formats are also heavily used.[25]

A comparable comprehensive account of the satellite and cable industries is not available for South and Southeast Asia. Generally speaking, satellite television came to Asia in 1992 with Star Television. Since the advent of Star, there have been a number of new entrants, such as Television Broadcasts (TVB) out of Hong Kong, Turner Broadcasting (which carries CNN), Home Box Office, ESPN, Discovery Channel, Viacom, and Time Warner, as well as Australian Broadcasting and Asia Business News.[26] Star is a major provider of programming content to India and Pakistan.

In the early years of the development of the South and Southeast Asian media market, cultural protectionism posed enormous trade barriers. Turner Broadcasting undertook an Asian version of TNT and the Cartoon Network to accommodate cultural protectionist sentiment, while Rupert Murdoch of Star TV created separate services for the three largest language groups to which Star provides service: Mandarin, Hindi, and Bahasa.[27]

Analysts of the Asian satellite and cable industry also warn that Western broadcasters planning to broadcast in English in Asia will face enormous difficulties due to the limited English fluency among the population. Moreover, illiteracy necessitates use of dubbing rather than the less expensive subtitling. Documentaries have been found to be particularly suited to dubbing. Perhaps the best example of localizing Western programming is MTV Asia on StarTV, which has been adapted locally in India and China.[28]

Information is scant about satellite and cable television in Indonesia. Cable television is available in limited areas of Jakarta and Surabaya as well as in Medan, Semarang, and Bandung. Satellite pay television has been available since 1994 through Indovision (Indonesia's first for-pay direct broadcast satellite provider)[29] and Indonusa (a cable television provider). While transmission previously relied upon a satellite requiring a 9- to 10-foot dish, Indovision now uses the Cakrawarta satellite that requires only a 30-inch dish. However, transmission from other countries is unavailable over the Cakrawarta satellite. The proliferation of satellite dishes in the Indonesian countryside does not mean that foreign programming is widely watched, as it would in many other places. It is simply a reflection of the inability of the government's television station (TVRI) to reach audiences much beyond Jakarta.[30] In fact, in a survey of programming that was taken in April 1993, 60 percent of the top 20 shows were composed of local Indonesian programming.[31] However, the Indonesian television market is huge: approximately 78 percent of Indonesians—more than 160 million people—watch television regularly.[32]

In the main, these data on the availability of satellite and cable programming demonstrate that the markets in the Muslim world are formidable in terms of both the percentage of households they reach in many countries and absolute numbers of potential viewers in any case. Also, there is a sizable void to be filled in content production for some service suppliers, which is often costly and resource-intensive to produce. This suggests that there are opportunities for effective long-term strategic communication to be carried out under the rubric of content development for regional broadcasters. Moreover, Arabic-language media should not be the only focus of U.S. strategic communication efforts. As the data presented here suggest, the huge markets in South and Southeast Asia, where the majority of the world's Muslims reside, mandates production in languages such as Bahasa, Urdu, and Bengali. At the same time, the various extant service providers have found that they must cater to a variety of specific tastes to be successful. This underscores the importance to U.S. strategic communication efforts of understanding in much greater detail than we do at present the interests, tastes, and preferences of the various demographic slices of the markets in question.

While the United States should consider ways of pairing up with local partners to produce content, there are other means of effectively leveraging the demand for content in various Muslim world markets to promote the achievement of U.S. long-term strategic interests. In 1997, when the author was serving as an intern at the American consulate in Mumbai, an officer on the mission staff was specifically tasked with engaging the Indian media industry. One of the objectives of this assignment was to attract Indian movie producers and directors to the United States to shoot their films, bringing work to American studios that have been hurt by the increasing tendency of U.S. producers to make their own movies on location in foreign countries. While the initiative being taken by the Mumbai consulate was driven primarily by business considerations, there are significant opportunities for pursuing U.S. strategic communications objectives through precisely this same kind of collaboration with regional filmmakers and television producers, not just with the Indian film industry but with those of Egypt and other regional countries as well. Movies and television are an important force in shaping social attitudes in the Islamic world, as they have been in the West, perhaps more important in the long run than the news programming on which strategic communications and public diplomacy efforts typically focus. This is one reason why Islamists who come to power often shut down movie theaters on grounds of immorality, as the Islamist government of Pakistan's Northwest Frontier Province has done in Peshawar. They understand the potential of film to subvert the narrow, rigid social perspective that Islamic fundamentalists seek to perpetuate. Promoting the growth of a vibrant cinematographic community in the Islamic world by supporting indigenous filmmakers' use of U.S. commercial filmmaking facilities, technical and artistic collaboration, and possibly subsidization of production costs could be an important means of reshaping public attitudes in the Islamic world without aggravating the backlash that has arisen against the export of "Western" entertainment. Clearly there would be a market for such productions, given the hunger for new and attractive programming content being felt by the region's burgeoning television industry.

Conclusion

This review of how people access information in Islamic countries highlights several notable findings. First, published literacy rates do not correlate in many countries with the actual availability of newspapers. This may cast doubt on the reliability of literacy statistics, which are often government-furnished. It also suggests that literacy rates should not be used as a simple proxy for the ease with which persons can access printed literature.[33]

Moreover, it would be wrong to assume that large numbers of newspapers correlate with notions of freedom of the press or variety of opinions. Iran is a case in point. Despite having some of the most impressive numbers of titles of newspapers and circulation figures, the lack of freedom of the press should caution one against assuming that these papers necessarily reflect an array of views.

Second, it should come as no surprise that people in different parts of the Muslim world have different degrees of access to different forms of media. This divergence needs to be taken into account in any communications strategy. The Internet, while limited in some places, is becoming increasingly accessible and affordable as new service providers come into new markets, as the technology becomes better and less expensive, and as Internet cafés and university computer labs continue to proliferate. Television globally attracts huge audiences, and many of the content providers servicing markets in the Muslim world are hungry for new and attractive content. Those Muslims with access to television receive their programming from a variety of providers, with satellite services dominating in some markets and cable or even traditional over-the-air broadcasting in others. The boom in access to television in the Islamic world creates enormous opportunities for U.S. strategic communications efforts, but the diverse ways in which programming is received require that the United States not place its entire focus on a single method of delivering its message. Moreover, radio and other lower-tech media should not be neglected. For instance, Afghanistan will remain a country where radio may be the most effective means of reaching audiences, given the low penetration of television and low literacy.

Finally, as a word of caution, this survey of information access in the Muslim world is by no means exhaustive. First, it does not address a wide array of outdoor media (for example, advertisements on buses, trains, kiosks, and billboards) that have traditionally been the mainstay of commercial, social, and political marketing in much of the Islamic world.[34] Gimmicks such as matchbooks, coffee mugs, shirts, and other such items are used in the Islamic world to promote products and messages just as they are elsewhere. While these are important means of conveying messages, there are no publicly available data sources that provide market breakdowns for these media, and therefore it was not possible to include these other media within this study. There may be proprietary data available in the advertising industry on these media; in any case, U.S. strategic communication efforts should not neglect this important sector, even if metrics on it are difficult to gather.

While reliable, comparable data on information access in the different countries comprising the Muslim world is hard to come by, it is clear that access to information varies from one country to another much more than it does from one language to another. Existing strategic communications and public diplomacy programs, which tend to be organized by language and not by country, may not adequately take account of the extreme diversity in how people who speak the same language but live in different countries most easily access information. In addition to the fact that people in different countries have significantly varying concerns and opinions, the fact that not all who speak a particular language can be effectively reached through the same media demands a more precisely tailored and targeted array of programming than that traditionally employed.

Notes

[1] Joseph Biden, Initiative 911, November 2001. For other references to this concept, see "The Message Is America: Rethinking U.S. Public Diplomacy," a hearing before the Committee on International Relations, House of Representatives, 107th Congress, November 14, 2001, available at <129.11.188.64/papers/pmt/exhibits/827/Themessageisamerica.pdf>. See also Duncan Campbell, "U.S. plans TV station to rival al-Jazeera," *The Guardian*, November 21, 2001, available at < guardian.co.uk/international/story/0,3604,604286,00.html>.

[2] While we have tried to ensure that tables 4–1 and 4–2 are comparable, there are some differences. For example, table 4–1 references West Bank and Gaza. Table 4–2 has data for the Occupied Territories. Table 4–2 in some cases does not have data for states listed in table 4–1 (for example, Afghanistan).

[3] Freedom House, *Freedom of the Press 2005* (New York: Freedom House, 2005), available at <freedomhouse.org/research/pressurvey.htm>.

[4] For a description of the criteria for such judgments and the arithmetic scheme employed, see Freedom House, *Freedom of the Press 2005*, discussion of "2005 Survey Methodology."

[5] Embassy of the United States of America, Jakarta, Indonesia, "Recent Economic Reports: Internet Slowly Moving Ahead in Indonesia," 2001, available at <usembassyjakarta. org/econ/Internet2001.html>.

[6] Ibid.

[7] Lonely Planet publishes a number of these travel guides. World66.com, an Internet-based travel guide, also publishes Internet café information for Africa, Asia, the Middle East, and elsewhere. There are extensive resources available about Internet cafés on the Internet, such as Arab Gateway, available at <al-bab.com/media/internetcafes.htm>; Pakistan Internet Cafes, available at <world66.com/world/asia/southasia/pakistan/internetcafes>; and Iran Tour, available at <irantour.org/intercafe.html>.

[8] For an account of this phenomenon in Nepal, see Pico Iyer, *Video Night in Kathmandu and Other Reports from the Not-So-Far East* (New York: Alfred Knopf, 1988).

[9] This figure excludes Yemen, as we only have data from 1990. Between 1990 and 1997, television penetration growth was only 10 percent. This figure includes the growth rate for Oman and the United Arab Emirates, which really are calculated for 1975 to 1997.

[10] Afghanistan has been excluded. The growth in television penetration tripled between 1980 (the first year for which we have data) and 1997. This increase was enormous because of the low penetration observed in 1980.

[11] Unlike the figure for television, this figure includes Afghanistan, for which we have data spanning 1970 to 1997.

[12] This figure excludes Yemen, for which we have data for 1990 to 1997. In this period, the growth in radio penetration was 58 percent.

[13] For a history of cable and satellite services in the Middle East, see Jon B. Alterman, "New Media, New Politics? From Satellite Television to the Internet in the Arab World," Policy Paper 49 (Washington, DC: The Washington Institute for Near East Policy, 1998), and Muhammad I. Ayish, "Arab World Television in Transition: Current Trends and Future Prospects," *Orient* 41 (2000), 415–434. While satellite dishes are increasing throughout the Arab countries, estimating the penetration of this technology is an inexact science. Alterman (1998) reports one estimate of satellite access according to which some two-thirds of the population of the Persian Gulf has access to satellite television, compared to 20 percent of the Palestinians and nearly 10 percent of the Egyptians and Syrians. Alterman's own estimates suggest that somewhere between 10 and 15 percent of Arabs in the Middle East regularly watch satellite broadcasts.

[14] See Ayish, 418. Ayish does not indicate whether this rating was due to some subjective notion of quality or to the number of its viewers.

[15] Ibid.

[16] See Peter Feuilherade, "Al Arabiya: A Profile," BBC News Online, November 25, 2003, available at <news.bbc.co.uk/1/hi/world/middle_east/3236654.stm>.

[17] For more information, see al Arabiya's Web site at <alarabiya.net/English.htm>.

[18] Ayish, 419.

[19] Ibid.

[20] Ibid. For more and recent information, see Orbit's Web site at <orbit.net/corporate/profile/DefaultEN.asp>.

[21] Ayish, 419–420. For more information about ART, see information provided by Allied Media at <allied-media.com/ARABTV/art.htm>.

[22] Ayish, 420. For more current information, see Showtime Arabia corporate profile at <showtimearabia.com/default.asp?id=8&l=1>.

[23] See Middle East Intelligence Briefing, "Dossier: Rifaat Asad," vol. 2, no. 5 (June 2000), available at <meib.org/articles/0006_sd.htm>.

[24] See Ayish, 420. Also see information about ANN provided through Mosaic at <linktv.org/mosaic/mosbroad.php3>.

[25] Juliana Koranteng, "Pan-Arab Audiences Turn to Lebanese TV for Entertainment," *Advertising Age International*, April 1997, I11; Ayish, 425–426.

[26] Jonathan Karp, "Cast of Thousands," *Far Eastern Economic Review*, January 27, 1994, 47.

[27] Karp, 48.

[28] Ibid.

[29] For more information, see the company's Web site at <indovision.tv/Company.php>.

[30] See the section titled "Television and Home Entertainment" at "Living in Indonesia," a Web site for expatriates living in Indonesia, available at <expat.or.id/info/televisi.html>.

[31] Karp, 48.

[32] See assessment by Indonesia media firm PT Jaring Data Interaktif at <jditeam.com/profile>.

[33] Other metrics may be useful, such as the publication of books, which is also available from United Nations Development Program; however, these data too are old.

[34] See Richard Earle, *Art of Cause Marketing: How to Use Advertising to Change Personal Behavior and Public Policy* (Lincolnwood, IL: NTC Publishing Group, 2000).

Chapter Five

Perceived Oppression and Relative Deprivation: Social Factors Contributing to Terrorism

Caroline F. Ziemke

A lively debate is evident in the current academic and policy literature concerning the degree to which social factors facilitate the spread of violent terrorist ideologies and the mechanisms by which they do so. Plenty of research exists to back up the notion that one's behavioral choices are powerfully influenced by one's social and political environment. An individual is, perhaps, more likely to become a terrorist in a repressive society in which exposure to violence, poverty, and political disempowerment is a regular occurrence than in a relatively free society in which legitimate outlets for rage and frustration and prospects for a better life exist. Yet the majority of people, even in the harshest of socio-political circumstances, do not become terrorists or give moral or financial support to terrorist organizations. Moreover, the vehement militant movements have generally emerged from relatively affluent quarters. As we have learned more about terrorism, terrorist organizations, and popular support for terrorists, some interesting paradoxes have emerged:

■ Editorial rhetoric notwithstanding, there is little empirical research that proves that poverty per se causes terrorism. None of the world's poorest societies have produced organized terrorist movements, and relatively few known terrorist operatives have come from grinding poverty. In fact, alleviating poverty generally leads to an upsurge in support for militant movements. One outcome of economic reform is usually a downward redistribution of wealth that leads to a relative decline in the economic and professional status of the generally politically volatile middle and merchant classes.[1]

■ Nor does illiteracy cause militancy. While promoting literacy and free speech is an unambiguous good with undeniable long-term advantages for every society, the transition to full literacy is a boon to illiberal as well as liberal ideologies. Teaching people to read does not necessarily make them wise or moderate.

■ No evidence suggests that terrorists and suicide bombers as a group suffer from any particular psychopathologies, and, at any rate, terrorism as a phenomenon is not caused by antisocial dispositions of single actors.

Group or social psychological factors, however, are extremely important facilitators of radicalization, terrorism, and support for terrorist activities. The dichotomy between individual and social psychology helps explain why public opinion polls can show that the majority says it condemns terrorism in the name of religion while tacit moral and financial support and popular adulation of terrorist masterminds and suicide bombers continue unabated.

■ While oppression is a common rhetorical theme of terrorist ideology and is another key element of the conventional wisdom, terrorist movements do not thrive (even underground) in truly repressive regimes. In fact, periods of liberalization and democratization are far more likely to see the emergence of militant groups and supporters than long periods of brutal repression. Terrorists do not emerge when nothing changes; they emerge when things change too slowly to meet rising expectations, or faster than people are able to adapt.

■ Radicalism and terrorism are as much symptoms of the Westernization and modernization of the Muslim world as reactions against them. The most dangerous militant Islamic ideologies (and, in fact, militant ideologies in most faith traditions) are surprisingly individualistic and probably would not have emerged in their current forms without significant cross-pollination from Western intellectual, religious, and philosophical traditions.

■ Religious fundamentalism is a modern phenomenon that appeals to modern mentalities, and some of Islamic fundamentalism's most influential theorists have come from outside the Arab core—especially British India and Pakistan. One of the most important dynamics contributing to militant ideologies and terrorism is the tension between an emerging "deterritorialized" brand of Islamic revivalism on the one hand and traditional cultural and national identities and orthodox religious traditions on the other.

The lesson of these paradoxes is not, of course, that the way to build a global antiterrorist environment is to promote poverty, spread brutal political repression, maintain widespread ignorance and illiteracy, and shut down contact between the Muslim world and the West. What they do demonstrate is that the social factors that contribute to terrorism are complex and intertwined in a way that means alleviating one evil can trigger a host of unexpected and unintended consequences, not all of which increase stability. Anticipating such unintended consequences will be a key challenge in building a durable global antiterrorist environment.

The landscape within which terrorist ideologies spread and the United States and its partners in the global war on terror attempt to prevent them from spreading is at least as complex. In rough outline, it consists of at least six concentric circles of Muslim identity. Those in each circle perceive the world, their role in it, the challenges of modern life, and the utility of extremist ideologies differently. Each circle also has its own historical, cultural, social, economic, and political contexts that shape both its sense of threat and the likelihood that significant elements of their populations may be inclined to see extremism as a viable solution to its problems. The six concentric circles are:

- the Arab core (including Arab North Africa)[2]

- the non-Arab "greater Middle East": Iran, Pakistan, Afghanistan, Turkey

- traditionally Muslim societies in the non-Arab periphery: Malaysia, Indonesia

- emerging Muslim nations: the Central Asian and Caucasian Republics, Bosnia, Albania, the Kurds[3]

- traditionally Muslim minorities with deep historical roots: Thailand, Singapore, Cambodia, the Philippines, China, Russia

- the Western Muslim diaspora: Western Europe, the United Kingdom, the United States, Canada, Australia, South America.

The goal of this chapter is to outline the links between the social factors underlying terrorism in general, and the relative importance they might play in the various concentric circles of Muslim identity. First, it outlines the six rings of identity focusing on the key differences in terms of unmet social needs and the role that Islam, militant or otherwise, might play in fulfilling them. Then it unpacks the paradoxes of social factors and terrorism in an effort to revisit some of the conventional wisdom that dominates discussions of the causes of terrorism. This analysis starts from the assumption that both everything and nothing explains terrorism. That is, each of the factors mentioned above contributes to the problem, but no single one contributes wholly, or even primarily, to it.

Social Landscape of the Global Antiterrorist Project

Formal religious and political rhetoric notwithstanding, there exists great diversity within the Muslim world that affects how, where, and to what extent militant Islamic movements can, or will, take root. Every Muslim society has a unique historical, cultural, and social context within which political phenomena, including militant Islam and terrorism, unfold. Each society is unique, but this is not the place to delve into that level of detail. Instead, we can tackle the problem more generally by revisiting the six concentric circles of Muslim identity—the Arab core, the non-Arab greater

Middle East, traditionally Muslim countries on the periphery, emerging Muslim nations, historic Muslim minorities, and the Muslim diaspora—and ask some general questions, the answers to which might provide insight into social approaches to building a global antiterrorist culture. What threats do people in each region think "Islam" can counter? What unmet needs might it fulfill? What national, ethnic, or other identities compete with militant Islam for loyalty? How strong are those identities? Who are the committed, charismatic influence elites who can tip opinion toward or away from support for terrorism? What kinds of messages are likely to resonate in each context? What is the social and cultural context within which an antiterrorist culture would have to emerge? What are the important sources of identity and cultural sensitivities? The answers to these sorts of questions provide important clues not only to how and why terrorism and support for terrorism might spread into a particular country or region, but also where effort might best be targeted to alleviate the discontents that facilitate the rise of militancy in order to build a global antiterrorist environment.

The Arab Core

The Arab world is the intellectual and spiritual homeland as well as the holy land of Islam, and hence the center of global Muslim identity. Muslims the world over will always look to the Arab core as an important source of religious identity and will continue to care deeply about political and social events that affect the three holy cities: Mecca, Medina, and Jerusalem (al Quds). In historic terms, the age of the Prophet, the rise of Islam to world power, and the cultural and intellectual flowering of the early caliphates—all of which took place in the Arab core—are seen as constituting the golden age of Islamic civilization. Theologically, the Arab core will always be influential because of its status as the birthplace of Islam and the importance Islamic teaching places on direct lines of authority from the Prophet, both in historical and familial terms. Linguistically, Arabic has traditionally been the lingua franca of Islamic intellectuals and the liturgical language of Muslims the world over.

The historic sources of Arab militancy are familiar: the decline of Arab-Islam from its cultural and strategic golden age, the subsequent humiliation of the Arab world at the hands of the West and Israel, the widespread disillusionment with secular nationalism, the economic and political stagnation of Arab societies under the influence of corrupt and incompetent ruling regimes, and the importance of Islam as the source of collective Arab identity. The specific desire to restore the historical glory and power of Islam through a resurrected global Islamic caliphate may be characteristic only of the rhetoric of global jihadists like Osama bin Laden, but even moderates express pain at the extent of the Arab world's fall from greatness.

Even in the theological realm, the Arab core has lost some of its former dominance. The intellectual center of gravity within Islam, whether militant or moderate, has been gradually shifting to the periphery, and most recently to the West. Increasingly, Muslim thinkers are writing as well as preaching in local tongues with an eye toward reaching a much broader audience among those for whom Arabic is merely a liturgical language. And just as Latin eventually lost its place as the liturgical language of the Catholic church with the grassroots shift toward the use of the vernacular in theological writing and preaching, so Arabic is increasingly being overtaken by English and other Western languages as the global *umma* (Muslim community) comes, increasingly, to rely on the Internet for interaction and exchange of ideas.

Two sets of social factors seem most important in contributing to cultures of terrorism in the Arab core: those related to humiliation (such as the loss of status of orthodox Islamic learning institutions, economic stagnation, and poor development prospects) and those related to disempowerment (lack of representative political institutions, lack of free speech, personal economic deprivation, and unemployment). At present, the opinion elites who capture the public imagination are those, like bin Laden, who can strike out against the oppressors and those who comfort the insecure by spinning elaborate conspiracy theories that externalize the Arab world's problems. To counter these factors, what is needed is a cadre of moderate voices of empowerment that can energize the Arab world—or, as in the case of Lebanon, crystallize and capitalize on the grassroots mood of empowerment—to look to the future, find a way to live peacefully with Israel, and take charge of and responsibility for its own fate. That might mean less U.S. influence in the near term, but it would lead to greater stability and prosperity in the region in the long run.

Non-Arab Greater Middle East

The non-Arab countries that are generally considered part of the greater Middle East—Turkey, Iran, Afghanistan, and Pakistan—have histories that are entwined closely with that of the Arab world, but they maintain clear, and often consciously diametrical, cultural and national identities. All regard Islam as central to their cultural identity, and all but Turkey (with its avowedly secular constitution and political culture) have attempted to some degree to structure their societies according to Islamic guidelines. But all are also careful to distinguish themselves, culturally and institutionally, from the Arab core. All of these groups also share a problematic historical relationship with the Arabs, owing to linguistic, sectarian, and cultural differences. In addition, Turkey and Iran have both long pursued strategic dominance of the region. These non-Arab societies are also, for the most part, less emotionally invested in the Arab-Israeli conflict than are their Arab neighbors. The Islamic Republic of Iran, which has been the most active and vehement opponent of the Arab-Israeli peace process, has adopted its hard-line stance at least in part to distance itself from the Shah, who was a de facto Israeli ally, and to build common cause with Arab public opinion, especially in Lebanon.

In addition, these countries' histories were shaped by their location on the borders between Muslim and non-Muslim civilizations. As a result, they have historically been less culturally homogeneous and somewhat more open to cosmopolitan influences than the Persian Gulf Arabs. Turkey has been strategically linked to Europe, Persia to Central Asia and Russia, Pakistan to Hindu India, and Afghanistan to Russia and the Indian subcontinent. Afghanistan has been, through most of its history, a world unto itself. While it became a primary base and staging area for global jihadist terrorism in the 1990s, it is important to keep in mind that al Qaeda was an import, not a native growth. While ideologically sympathetic, the Taliban did not necessarily share al Qaeda's global jihadi ambitions. The Afghans, through most of the period during which militant revivalist Islam emerged, were too busy fighting among themselves to think about exporting jihad. They draw a fairly clear distinction between their Islamic and cultural identities and those of the "Afghan Arabs," who injected themselves into the war against the Soviet Union and then, like bad houseguests, refused to go home.

Within this circle, the terrorist culture is strongest in those societies—Afghanistan and Pakistan—that have weak unifying identities. Both countries are constantly teetering on the verge of becoming failed states. In both cases, relative deprivation and disempowerment are the social factors that contribute most directly to cultures of violence. The best hope for building a durable antiterrorist culture in these two societies is for them to forge unifying national visions that define the role of Islam in national life and political culture in a positive and relatively inclusive way. Pakistan's national vision has always been "Islamic," but it has never gelled into something more unifying and defining than being Pakistanis because they were not Hindus. The emergence of viable national visions, in turn, will depend on the emergence of charismatic leaders and civil institutions that can build a foundation for assimilation and integration of national identity based on a sense of pride and empowerment, but not necessarily cultural homogeneity. Both are countries that have too long been held together by external threats: Russia for Afghanistan, and India for Pakistan. In both societies, the charismatic leaders and institutions that are most likely to be able to build such an identity are religious in orientation, for the simple reason that civil cultures and institutions have been weak, corrupt, or nonexistent. In Iran and Turkey, the long-term prospect for building an antiterrorist culture will depend on the emergence of moderate Islamic voices and the ability of those voices to speak freely and openly challenge the status quo.

The Traditionally Muslim Periphery

The further Islam spread from its center on the Arabian Peninsula, the more diverse it became as local custom, religious practice, law, and superstitions were folded into the local versions of the faith. While the Arab core maintained its doctrinal and intellectual influence, which it periodically reasserted through reformist movements like Wahhabism, the Muslim world through most of its history lacked a strong social and cultural center. The salafist movement, whose name derives from the Arabic expression for "the pious ancestors," advocates strict adherence to the letter of Koranic teaching and Islamic law as it is believed to have been practiced at the time of the Prophet and his companions. This movement is at the core of militant Islamism on the periphery. Reformist movements that attempted to purge the remnants of local pre-Islamic custom have surfaced periodically in these regions, but the current emphasis on outward cultural uniformity across the global *umma* is a relatively recent phenomenon. In fact, the global *umma*, insofar as it sees the Muslim world as a single cultural entity, is itself a product of the globalization era.

Through most of their history, Muslims on the periphery have been culturally, historically, and geographically remote from the historical caliphate and the glory days of Arab political power. The demise of the political caliphate had few practical consequences outside the greater Middle East. The shifting of trade routes away from the Mediterranean and the ancient Silk Road, which marginalized the Arab world and undermined its former economic power, had the opposite effect on Muslim societies in South and Southeast Asia, which became the new crossroads of trade in the modern era, especially after the discovery of oil in Southeast Asia. The awareness of Islam's "humiliation" at the hands of the West has symbolic importance for these societies, but it lacks the power of a shared historical trauma that it has in the Arab core.

The social and political challenges that have shaped the political cultures of these traditionally Muslim societies of the periphery are legacies of decolonization and military dictatorship. Resentments tend to be focused on Western and global institutions that carry the stigma of colonialism or cultural and economic imperialism, particularly the World Bank and the International Monetary Fund. Islam has always been an important source of unity in these heterogeneous societies. In the years since independence and, especially in Indonesia, the more recent era of liberalization, Islamic identity provides a symbolic departure from both the frustration of colonial rule and the corruption of postcolonial secular regimes and martial law. In

Malaysia, Islam has been integrated into the secular political culture from the beginning, and since 1999, Indonesia is seeing the emergence of a political culture (albeit a sometimes turbulent one) in which Islamic and secular nationalist parties work peacefully and effectively side by side. In most of these peripheral societies, the extreme tension between Islam and modernization has been less widespread, and the taste for puritanical fundamentalism is fairly localized. Indeed, by providing reliable cultural and social touchstones, Islam in some respects makes modernization, economic development, and, most recently, political reform safe.

The Muslim periphery has produced its share of militant Islamic revivalist movements, and both Indonesia and Malaysia have become centers of al Qaeda and Jamaah Islamiya activities. Nevertheless, the popular taste for militancy seems to be limited, although a lack of continued progress on economic and social justice could tip the balance in favor of militant views. Attitudes toward the West in general, and the United States in particular, are volatile in these societies and can respond quickly and negatively to events in the Middle East and U.S. actions in the war on terror that are perceived as anti-Islam. On the other hand, attitudes toward the United States saw dramatic improvement following military humanitarian operations in the wake of the 2004 tsunami (especially since U.S. forces were willing to deliver aid to regions that national governments had neglected, such as Aceh in Indonesia). In these societies, it is especially important not to conflate anti-Americanism with support for terrorism.

It is also important, in working with regional governments in building an antiterrorist environment, not to link counterterrorism cooperation and aid to open endorsement of U.S. policy. For a host of domestic political reasons, regimes are unlikely to declare themselves allies of the United States or embrace the global scope of the U.S. counterterrorism strategy. For them, terrorism is a local, internal security problem.[4] Despite dire predictions in the late 1990s and the rise of anti-U.S. sentiment since the 1997 economic crisis, Indonesia's democratic evolution seems to be moving toward moderate Islamism rather than either political collapse or "Talibanization," as some predicted. The charismatic leaders in these peripheral Muslim societies tend to be pious populists who preach a message of political empowerment and self-sufficiency.

The Emerging Muslim States

Most of these states, like the states in the greater Middle East, have histories deeply entwined with the Arab core, but they are histories whose continuity was broken by conquest and occupation. Bosnia and the emerging Muslim republics in the former Soviet Union have, through most of their modern history, found their social, political, and strategic interests closely linked with those of non-Muslim societies. The Kurds have struggled to maintain their unique ethnic identity under the domination of three Muslim states—Iraq, Iran, and Turkey—and have never achieved full national independence. As all these states regain their autonomy and strive to build new national identities, Islam is an important source of cultural and historical identity, but it has never been bound up with the way people defined either their ethnicity or their political culture as it was in much of the Arab core and the greater Middle East. Central Asia, moreover, has its own historical tradition as a cultural and intellectual center of Islam and does not, as do some of the peripheral Muslim states, look to the Arab core for guidance on how to live as Muslims. For the majorities in these societies, militant revivalist Islam is too severe, too destabilizing, and, most importantly, too "Arab" to gain widespread support or sympathy.

The danger in these societies, especially those in former Soviet Central Asia, is that political and economic reform will move too slowly under the current generation of post-Soviet despots, presenting militant preachers and groups, who so far have found limited and localized support, with an increasingly target-rich environment as impatience rises. The cynical tendency of secular regimes in the region to use the specter of "Islamic extremism" as an excuse to crack down on political and economic opposition could further polish the image of Islamism in the eyes of a fed-up population.

For the United States, the challenge in these areas is less to foster a new antiterrorist culture than to capitalize on what seems, for now, to be a relatively benign public perception of the West, the United States, and the forces of modernization and to prevent corrupt and repressive regimes from poisoning the well. If the still-repressive post-Soviet regimes do not reform voluntarily, popular uprisings to force liberalization and democratization are likely, and as events in Uzbekistan in the spring of 2005 clearly demonstrated, regime reactions could trigger significant violence. But as things stand, outbursts are more likely to follow the political models of Ukraine or Kyrgyzstan—secular, populist uprisings to end political and economic corruption—than the rigid and extreme Islamist model of Afghanistan. Charismatic leaders with a message of secular nationalism and political and economic reform in a Muslim context will find willing audiences in these countries, but these emergent political cultures are still vulnerable, and militant groups like the Hizbut Tahrir are poised to step in if reform comes too slowly.

Historic Muslim Minorities

Scattered throughout Asia are pockets of Muslim minorities who, by the fortunes of history, find themselves outside the boundaries of neighboring majority Muslim states. In many cases, their existence is an irritant to the dominant societies in which they find themselves. For these groups, the social factors that shape their attitudes toward militant revivalist Islam, and hence have the potential to foster in them a pro-terrorist culture, are simple and primal: physical and cultural security. Each of these groups sees (or has, at some time in the recent past, seen) itself under cultural siege because of its religious identity. Muslims in India, the Pattani Muslims in Thailand, and the Moros of the Philippines have all described themselves as victims of attempts at cultural genocide at the hands of religious majorities. In a few cases, the use of "genocide" is particularly fitting. The tiny Cham Muslim minority in Cambodia was virtually wiped out by the Khmer Rouge: no mosques and only a handful of *ulamas* survived the purge. The Cham have long been isolated from the mainstream Muslim world. They developed their own, unique style of Muslim religious practice, which includes elements of Buddhist and other local religious tradition, and have only recently gained the attention of revivalist Islamist missionaries. In other cases, such as the Moros in the Philippines, the Uighurs in China, and the Chechens in Russia, resistance to political and cultural domination has been longstanding.

These Muslim minorities, for the most part, suffer from real economic and political marginalization and limited educational opportunities. Many lost their traditional livelihoods when agricultural lands were seized by central governments, and most found themselves isolated from their traditional economic and trade systems. In many cases, these minority Muslim populations reside in regions rich in natural resources that are exploited solely for the benefit of central governments, corporations, or agricultural conglomerates. In some cases, such as the Moros, the Uighurs, and the Chechens, government efforts to "assimilate" Muslim minorities stem primarily from economic motivations; but the rise of Islamist political theory in the early 20th century gave what had been a battle between local elites and colonial or government authority a new ideological and religious authority. And as has been the case in Central Asia, governments in China and Russia have used the "threat" of Islamist extremism as an excuse to step up their "assimilation" and crack down on resistance with minimal criticism from the West.

The emotionally empowering and charismatic messages of militants—even those who, like the Abu Sayyaf group in the Philippines, straddle the line between ideological and criminal terrorism—have great emotional appeal. In the Philippines, a new movement has emerged, the Rajah Solaiman Movement, devoted to the "re-Islamization" of the country. It has met with surprising success in converting Filipinos to Islam, at least in part by tapping into dissatisfaction with the status quo and presenting a revolutionary vision of Islam as a force for building social and economic justice. The jihadist groups have also become an important source of operational training, technology, and logistical support (witness the recent appearance of al Qaeda–style improvised explosive devices, remote triggers, and coordinated attacks in Thailand and the Philippines, for example).[5] It is less clear that the regional or global jihadi agendas of these militant groups have much political appeal with Muslim minority populations. For the most part, the militant groups among Muslim minorities fight for local interests—political and cultural autonomy and economic justice—and not for some abstract notion of a global Islamist caliphate. What these communities need and want is respect and security. Even in those cases in which autonomy is not a realistic option, the governments and minorities have to find a common ground of tolerance upon which to build and sustain an antiterrorist culture. The messages that resonate with these groups are social autonomy, the right to live according to their Islamic values and mores, and cultural survival.

The Muslim Diaspora

Like the Muslim minorities, a portion of the Muslim diaspora in the West sees itself as a group under cultural and social siege. Unlike the indigenous minority communities in Asia, however, the Muslims in the West often lack the strong sense of communal and cultural identity that can root a group to a specific tradition and place. Relative economic deprivation (in most Western European countries, Muslim populations remain disproportionately poor, less well educated, and politically underrepresented, even though they are, for the most part, better off than those who stayed behind in their homelands) breeds in them a sense of humiliation and resentment, and discrimination adds an additional dimension of personal humiliation. Alienated Muslims in Europe, in short, share many of the perceived grievances of Muslim minorities elsewhere (cultural and religious hostility, economic injustice, political inequality, limited opportunities, and no political voice) without the strong communal identity (*I am a member of a proud and cohesive community that has a strong historical identity; and I must conduct myself in a way that is consistent with the values and well-being of that community*) that is necessary to make progress (either by peaceful or violent means) toward improving their future.

For these Muslims, a new sort of Islam has evolved to provide a source of identity that unifies individuals from diverse cultural, ethnic, and social backgrounds. As the experience of Hassidic Judaism demonstrates, the de-territorialization of religious identities is an extremely effective way of reviving and maintaining religious identity and holding modernization and cultural assimilation at bay among a people in diaspora. Ultra-Orthodox Jews are virtually indistinguishable culturally (including their dress, manners, and use of the Yiddish language) wherever they live in the world (since the Holocaust, primarily in North America and Jerusalem, where they tried to rebuild their devastated communities). Individual Hassidic communities draw their identity from the *rebbe* (spiritual teacher) who leads them, and the divisions within the movement are sometimes bitter. Because the community identifies with its leader rather than with a particular place, the community is wherever the leader is. Salafist Islam in the West has developed a similar enclave culture. Followers of particular sheiks (teachers, preachers, and spiritual leaders who may or may not have formal religious educations) live in closely knit and culturally quarantined self-segregation. And just as Yiddish replaced Hebrew as the language of Jews in diaspora in the 18th century, under a combination of influences (the Internet, the emergence of second- and third-generation European Muslims for whom Arabic is merely a liturgical language, the multicultural nature of the global Islamic revivalist movement, and the concentration of some of its most charismatic sheiks in the United Kingdom), English is replacing Arabic as the lingua franca of the global Muslim revivalist movement.

It is important to draw a distinction between those Muslims—in most countries a minority of the Muslim community—who still regard themselves as outsiders in exile in a hostile, or at least alien, land and those who have assimilated into Western society to some degree and think of themselves as European Muslims or Muslim Americans. Pakistanis and Bangladeshis remain the most segregated ethnic communities in the United Kingdom, for example, but they are becoming increasingly economically assimilated and have even begun participating in politics at the local level.[6] Even the most segregated revivalist Muslim enclaves in Europe are largely not involved in political violence (most, in fact, shun political involvement of any kind). Perhaps more than in any other ring of the Muslim community, it is vital that the United States and its allies focus a great deal of effort and thought on expanding the antiterrorist culture across the Muslim diaspora. Often lacking traditional community, extended family, and religious ties, this group is vulnerable to the messages of individual spiritual renewal, belonging, shared identity, and righteous destiny preached by militant revivalist missionaries from the Arab core and the greater Middle East. Encouraging moderate voices from within the Western Muslim community (including traditionalists and even revivalists) and reaching out to the disaffected and deprived immigrant communities in large Western cities will be crucial to the overall effort to fostering a global antiterrorist environment. The difficulty in building a sense of patriotic identity among European Muslims is attributable as much to the nature of European societies as of the Muslim communities themselves. Unlike the United States, where patriotic assimilation is the foundation of national identity and cultural differences are accepted so long as a community embraces the dominant civic values, European countries have little history of assimilation upon which to build. For them, the presence of "foreign" communities that cling to external signs of cultural difference is new and threatening to their historical identities. The challenge for Europe is to find ways to cultivate a stronger patriotic identity among its Muslims that does not necessarily require them to submit to total cultural assimilation.

Social Paradoxes of Terrorism

Having considered the characteristics and concerns of the populations of each of the six concentric rings of Muslim identity, it is now necessary to examine the specific social factors within each ring that contribute to participation in and support for terrorism. As noted at the outset, the mono-causal relationships that are often posited between such factors as poverty, illiteracy, oppression, psychopathology, and religious fundamentalism on the one hand and terrorism on the other are not able to withstand serious scrutiny. Nevertheless, these factors do have a bearing on the way each ring of the Muslim community relates to the terrorist phenomenon, often in some quite unexpected ways.

Poverty

One of the most surprising elements of the September 11, 2001, terrorist attacks in New York and Washington was the fact that the terrorist entrepreneurs who planned the plot and the pilots who carried it out came from relatively well-off, middle-class backgrounds. The 13 "muscle hijackers" who subdued passengers came from less affluent circumstances, most from the underdeveloped tribal hinterlands of Saudi Arabia. All were young, unemployed, and all but two had no more than high school educations. None came from grinding poverty, but all had seen the economic well-being of their families and tribes decline from the heyday of Saudi economic largesse.[7] It has long been an axiom of the "addressing root causes" school that terrorism is a product of the roiling frustration and rage of chronically underprivileged and economically deprived people. In truth, in the traditionally Muslim world, poverty turns out not to be a particularly strong indicator of radicalization. The assumption of a link between poverty and terrorism stems, in part, from the fact that the rise of militant Islam in the Muslim world, and especially among Muslim minorities in the West, coincided with the mass migration of Muslims from rural to urban areas, and from their homelands to Europe and North America in search of gainful employment. This migration resulted in a dramatic and visible increase in the number of people living in abject poverty in cities like Cairo and the rise of expanding ghettos of underprivileged, semi-assimilated Muslim minorities in the cities of Europe and North America.[8]

Dislocation stemming from mass migration and the resulting cultural and social alienation are, to be sure, important contributing factors in the rise of militant Islamic movements. But it is not poverty, per se, that causes it.

In fact, none of the world's poorest societies have produced terrorist movements or even contributed significant numbers of their citizens to terrorist organizations. It is more the sense of disempowerment that contributes to the sort of rage that leads a person to follow a terrorist or jihadi leader. Two other concepts are more useful in thinking about the links between socio-economic factors and terrorist activity and support: harshness and relative economic deprivation. Graham Fuller explains that "harsh conditions will routinely produce a higher degree of violent individuals than do comfortable societies."[9] Harsh societies are, of course, often characterized by widespread poverty and fear, and living in such societies surely contributes to the creation of a militant. Cultures of violence—collective worldviews, values, and habits of thought that condone or even celebrate violence as a means of vicarious empowerment—are the natural outgrowth of such harshness. This is almost certainly the case in the refugee camps of Palestine, Afghanistan, and Pakistan, where grinding poverty is endemic. Likewise, among separatist Muslim communities in Aceh (Indonesia) and minority enclaves in the Philippines, Thailand, and Cambodia, poverty and fear are certainly part of the harshness of life and contribute to often longstanding separatist aspirations.

Relative economic deprivation is an important factor in understanding the social origins of terrorism on both a macro and a micro level. At the macro level, many in the Islamic world perceive that globalization and Western (read: U.S.) cultural and economic imperialism have malign influences on Muslim societies. According to this worldview, these societies are failing to keep pace economically with the West and Asia because of corrupt and incompetent regimes shored up by a rapacious West that seeks to plunder Muslim societies (particularly their oil) and keep them economically dependent for its own economic benefit and material well-being. In the Arab world, the sense of relative decline can be traced to the 1967 Arab-Israeli War, when Arab regimes were humiliated by Israel and lost control of Jerusalem and the West Bank. At about the same time, the fundamental feebleness of Arab statist economies became undeniable, and economic development stagnated. In Southeast Asia, the resentments have emerged more recently and have intensified since the 1997 Asian economic crisis. Most Indonesians and Malaysians believe their collapse from the economic boom days of the "Asian Tigers" in the early 1990s was triggered by the predatory lending practices of the International Monetary Fund and World Bank.

On the micro level, individuals in many Muslim societies—particularly in the Arab world—perceive their present economic and social status as out of line with their education, capabilities, family tradition, and customary social status. Among historical Muslim minorities, the sense of deprivation often stems from three additional factors: the loss of historical status as independent communities, the disruption of traditional economic and trade structures, and the economic exploitation of local resources by non-Muslim elites and regimes that often leaves Muslim communities in poverty. The result is a class perception of relative social and economic decline, especially in the lower-middle and merchant classes. At all levels, fear of becoming economically and socially marginal is keen. In this sense, Islamist terrorists come from the same socio-political environment that produced fascism and other religious extremist movements: the lower-middle class, petty merchant class, and actual or former peasantry. These groups have historically been, and continue to be, the ones that live in constant fear of economic marginalization and stand to lose the most in the downward redistribution of wealth that often results from economic modernization. Terrorist and jihadi movements impart to the insecure sons of the middle class, many of whom have had to delay marriage and family for economic reasons, the notion that they have a vital role to play and mission to fulfill in a cosmic war between good and evil. In a world in which their milieu and their futures seem increasingly beyond their control, these men, mostly young, find for themselves a glorious destiny and values other than economic achievement that separate them from the crowd and, often, from what they see as the dreary, spiritually empty lives of their petit-bourgeois parents.

Education and Literacy

The widely held premise that high levels of literacy can be a barrier to the spread of militant ideology is true—sometimes. Militant Islam has been relatively slow to catch on in the emerging Muslim republics of Central Asia and in Bosnia, in no small part because of the nearly full literacy of those states—a legacy of the Soviet era. In these cases, not only does literacy inoculate the public mind against the simplistic messages of many militant groups, it also enables citizens interested in learning more about Islam or national affairs to gather and compare information from a number of different sources.[10] Moreover, Central Asia's own long history as an intellectual center of Islam has become an important part of the national myths of these emerging nations. Despite a century of Russian and then Soviet cultural imperialism, Central Asian Islam managed to maintain a strong sense of its identity. Ironically, Soviet literacy policy (designed to facilitate the propagation of socialist ideology) enabled underground mosques and Islamic study groups to keep the study of Islamic texts alive and even vibrant in Central Asia. In the post-Soviet period, Central Asia has not proven the ideological and religious tabula rasa that many assumed it would be. Its Islamic intelligentsia regards itself as fully capable of guiding its own faith community and has been highly resistant to the "Arabization" of Central Asian Islam.[11]

Meanwhile, much has been made in the post-9/11 terrorism literature of the role of radical *madrassas*, many Saudi-funded, in cranking out semiliterate, zealous, radicalized prototerrorists burning to take up the sword of jihad (or the vest of the suicide bomber) against Israel and the West. These institutions are a legitimate source of deep concern and present a particular challenge in the stabilization of fragile moderate regimes in Afghanistan, Pakistan, and parts of Southeast Asia. It is imperative that the creation of a public education system worthy of the name, that teaches a moderate and modern curriculum to boys and girls, be a key component of any project to build a durable antiterrorist environment. Through the 1980s and 1990s, the only funding for religious education (or, too often, for education of any kind) in the Afghan refugee camps, among the tribal populations of Western Pakistan, in remote provinces of Indonesia, and among Muslim minorities in the Philippines came from Saudi Arabia or militant, often jihadi, Muslim charities.

The tragic irony is that these Saudi-funded *madrassas* gradually devolved into a virulent variety of Islamic militancy that is not even tolerated inside the puritanical Saudi Kingdom. In the majority of these institutions, students (all boys) study only Islam—no math, no science, no world history or literature. The boys learn by rote, memorizing the Koran and reciting the Hadith, and are inculcated with a dread of modernity and fear and hatred of the United States as the Great Satan, a mortal enemy dedicated to the destruction of Islam and of all Muslims. In Pakistan alone, some 7,000 *madrassas* feed, house, and teach hundreds of thousands of boys and young men who will graduate with an intellectual command of nothing but militant Islam, no understanding of the outside world, no analytical or technical skills to function in a modern economy, and a belief that martyrdom for their faith would be the highest achievement within their reach.[12] In Southeast Asia, religious schools (known there as *pesantrens*, *pondoks*, or *pusakas*) have a long history of principled resistance to local and imperial authority, but their agendas have not necessarily been coopted by the jihadists. Individual militant ringleaders have come out of such schools, but the numbers are small; one survey conducted out of Singapore concluded that only 10 of 40,000 such schools monitored had avowedly militant Islamist or jihadi curricula, and most of those had been closed or reformed.[13] The governments in the region monitor the curriculums of these institutions, but express concern about the "hidden curriculum"—the culture of hatred and radicalism—that is promoted in small social and study circles outside the classroom.

In respect to the global jihadi threat, however, an equally serious problem has emerged in higher education in much of the Muslim world, including (and perhaps especially) among Muslims educated at Western universities. Public education in the Muslim Middle East has traditionally been state-sponsored and designed to serve state interests. It does little more than crank out aspiring mid-level bureaucrats for whom the state can no longer provide meaningful employment. With the exception of a very few Western-sponsored institutions of higher learning (such as the American universities in Beirut and Cairo), there are no private universities to challenge state schools or introduce principles of critical thinking in the intellectual traditions of the region.[14] In much of the greater Middle East, religious schools provide the only alternative to deficient public education. As a result, the number of students pursuing advanced degrees in religious studies has increased dramatically, in some places outstripping the other social sciences and humanities. These graduates, in turn, enter the job market in their homelands and demand the Islamization of public education in order to improve their own job prospects. The Saudi export of *madrassas* during the era of "Petro-Islam" in the 1970s and 1980s provided a valuable alternative job market for religious teachers who might otherwise have posed an internal stability threat to the Saudi regime.[15] But the problem is not just a Middle Eastern one. European Muslims seeking advanced religious education have few options, as there are no Islamic universities in Europe. The emergence of an indigenous, moderate European Muslim identity will depend, in large part, on the ability of European governments and Muslim leaders to cooperate to provide educational alternatives to the foreign, and too often militant, *ulamas* and *imams* sent from Saudi Arabia, Egypt, or Yemen to teach Islam to young Europeans.

Graduates of Middle Eastern Islamic studies programs who find their prospects limited at home (due to lack of connections or of skill) have taken their diplomas on the road (often with financial support from their governments or from Islamic nongovernmental organizations), establishing their own *madrassas* in distant Muslim communities in need of "reform" or "Islamic revival." At first, these itinerant Islamic "scholars" settled in the Muslim hinterlands—the Afghan refugee camps of tribal Pakistan, the remote islands of Indonesia, tribal Sudan—but in recent years they have found a burgeoning market among the Muslim minority communities of Southeast Asia and Western Europe, the United Kingdom, and North America. Global radical and jihadi movements are growing fastest among relatively well-educated Muslims, many of whom have been schooled, employed, and often radicalized in the West. The result of this export of Islamic studies graduates is the emergence of a new, globalized brand of Islam that has taken on a distinctly fundamentalist/revivalist and salafist tinge. The movements have thrived and reached their ideological peak in the West largely as a result of two factors: the greater academic and religious freedom of Western European and American societies, which allows militant sheiks to teach and preach more or less unimpeded (especially in Britain and Spain, a source of some tension with their European Union partners),[16] and the tendency of Muslims studying in the West to pursue technical and engineering programs in which they are less likely to be exposed to Western traditions of critical thinking and challenging intellectual authority.

The driving force of this brand of radicalization is not illiteracy and ignorance but the intense anti-intellectualism that characterizes fundamentalist movements of all faith traditions. Historian Richard Hofstadter identified three pillars of anti-intellectualism in America that clearly apply as well to the Muslim world: evangelical (or revivalist)[17] religion, pragmatism, and populism. Anti-intellectualism is suspicious of moral relativism and specialized knowledge, especially in the realm of faith and theology. Most movements in the West have grown on the backs of religious "entrepreneurs" who are brilliant businessmen and charismatic religious figures. Few sell themselves as scholars of their faith; rather, they preach an emotional "old-time religion" and sow suspicion of religious as well as secular "eggheads."[18] Bin Laden is, by all credible accounts, just such a modern, anti-intellectual revivalist leader. He is a capable civil engineer, a pragmatic and effective man of business, and an untrained but charismatic preacher whose faith and piety are emotional rather than intellectual and have been legitimized by a deep commitment to jihad in defense of the faith rather than formal religious education.[19]

Fundamentalist religious education does not encourage critical thinking. A strict emphasis on the letter of scripture and religious law does not encourage questions, alternative interpretations, or the incorporation or tolerance of other religious and intellectual approaches. This ideological rigidity and absolute certainty serve these movements well in the recruitment of young people. Militant ideologies have spread most readily among young Muslims raised in urban environments by middle-class, professional parents. They received secular education but little or no traditional religious training and, as young adults, find their professional prospects limited and seek spiritual meaning in their lives. Those who do not want to commit to the years of study and seeking necessary to earn genuine religious enlightenment are seduced by the emotional intensity and instant gratification of the revivalist movements. The simple, immediate answers and absolute truths of revivalism appeal to both their youthful impatience and their often technical educational backgrounds.[20]

Oppression and Liberalization

History shows that the only guaranteed cure for terrorism is oppressive authoritarianism. In truly repressive societies, the downtrodden masses develop a degree of fatalism. They may blame their government for their sad lot in life, but they are also likely to accept it as the will of God, or the natural order of things. "Untouchables," as Crane Brinton, the dean of historians of revolution, wrote, "very rarely revolt against God's authority."[21] Organized terrorist movements were almost nonexistent in Nazi Germany, Fascist Italy, the Soviet Union, Fascist Spain, or Saddam Hussein's Iraq, as they are in North Korea today. As historian Walter Laqueur has explained, the reasons for this apparent paradox are fairly obvious: "terrorism [does] not stand much of a chance against political regimes able to use unrestricted force against them [sic], unhampered by laws, considerations of human rights, and public protests."[22] To put it another way, when the government itself is a terrorist organization, amateurs stand little chance of entering the market and being competitive.

Still, if actual oppression is not a factor in the rise of terrorism and public support for it, perceived oppression certainly is. At the heart of the ideology of every terrorist movement is the theme that the community the terrorists purport to represent is under mortal attack. In the most extreme cases of millennial terrorist ideologies—those of al Qaeda and Aum Shinrikyo, for example—prosaic political conflict is magnified and transformed into cosmic spiritual confrontations. It ultimately does not matter if the perceived oppression reflects reality, or even if the communities the terrorists claim to protect actually believe themselves in need of rescue, let alone see the terrorists as legitimate agents to act on their behalf. Militants and terrorists, especially those who believe their mandate comes from God, will continue to act as though they and their use of violence have popular legitimacy. The more successful their actions are, especially actions against a broadly resented target such as the United States, the more legitimate they become in the eyes of the disgruntled and alienated.

The most dangerous periods in the rise of major, influential militant revivalist movements and, in particular, in the emergence of terrorist organizations with significant popular support are periods of transition: either the collapse of an authoritarian regime (the dissolution of the Soviet Union in the mid-1990s and the overthrow of Saddam Hussein in Iraq in 2003) or the liberalization of an existing regime in response either to internal (Latin America in the 1980s and 1990s) or external (Iran in the late 1970s and Palestine in the early and mid-1990s) forces. Under authoritarian regimes, the rules of the political game are fixed to ensure the continuation of the status quo, and for all but the most extreme and zealous opponents, the risks of open resistance are too high. That does not mean, of course, that reformist sentiments do not exist. Soviet Central Asia is a case in point.

During the Soviet era, Moscow suppressed the free and open practice of Islam, and Islamic political groups were officially forbidden. But a devoted cadre of Central Asian Muslims met and studied underground and stood ready to capitalize on liberalization when it finally did occur. Moreover, when the pressure of repression is finally lifted, even a little, the opening stages are likely to be characterized by a chaotic ideological landscape in which extremists compete fairly effectively, at least initially.

Historians of revolution have long understood that the most danger-ous periods in the political evolution of nations are not when the society is burdened with widespread poverty. They come when people's lives are get-ting better but an inept regime is unable or unwilling to ensure that change keeps pace with popular expectations. Revolutionary movements are born of hope and rising expectations: it happened to the regimes of George III and Louis XVI, to Tsar Nicholas II, and to the Shah of Iran—each of whom responded to national crisis by making symbolic but wholly inadequate concessions to moderate reformers. But history would indicate that a coun-try cannot be a little bit democratic. As Brinton put it, in societies that have experienced revolutions, "the governments seem to have been relatively in-efficient, and the governed relatively impatient."[23] Especially in the modern age of instantaneous communication, greater openness is likely to afford populations unprecedented access to the outside world, resulting in a sense of relative deprivation even where economic and political realities at home are improving dramatically, as was the case in the Peoples' Republic of China in the period leading up to the Tiananmen Square massacre. The difference between Iran and China was that, unlike the Shah, the Chinese Communist Party leadership was able and willing to give the Chinese people the changes they wanted—economic and social liberalization—while keeping the lid on expectations regarding political change. One cannot help but wonder whether some of the nostalgia for the old communist order in places like Russia and East Germany stems at least in part from a desire to return to the relative innocence that comes from repression.

Another factor in the rise of militant sentiments is the displacement of responsibility—the tendency to blame political authorities and foreign manipulation for hardships rather than accepting personal or community responsibility for disappointments and setbacks. This sort of displacement of responsibility is fairly common in Western democracies and is a major trigger for the anti-globalization and anti-immigrant movements that have developed increasingly high profiles, even in one of the most self-consciously tolerant of Western countries: the Netherlands. In societies undergoing sig-nificant political and economic reform with little historical experience of the vagaries of the process, during which expectations escalate quickly and inevitably overtake real progress (which is often halting, at best), it is virtually inevitable.[24] Militant movements are well placed to capitalize on the smoldering resentments of a disappointed or impatient populace.[25] Moreover, the intense religious group identity that usually characterizes such movements provides a comforting sense of roots and collective identity for societies in transition. In the past decade or so, that frustration has been channeled into public support for militant fundamentalist and Islamist movements and, to a somewhat lesser degree, for terrorist figures. In a more representative Middle East, political parties—whether Islamist or not—will find the temptation to capitalize on that long-smoldering anti-U.S. sentiment irresistible come campaign time. Add to this already unstable mix the fact that the religious revivalism underlying many radical and reformist movements is characterized by hyper-emotionalism, and it seems surprising that popular support for the militant agenda is not greater across the Muslim world than it is.

So why isn't it? The reason seems to be that there is a natural ceiling to the amount of political capital that terrorists and militants can garner through devastating but still largely symbolic terrorist attacks against distant Western targets. Michael Scheuer, among others, has made a persuasive (although not yet conclusive) argument that al Qaeda and bin Laden are waging not a terrorist campaign but a global Islamist insurgency with the strategic aim of forcing the West out of the Muslim world and establishing a global Islamic caliphate.[26] He is almost certainly correct in his contention that there is virtually nothing the United States can do through "public diplomacy" to change negative public perceptions of the United States in the Muslim world or the surges of bin Laden's and al Qaeda's popularity when terrorists succeed in striking Western targets. But his justifiably pessimistic assessment of the situation misses one subtle but potentially important factor. Historically, the committed support base for militant movements like al Qaeda has been significant, but not widespread. Beyond that committed base, public support for the militants is soft—at best tacit, and at worst little more than temporary band-wagoning.

In order to achieve any long-term strategic aims, militant groups have to move out of the shadow world of global terrorism and earn (or seize) domestic political power. And given their almost universal lack of peaceful political experience, the only way militant terrorist groups have seen to gain power is to bring the terror campaign home. Yet in every recent case—in Egypt in 1997, in Saudi Arabia in 2004, and in Lebanon in 2005—the result of a major, high-profile campaign of terrorist violence in the homeland was exactly the opposite of what the militants hoped for. In each case, it led to a virtual evaporation of "soft" public support for the terrorists and the militant movements they represent. Destroying Western embassies, hotels full of Israeli tourists, and even the Pentagon and World Trade Center may be interpreted as giddy symbolic victories against a perceived evil oppressor, but destroying economic infrastructure and killing innocents and beloved public figures at home has turned out to be a bridge too far. This is wholly consistent with history. Militant extremists want to reform society and the hearts of men to build a moral and political "heaven on earth." But humans and their society are not so malleable. Militant attempts to force change through strict legal enforcement, terror, and physical extortion ultimately fail, and power eventually settles somewhere well short of the extreme. In the long run, in Brinton's words, "the constant prevails."[27]

Psychopathologies and Social-Psychological Contagions. For decades, psychological researchers have sought to explain why individuals become terrorists or join terrorist movements. Aside from identifying the odd paranoid schizophrenic (such as Shoko Asahara, the founder and leader of Aum Shinrikyo) among the ranks of terrorists, psychology has found no convincing evidence that terrorists show any greater tendency toward mental illness or instability than the general population. In fact, quite the opposite is the case. Terrorist organizations like the Irish Republican Army and al Qaeda carefully cull mentally unstable recruits because their lack of impulse control could undermine operational security. The mentally less-than-stable may be somewhat more common in the rank and file, particularly among the ranks of suicide terrorists, but these individuals (like Richard Reid, the so-called shoe bomber, and some of the Palestinian suicide bombers) are generally walk-ins or last-minute recruits who are kept on the periphery of the movement, isolated from operational planning.

Terrorists, and particularly terrorist elites, do share some basic similarities in their social and psychological development. Most are well educated, often in technical and professional disciplines (engineering seems especially common), and are frequently radicalized while still in school (most often in their mid-20s to early 30s). They are highly idealistic but in an abstract way—most show little remorse or pity for the real people whom they injure or kill—and they see themselves not as murderers or criminals but as agents of justice and/or righteousness. Many hold the conviction that they are avenging wrongs done against their parents and grandparents, and, in this sense, their acts of violence can be quite personal.[28] While most feel deep alienation from society, sometimes bordering on (or crossing the line into) sociopathology, they seldom display any outward signs of their rage or of their violent predilections.[29] Others harbor a deep conviction that they are divinely guided and often possess the ability to convince others of their unique contact with the divine.

Whether acting out of vengeance or divine guidance (or both), terrorist elites and their followers dehumanize and demonize the "other"—the societies against which they aim their violence—as embodiments of evil in a great cosmic confrontation. The function of dehumanization is twofold. First, it transforms a prosaic enemy into a cosmic threat and thus a target worthy of violence and undeserving of mercy or pity. Second, it creates a stronger sense of membership in an elite and righteous in-group.[30] Jerrold Post, among others, has developed detailed psychological profiles and analyses of terrorist elites like Osama bin Laden that provide insights into their individual motivations, but these offer few insights that are generalizable to the broader movement, let alone to the terrorists' popular support base. They are thus of limited utility in understanding the landscape of social factors that lead to the culture of terrorism.

Terrorism, as Mark Juergensmeyer and others have pointed out, is seldom a solitary act. Even if individual masterminds are sociopathic or mentally ill, they must have sufficient social skills to identify and capitalize on shared anxieties and traumas and enlist and sustain a support structure. Thus, most terrorism is the product not of individual psychology but of what Clifford Geertz calls a "cultural system": underlying patterns of thought, worldviews, and the ideological or religious meanings that groups attach to their actions.[31] It is important to keep in mind that most of the rank and file of terrorist organizations consists of young adult men, ranging in age from late teens to early thirties. Apparently they join jihadi groups for the same reasons young adult men forge other social relationships: in pursuit of social status, glamour, power, prestige, brother- or sisterhood, and perhaps for the financial compensations sometimes promised to their surviving families.

Alienation, dislocation, desire for meaning in one's life and actions, and humiliation—common denominators in the cultural systems of terrorists—can be found among young adults in almost any society. Social psychologists have long understood that while individual character traits predispose some people to violence, those traits do not in and of themselves explain violent behavior. More important, however, social psychology also provides useful insight into how social contexts lead otherwise mentally stable and even highly moral individuals who would normally abhor violence to take part in, or tacitly condone, heinous acts of violence even against innocents. Group-think and authoritarian pressure (whether real or perceived) consistently lead to riskier, crueler behavior and a greater willingness to commit or at least accede to violent acts than individuals would ever undertake on their own. As social psychologist Stanley Milgram warned in 1974: "The social psychology of this century reveals a major lesson: it is not so much the kind of person a man is as the kind of situation in which he finds himself that determines how he will act."[32]

What are the social contexts that account for the rise in some societies of larger, more complex terrorist organizations and, more important, widespread popular tolerance, support, and sometimes adulation of them and their actions among individuals who would otherwise abhor or at least not embrace violence? If we must accept that in any society at any time, there will be some individuals who act on a predisposition to violence by committing terrorist acts, how can we identify the tipping point for the emergence of broader terrorism and terrorist support? Why is it that a society can live in relative poverty and political repression for years, or even decades, and then suddenly produce a mega-terrorist movement with widespread social support?

Three key factors contribute to the rise of social epidemics.[33] The first is the rise of a cadre of committed individuals with particular social gifts: they are well and widely connected (through educational, social, political, and/ or religious networks); they are outgoing and eager to talk to their friends, families, and acquaintances one to one or in small groups about their ideologies; and at least a few of them are particularly persuasive and are able to convince the uncertain that their ideologies are reasonable, attractive, and satisfying. The second factor is the emergence of a message that lingers in people's minds. Instead of simply raging at injustice, for example, Osama bin Laden and Hamas have propagated an empowering, jihadist message of action—what 19th-century anarchists called the "propaganda of the deed."

The final factor is the context within which the message spreads. Context refers to not only the broad social environment (although that is important), but also the social and political networks within which the ideology is propagated. Intentionally or not, the cellular structure of most radical Islamic and terrorist groups is ideally suited to starting and sustaining a social epidemic. According to the "Rule of 150," borrowed from marketing, it is more effective to establish a network of small, targeted movements in groups of less than 150 individuals than to attempt to reach an entire society with a single message.[34] The Rule of 150 is important in the rise of radical movements for two reasons: first, 150 seems to be the largest group within which individuals can exchange and absorb information effectively; second, it seems to be the largest group over which a leader can exercise ideological influence and discipline. In this sense, the traditional social and religious structures of the Muslim world (especially the tendency for believers to affiliate themselves with a specific religious teacher based on the congeniality of his message rather than, as in most Christian denominations, based on geographic parish boundaries)—even as they have been adapted and mutated in the West—lend themselves to the propagation of radical ideologies.

Identity Crises. A reason for the apparent glass ceiling that limits committed popular support for militant Islamic movements in most of the traditionally Muslim world is that even the highly emotional Muslim revivalist identity must, in Muslim homelands, compete with a hierarchy of identities that are often more deeply ingrained: sectarian, national, tribal, ethnic, and linguistic, to name just a few. In the majority of cases, conflicts—whether political or military—historically have had more to do with those traditional identities than with purely religious ones. One of the main reasons pan-Arabist and pan-Islamist movements have consistently failed in the past, despite their rhetorical and emotional appeal, is that neither could overcome the centrifugal forces of national and ethnic identities. Even in those areas, such as Iraq, where the internal political landscape is in turmoil, terrorists and militants risk undermining their own cause when they are seen to be a threat to those older and broader identities.

In the January 2005 Iraqi elections, for example, a surprising number of ordinary citizens demonstrated an unexpected degree of patriotism in their stubborn and courageous resistance to the insurgents' attempts to disrupt and delegitimize the democratic process. Politically successful Islamist parties—including the most extremist ones like Hezbollah in Lebanon and the clerical conservatives in Iran—continue to operate almost exclusively in the context of national politics, pursue largely nationalist agendas (as they define them), and do not embrace an international caliphate as part of their political agenda. Even in the case of Afghanistan, the distinction must be drawn between the Taliban, which seemed content to inflict its miserable brand of puritanical rule only on its fellow Afghans, and al Qaeda, their invited but ultimately catastrophic Arab guests.

This rule of multiple competing identities does not seem to apply among Muslims in the West, particularly young second- and third-generation children of immigrants. While they may retain a superficial identification with the homelands and native cultures of their parents, they have no roots there. Unfortunately, large numbers of young Muslims in the West are not fully established in their adopted home societies either. Even where governments have made concerted efforts to facilitate assimilation, such as in the Netherlands and France, success has been limited, and the effort as often results in friction as in mutual understanding. While there are, of course, many individual success stories in Western Muslim communities, the hard reality is that Muslims in the West, particularly in Western Europe, suffer relative economic, educational, and political deprivation.

This identity crisis sets up a target-rich environment for militant clerics and sheiks looking for recruits to their anti-Western and anti-secular cause. Increasingly, young Muslims are isolating themselves in ideological ghettos in large European cities, which makes them both less likely to assimilate successfully and more likely to embrace violent militant ideologies. The sense of being downtrodden that derives from poverty or low socioeconomic status is aggravated by a lack of self-identity.[35] The first waves of migration—from either rural to urban or Muslim to non-Muslim societies—were not, for the most part, meant to be permanent but were seen as temporary economic expedients. This self-defined temporary status, combined with the hostility or indifference of host societies, prevented assimilation, but as their economic roots deepened, it became more difficult to return home. As a result, the second generation had a foot in both worlds. They identified with their "homelands" religiously and politically, but had no real experience of living in Muslim society (or, in some cases, of even living as Muslims). Those who tried to return often found themselves as out of place "at home" as they were in their birthplaces in the West.

The Islamic revival movements from which the terrorist and jihadi groups have emerged provide culturally rootless young Muslims a source of identity.[36] Their conspicuous piety gives dislocated and alienated youth a place to fit in and a sense of spiritual and moral superiority over a society that they believe has acted disrespectfully toward them, their parents, and their faith. The sense of alienation and deprivation is not limited to Muslim minorities, and revivalist Islam can be a means of escaping empty lives and finding brotherhood and a sense of destiny for lost souls of any ethnicity.[37] In the West, militant Islamic movements recruit young adherents in much the same way that the religious cults of the 1970s and 1980s recruited disillusioned young Americans: they embrace alienated young people (they have even had surprising success in converting non-Muslims such as Richard Reid and Jose Padilla) and make them part of a small, close-knit group that provides brotherhood, support, and status, and enforces ideological conformity; they impose an intricate and all-encompassing moral and behavioral code that provides meaning to day-to-day life and breaks down individuality; and they instill a degree of self-righteous paranoia in which the insiders are the guardians of virtue and the outside world is a threatening realm of corruption and evil. In contrast to the traditionally Muslim world, these young Western Muslims have little or no grounding in more orthodox religious and social structures to counter the influence of the militant groups. They are, in a sense, ideological free agents.

Fundamentalism and Revivalism. The rise of revivalist religion throughout the world has added a dimension to terrorist movements and their support base that the national liberation movements that emerged through the 1970s and 1980s did not demonstrate. Increasingly, revivalist religious movements have translated social unease and insecurity in the face of modernization and globalization into charges of oppression and persecution at the hands of secular society. Secular society is portrayed as corrupt, sinful, stagnant, and hostile to faith. In contrast, the revivalist fundamentalist movements promote faith as the road to empowerment. The most radical and demanding of the religious revivalist movements are creative and vibrant and make great demands on the individuals and societies that embrace them. The struggle and the sense of righteousness in the face of a hostile "world" give life and hardship meaning.[38] This phenomenon is not unique to observant Muslims; in the last few decades, virtually every major world faith has produced at least one radical revivalist movement that has, at least on its fringes, embraced terrorism. For these millennial groups—including extreme right-wing Christian and white supremacist movements in the United States—the force of evil oppressing the people is a demonic, irreligious secular national government. The illegitimacy of secular regimes extends to official religious hierarchies, which, because of their dependence on the largesse and good will of the state, the militants see as corrupt, impotent, and intellectually and spiritually bankrupt. In the United States, militant Christian revivalists (the Army of God, the Christian Identity Movement, and the Reconstruction Movement, for example) see themselves as fighting to free society and establish a new order rooted in Biblical law and a spiritual rather than secular social order.[39] In the Muslim world, the appeal of violent revivalist movements appears to be more widespread, and the hierarchy of evil is more complex. While militant revivalist movements see their own governments as apostates and enemies of faith and righteousness, the ultimate cosmic enemy is the West and, usually, the United States. The militants see America as the real power behind their corrupt and yet typically inept local regimes.

As a result, Islam is not the only faith to have produced violent militant fundamentalist movements, but so far, it is the only one that has produced militants who conduct their terrorist campaigns and entertain strategic ambitions beyond a domestic or regional context. Religious fundamentalism is a modern phenomenon that could not have existed prior to the scientific, rational age. Fundamentalists, unlike members of orthodox faiths, undertake to directly battle the twin evils of scientific rationality and modernism (especially individualism) by embracing the methodologies of the enemy. The fundamentalists have transformed religious teaching into literalist dogma and have challenged the authority of traditional religious hierarchies (be they priests or *ulamas*) as the sole legitimate interpreters of scripture and religious law. As a result, fundamentalist sects are most often led by "enlightened" amateurs: individuals whose knowledge of religion comes from sources other than formal religious education.[40] In the most extreme cases, such as the Taliban, the line between the sacred and the profane disappears, and every aspect of every individual's life becomes a matter for religious law.

Fundamentalists (of any faith) are, by definition, militant in the sense that they challenge both the dominant secular culture and traditional religious establishments. The University of Chicago Fundamentalisms Project defines fundamentalism as "a discernible pattern of religious militancy by which self-styled 'true believers' attempt to arrest the erosion of religious identity, fortify the borders of the religious community, and create viable alternatives to secular institutions and behaviors."[41] They believe they are warriors for God, condemning accommodations to secularism or ecumenicalism. That said, they are not necessarily a threat to national and international security.[42] Common features of the most extreme revivalist movements, such as the salafist schools in Islam, the ultra-Orthodox Jews, and some fringe millennialist Christian groups, are the twin goals of quarantining the community of the righteous from contamination by the outside world and deterritorializing their religion. Their goal is not necessarily to reform national governments to bring them in line with religious law, but to divorce the community from governmental institutions (which, because they are products of man's rather than God's will, are by definition profane) altogether.[43] Many ultra-Orthodox Jews condemn Zionism and have refused to accept the Israeli state (in fact, some have refused to emigrate to Israel) because they believe only God can restore the Jewish nation. For man to attempt to do so usurps God's authority and requires too many compromises with the secular world.[44]

The Tablighi Jama'at, one of the leading Islamic revivalist organizations operating in Europe today, sends itinerant preachers to Muslim communities in Hijra to purify them of accommodations to local culture. Founded in 1926, the Tablighi aimed to cleanse Indian Muslims of Hindu influences. Today, its missionaries are active in the West, instructing their followers to stay out of local politics, veil their women, resist coeducation, and avoid social interaction with non-Muslims. They do not, however, advocate violent jihad or any other attempt to overthrow the status quo.[45] Even the most recent revivalist movements, as a rule, have no interest in social structures and government infrastructures but focus purely on individual piety as the means to building a righteous and prosperous society. If every individual lives righteously in a way that pleases God, the result will be a peaceful and just society that will have no need of governments.

The deculturation and deterritorialization of Islam, which has been particularly (and primarily) effective in the Muslim diaspora, speaks directly to displaced and alienated young Muslims all over the world, but especially in the West. Part of the reason its allure is strongest in the West is that it appeals to the Westernized sensibilities of second- and third-generation children of Muslim immigrants who have never developed attachments to particular local Islamic traditions. It reduces Islam to pure religion with no meaningful cultural accretions. More important, it focuses on piety as the route to individual salvation. Islamic law and the traditions of the Prophet provide the basic blueprint for Muslim society but leave deeper interpretations of the meaning and implications for individual spirituality open to the diverse views of individual missionaries and preachers. Just as important, it insists on complete moral and cultural separation from the surrounding society and establishes identifying marks of piety—*hijab*, personal grooming, religious rituals, and so forth—that further quarantine its followers from their cultural surroundings and reduce their receptivity to alternative views.[46]

In the end, this revivalist emphasis on Islam as a road to individual identity and spiritual fulfillment—what Olivier Roy has called the "Protestantization" of Islam—may be the most important key to understanding the social origins of terrorism. Not only has it freed the individual from the traditional hierarchies and social strictures of orthodox Islam (both Sunni and Shia), but it also has devalued the traditional clerical and intellectual elite and opened the door to individual and iconoclastic interpretations of sacred texts by self-appointed religious experts like Osama bin Laden and Ayman al Zawahiri. This decoupling of religious piety from its historical, cultural, and social base is not unique to Islam; globalization, and particularly the rise of the unregulated Internet, has created a true free market of ideas for religious entrepreneurs and extremists of every stripe. It has also provided Islamic terrorist organizations with their richest recruiting base: like Mohammed Atta, much of the brain trust of global jihadism came from relatively secular families, and many were radicalized while receiving secular educations, either in their homelands or in the West. In fact, experience with Western languages and culture is a prerequisite for participation in complex terrorist operations in the West, since operatives who cannot pass for an assimilated immigrant run too great a risk of detection and capture.

In this sense, unfortunately, Westernization may have succeeded to a fault, creating a new *umma* of fully autonomous individuals with few ties to their societies of origin and the freedom to recreate Islam in their own ideological image and in service to their own spiritual and psychological needs.[47] Historically, the impetus for ideological change and evolution of Islamic mores has most often come from the periphery: first Spain and Persia, later Central Asia, and most recently, from Muslim India (Pakistan). This trend accelerated through the 1960s and 1970s as Islamic identities on the periphery strengthened while they seemed to be undermined by secularism and nationalism in the Arab core.[48] The turn of the millennium saw the dawn, perhaps, of a new stage in which the West is fast becoming the new center of Islamic thought, on both ends of the spectrum—a trend that promises to accelerate in the years ahead.

Notes

[1] Scott Atran, "Genesis of Suicide Terrorism," *Science* 299, no. 5612 (March 7, 2003), 1534.

[2] This chapter does not deal explicitly with the social context of terrorism in Palestine. Regardless of whether one sees the Palestinian intifada as a legitimate war of national liberation, it is clear that the superheated political context of the Palestinian quest for autonomy and the Israeli occupation sets it outside any useful generalizations that could be made about the social factors contributing to terrorism elsewhere in the Muslim world.

[3] The Kurds are not easily categorized, but their essentially ethnic rather than religious sense of identity bears the greatest similarity with the emerging independent Muslim nations; also, as a minority seeking autonomy, the Kurds share some characteristics with the traditionally Muslim minorities—in particular, the fear of cultural and social absorption by the ruling majority.

[4] Dato Zainal Abidin Mahamad Zain, Director General, South East Asia Regional Counter Terrorism Center (SEARCCT), address to Institute for Defense Analyses (IDA)/SEARCCT Seminar on the Dynamics and Structure of Terrorist Threats in Southeast Asia, Kuala Lumpur, Malaysia, April 18, 2005.

[5] Rommel Banlaoi, "Leadership Dynamics in Terrorist Organizations in Southeast Asia: The Abu Sayyaf Case," paper delivered at the IDA/SEARCCT Seminar on the Dynamics and Structure of Terrorist Threats in Southeast Asia, April 20, 2005.

[6] "Special Report: Dim drums throbbing in the hills half heard," *The Economist* 364, no. 8285 (August 10, 2002), 21.

[7] National Commission on Terrorist Attacks Upon the United States, *The Complete Investigation: The 9/11 Report* (New York: St. Martin's Paperbacks, 2004), 323–335.

[8] Richard W. Bulliet, *Islam: The View from the Edge* (New York: Columbia University Press, 1994), 202; Gabriel A. Almond, R. Scott Appleby, and Emmanuel Sivan, *Strong Religion: The Rise of Fundamentalisms around the World* (Chicago: University of Chicago Press, 2003), 128.

[9] Graham E. Fuller, *The Future of Political Islam* (New York: Palgrave Macmillan, 2003), 93.

[10] Review of James Thrower, *The Religious History of Central Asia from the Earliest Times to the Present Day* (Edwin Mellen Press, 2004), August 11, 2005, available at <wordtrade.com/religion/islam/centralasiaR.htm>.

[11] Zamira Eshanova, "Central Asia: Are Radical Groups Joining Forces?" *Eurasia Insight*, February 25, 2005, available at <eurasianet.org/departments/insight/articles/eav101102.shtml>.

[12] Jeffrey Goldberg, "The Education of a Holy Warrior," *The New York Times Magazine*, June 25, 2000, 32. See C. Christine Fair, "Religious Education in Pakistan: A Trip Report," U.S. Institute of Peace (March 20, 2006), available at <usip.org/events/2006/trip_report.pdf>, for a reexamination of the statistics of *madrassa* attendance in Pakistan.

[13] Rohan Guanaratna, paper delivered to the IDA/SEARCCT Seminar on the Dynamics and Structures of Terrorist Threats in Southeast Asia, April 18, 2005.

[14] Bulliet, 198.

[15] Olivier Roy, *Globalized Islam* (New York: Columbia University Press, 2004), 92–93.

[16] See, for example, John Kampfner, "Why the French Call Us Londonistan," *The New Statesman* 15, no. 736 (December 9, 2002), 18; and Stephen Ulph, "Londonistan," *The Jamestown Foundation: Terrorism Monitor* 2, no. 4 (February 26, 2004), 1.

[17] This paper uses two terms in characterizing militant Islamic movements: *fundamentalist* and *revivalist*. Fundamentalism refers to the various schools of Islamic thought and practice that seek to impose a literalist interpretation of Islamic religious and social laws in society, but which may or may not pursue a broader political and ideological militant agenda. I use revivalism to refer, more narrowly, to that subset of fundamentalism that actively proselytizes, politically and religiously, and sees religious revival as the key to social and political empowerment for the global Muslim *umma*. Islamic revivalism is closely tied to jihadi movements that have dedicated themselves to the purification of the *umma* and the restoration of the imagined golden age of Islamic supremacy.

[18] Todd Gitlin, "The Renaissance of Anti-Intellectualism," *The Chronicle Review*, December 8, 2000, available at <chronicle.com/free/v47/i15/15b00701.htm>.

[19] See *Through Our Enemies' Eyes: Osama bin Laden, Radical Islam, and the Future of America*, ed. Michael Scheuer (Washington, DC: Potomac Books, 2003), 69–73.

[20] Roy, 169.

[21] Crane Brinton, *The Anatomy of Revolution* (New York: Vintage Books, 1965), 251.

[22] Walter Laqueur, *No End to War: Terrorism in the Twenty-first Century* (New York: Continuum, 2003), 14–15.

[23] Brinton, 36, 250–251.

[24] The classic work in this genre is Crane Brinton's *The Anatomy of Revolution*. More recently, Fareed Zakaria has given the thesis of the destabilizing effects of democratization a more contemporary spin in *The Future of Freedom: Illiberal Democracy at Home and Abroad* (New York: W. W. Norton & Co., 2003).

[25] Mark Juergensmeyer, *Terror in the Mind of God: The Global Rise of Religious Violence* (Berkeley: University of California Press, 2000), 210.

[26] See *Through Our Enemies' Eyes*; and Michael Scheuer, *Imperial Hubris: Why the West is Losing the War on Terror* (Washington, DC: Potomac Books, 2004).

[27] Brinton, 246, 254, 262.

[28] Vamik Volkan, *Bloodlines: From Ethnic Pride to Ethnic Terrorism* (New York: Farrar, Straus and Giroux, 1997), 43–48.

[29] See, for example, Edgar O'Ballance, *The Language of Violence: The Blood Politics of Terrorism* (San Rafael, CA: Presidio Press, 1979); and Charles A. Russell and Bowman H. Miller, "Profile of a Terrorist," in John D. Elliot and Leslie K. Gibson, *Contemporary Terrorism: Selected Readings* (Gaithersburg, MD: International Association of Chiefs of Police, 1978), 81–95.

[30] Juergensmeyer, 116–117.

[31] Cited in Juergensmeyer, 13.

[32] In explaining his notorious obedience experiments, Milgram wrote that

with numbing regularity good people were seen to knuckle under to the demands of authority and perform actions that were callous and severe. Men who are in everyday life responsible and decent were seduced by the trappings of authority, by the control of their perceptions, and by the uncritical acceptance of the experimenter's definition of the situation, into performing harsh acts. . . . A substantial proportion of people do what they are told to do, irrespective of the content of the act and without limitations of conscience so long as they perceive that the command comes from a legitimate authority.

Quotes available at <stanleymilgram.com/quotes.htl.php>.

[33] This discussion of social epidemics is based primarily on Malcolm Gladwell, *The Tipping Point: How Little Things Can Make a Big Difference* (Boston: Little, Brown and Company, 2000).

[34] Ibid., 175–182.

[35] Roy, 269–274.

[36] Bulliet, 204–207.

[37] Roy, 317.

[38] Juergensmeyer, 225.

[39] Ibid., 23.

[40] Karen Armstrong, *The Battle for God* (New York: Alfred A. Knopf, 2000), ix–xvi.

[41] Almond et al., 17.

[42] Ibid., 14–17.

[43] Roy, 232–234.

[44] Samuel Heilman, *Defenders of the Faith: Inside Ultra-Orthodox Jewry* (New York: Schoken Books, 1992), 29–30.

[45] Roy, 235.

[46] Giles Kepel, *The War for Muslim Minds: Islam and the West* (Cambridge: Belknap Press, 2004), 256–257.

[47] Roy, 265–269, 302, 308.

[48] Bulliet, 195.

Chapter Six

Madrassas, Pesantrens, and the Impact of Education on Support for Radicalism and Terrorism

Kumar Ramakrishna

In late October 2003, in an internal memorandum to senior Pentagon officials, Secretary of Defense Donald Rumsfeld expressed concern about whether radical Islamic education was producing new generations of terrorists filled with violent hatred for the United States and its allies. He wondered if the United States was "capturing, killing, or deterring and dissuading more terrorists every day than the *madrassas* [Islamic religious schools] and the radical clerics are recruiting, training and deploying against us?"[1] Rumsfeld's concern was and is not without foundation. At this juncture in the war on terror, education is well recognized as a key factor in generating systemic, long-term support for radicalism and terrorism.

In Pakistan, for instance, some estimates place as many as a million students studying in over 10,000 *madrassas,* although other analyses have raised serious questions about these numbers.[2] More important than the total numbers, however, is the fact that, for a variety of reasons, the largest concentration of *madrassas* is now in the Pushtun belt of the Northwest Frontier Province, the area in which radical Deobandi Islam has had the strongest following. As a result, many of these institutions have been used as "incubators for violent extremism." Such *madrassas* allegedly have had links with both the ousted Taliban and al Qaeda.[3]

Furthermore, schools in Saudi Arabia, which are among the most highly developed in the Arab world and consume some 30 percent of the country's national budget, follow an extremist Wahhabi religious curriculum that takes up one-third of the average school day. The Wahhabi mindset is suggested by a passage from *Geography of the Muslim World,* an eighth-grade text that, in spite of its relatively innocuous title, clearly propagates a virulent, binary, us-versus-them worldview:

> There is no doubt that the Muslims' power irritates the infidels and spreads envy in the hearts of the enemies of Islam—Christians, Jews and others—so they plot against them, gather [their] force against them, harass them, and seize every opportunity in order to eliminate the Muslims. Examples of this enmity are innumerable, beginning with the plot of the Jews against the Messenger

and the Muslims at the first appearance of the first light of Islam and ending with what is happening today—a malicious Crusader-Jewish alliance striving to eliminate Islam from all the continents. Those massacres that were directed against the Muslim people of Bosnia-Herzegovina, the Muslims of Burma and the Philippines, and in Africa, are the greatest proof of the malice and hatred harbored by the enemies of Islam to this religion. [4]

The theme embedded in the above passage—of a global Islamic community or *umma* being subjected to vicious oppression by the "Crusader-Jewish alliance"—is one that animates the radical Islamist ideologies driving terrorist networks such as al Qaeda. This chapter seeks to analyze the ways in which both secular and religious forms of education lay the cognitive groundwork for the eventual emergence of such radicalized binary worldviews. Due to space constraints, the chapter will focus on how education generates support for Islamic radicalism in particular, drawing on cases from across the Muslim world. A religious radical in this chapter will be taken to mean a religious fundamentalist who, dispensing with an evolutionary, gradualist program for actualizing his socio-religious agenda, opts instead for a more revolutionary strategy for profoundly transforming society from the roots up and in as short a time as possible, through religiously legitimated social and political agitation, including violence.

The Socio-Cultural Backdrop

Any analysis of the impact of education on radicalism cannot be divorced from the wider sociocultural context. Olufemi A. Lawal, drawing on anthropological research, identifies a few dimensions of culture that can be used to analyze different societies, including power-distance, uncertainty avoidance, and individualism/collectivism.[5] Lawal notes that in high power-distance societies, "peoples accept as natural the fact that power and rewards are inequitably distributed in society."[6] In collectivist societies, individuals are expected to be loyal to the ingroup and subordinate personal goals to those of the collective. Moreover, such individuals may feel particularly "threatened by uncertainty and ambiguity."[7] Following Lawal, it may be hypothesized that individuals in high power-distance, collectivist, and ambiguity-intolerant milieus may be relatively more likely to gravitate toward radicalized educational environments. Three tentative reasons may be offered for this position. First, individuals in such societies, as Lawal suggests, would accept fairly readily that all authority and "power has been naturally concentrated" in the hands of a religious leader who may or may not espouse radical views.[8] Second, being cultural collectivists, they would tend to regard it as psychologically satisfying and their individual duty to demonstrate loyalty to the group. Third, being ambiguity-intolerant, they would be willing, relatively uncritically, to accept that leader's clear and unambiguous interpretations—couched possibly in religious language—of wider sociopolitical developments.[9]

Lawal's cultural dimension of ambiguity intolerance is of direct relevance for our purposes and deserves elaboration. Psychologists argue that in general, people have a tendency to organize the environment according to simple cognitive structures. More than that, humans, from childhood, seem to possess a need for "cognitive closure"; they desire a definite answer to a particular topic "as opposed to confusion and ambiguity."[10] This natural human quest for cognitive closure, particularly but by no means exclusively in non-Western, collectivist societies (which form 70 percent of the world population), has been greatly intensified by the psychosocial dislocations caused by globalization. Globalization has been usefully characterized as "worldwide integration through an ongoing, dynamic process that involves the interplay of free enterprise, democratic principles and human rights, the high-tech exchange of information, and movement of large numbers of people."[11] While "the juggernaut of free enterprise, democracy, and technology offers the best chance of wealth creation," the key to "improving the human condition"—globalization—has other implications.[12] By privileging "individualistic, impersonal, competitive, privatistic, and mobile" values and attitudes, globalization processes have inadvertently undermined traditional social units such as the family, clan, and voluntary association.[13] More precisely, globalization, which to many non-Western societies is synonymous with Westernization, is destabilizing because it promotes the de-sacralization of society; encourages religious and moral relativism; places the onus on the individual to determine his "values, career, life style, and moral system"; and, most disconcertingly, undermines traditional ideas about sexuality and the status of women.[14] Michael Stevens captures this well:

> For communitarian societies, keyed to historical continuity, group coherence and security, personal rootedness, and the affirmation of moral righteousness, empowering the individual is equated with rending society asunder.

Globalization may thus inadvertently precipitate socio-cultural dislocation at the aggregate level, and psychosocial dysfunction at the unit level.[15] Charles Selengut adds that to "follow the West is to become spiritually and psychologically homeless, without a transcendental anchor to provide security and safety during life's journey."[16]

Even within non-Western, collectivist, relatively ambiguity-intolerant societies, one should not imagine that everyone senses or perceives the world, and responds to any cognitive dissonance generated by contact with the world, in exactly the same way. Personality theorists have postulated two basic types of individual: the abstract/intuitive (intuitive) and the concrete/objective (concretist). According to Ronald Johnson, the intuitive individual tends to be creative in solving problems; is willing to explore hunches and new ideas; is imaginative; likes change; and is problem-oriented and subjective. Concretists, on the other hand, tend to "prefer a concrete way of perceiving the world, are down-to-earth; perhaps simple and possibly simplistic," and strongly "solution-oriented." Thus, while intuitives see "what could be," concretists see "what is."[17] The upshot of this is that non-Western, collectivist, ambiguity-intolerant societies undergoing accelerated Westernization may well produce individual concretists who are vulnerable to possible psychosocial dysfunction. Quite simply, in comparison to intuitives, they would be relatively less equipped cognitively to cope with what Jessica Stern calls "a surfeit of choice." For concretists, too much choice, "especially regarding identity, can be overwhelming and even frightening."[18]

This is precisely why religious fundamentalism, for example, is so attractive to many concretists. Charismatic fundamentalist leaders "offer their constituencies clear, objective, practical, and absolute directives for their lives and answers for their theological questions."[19] From the perspective of the unsettled concretist, relinquishing "one's autonomy in return for absolute ideological security is a powerful motive."[20] Interestingly, several Singaporean militants of the al Qaeda-affiliated Jemaah Islamiyah (JI) organization turned to leaders like Singapore JI spiritual leader Ibrahim Maidin because—like classic concretists—they wished to "free themselves from endless searching as they found it stressful to be critical, evaluative, and rational."[21]

Understanding why absolute ideological security can be so important to concretists requires a brief incursion into the burgeoning new field of psychobiology.[22] Neuroscientists tell us that the seat of human emotions and motivations lies in a primitive area of the brain called the limbic system, comprising the hypothalamus and the amygdala. The grape-sized amygdala is linked to the human sensory systems and constantly scans the information flowing through them, looking for signs of "threat or pain, whether physical or mental." Researchers have found that the amygdala plays a role in many emotions including hate, fear, joy, and love, and "serves as an emotional and behavioral trip wire, capable of automatically triggering a response before we consciously realize what is happening."[23]

The amygdala is interconnected with another area of the brain associated with aggression and defense: the hypothalamus, a small organ that regulates many of the body's automatic, stereotyped responses to external stimuli. When the amygdala senses danger, the hypothalamus activates the pituitary gland lying just below it; the pituitary releases an emergency hormone into the bloodstream that flows to the adrenal glands, prompting the latter to release stress hormones that galvanize the body for action—be it fight or flight.[24] The limbic system is very important in our analysis of the psychological (or psychobiological) makeup of hard-core concretists. Rush W. Dozier, Jr., explains:

> Our limbic system has evolved a powerful tendency to blindly interpret any *meaning system* [emphasis added] that we deeply believe in as substantially enhancing our survival and reproduction. Someone who wholeheartedly converts to a particular religion or political ideology, for example, is likely to experience strong primal feelings of joy and well-being coupled with an exciting new sense of purpose. This is true even if the belief system has elements that are bizarre or self-destructive.[25]

Dozier rightly points out that this tendency of the primitive limbic system to identify particular meaning systems as congruent with personal well being and survival can result in individuals "decoupling" their behavior from "objective criteria of survival and reproduction."[26] This insight may shed light on the motivations of suicide bombers, for instance.

This brings us back to the attraction of the dualistic, black-and-white certitudes of religious fundamentalism for concretists. The concretist personality, immersed in a rapidly globalizing non-Western sociocultural milieu, in search of cognitive closure in the midst of moral and spiritual uncertainty, would largely be "limbicly" hard-wired to want certainty and closure. Once the concretist has discovered ideological security in a particular fundamentalist religious system, he or she is likely to defend the new beliefs with "great emotional intensity."[27] In this respect, scholars like J. Harold Ellens regard fundamentalism less as a system of beliefs than as a highly problematic thinking or cognitive style. Ellens, to be sure, sees fundamentalist cognitive styles not just within religious systems, but also in "political movements, ethical systems, scientific perspectives, and every type of profession in which humans engage."[28]

Is Education the Cure for Concretists?

If the problem is the concretist cognitive style, could education be a solution? This issue needs to be approached with care. Much evidence suggests that certain types of education—even higher tertiary education—may be positively associated with religious radicalism. Daniel Pipes notes that many

Islamists have "advanced education" while a "disproportionate number of terrorists and suicide bombers" possess a "higher education, often in engineering and the sciences."[29] Nor is anecdotal evidence of a connection between science/technical education and radicalism hard to find. Ramzi Yousef, the al Qaeda operative who planned the 1993 World Trade Center attack, for instance, studied computer-aided electrical engineering in Swansea, Wales.[30] Some JI members are similarly well educated in technical fields. Indonesian Islamist Agus Dwikarna, who has had associations with JI, is a civil engineer by training.[31] Malaysian JI operative Shamsul Bahri Hussein read applied mechanics at Dundee.[32] Yazid Sufaat, who apparently tried to acquire anthrax and develop biological weapons for al Qaeda, was a 1987 biochemistry graduate from California State University.[33] Also of note is the late Malaysian Dr. Azahari Husin, the top JI bombmaker who wrote the organization's bomb manual and was involved in the Bali, Jakarta Marriott, and Jakarta Australian embassy bombings.[34] Husin studied in Adelaide for 4 years in the 1970s, secured an engineering degree in Malaysia, and later received a PhD in statistical modeling from Reading University in the 1980s. He taught at Universiti Teknologi Malaysia before going underground in 2001.[35] This is by no means an exhaustive list.

Is any alleged correlation between a technical and hard sciences education and radicalism a wildly simplistic and even irresponsible assertion to make? Bahai scholar Moojan Momen suggests, perhaps counterintuitively, that "when scientists (especially from the physical sciences) and engineers become religious, they often tend towards fundamentalist religion."[36] Psychological research has shown that natural or physical scientists in fact tend to be *more* religious than social scientists such as sociologists and psychologists. This has been explained by the so-called scholarly distance thesis:

> The reason, in psychological terms, is that the natural sciences apply critical thinking to nature; the human sciences ask critical questions about culture, tradition, and beliefs. The mere fact of choosing human society or behavior as the object of study reflects a curiosity about basic social beliefs and conventions and a readiness to reject them. Physical scientists, who are at a greater scholarly distance, may be able to compartmentalize their science and religion more easily.[37]

The scholarly distance thesis could explain the strikingly high proportion of Islamist activists worldwide with backgrounds in the hard sciences and engineering. For example, on university campuses in Iran and Egypt, such activists constitute "25 percent of humanities students, but 60–80 percent of students in medicine, engineering, and science."[38] Islamic scholar Khalid Duran has commented on the "odd" fact that "Islamic fundamentalism" has always had "its strongest appeal among engineers." He observes wryly that in Egypt, "they always say the Muslim Brotherhood is really the Engineering Brotherhood."[39] Duran offers his interpretation of this phenomenon:

> Engineers don't exercise their fantasy and imagination. Everything is precise and mathematical. They don't study what we call 'the humanities.' Consequently, when it comes to issues that involve religion and personal emotion, they tend to see things in very stark terms.[40]

This leads the certainty-seeking (concretist) Islamist scientist/engineer to engage in what Malise Ruthven calls "monodimensional or literalist readings of scripture," as compared to their "counterparts in the arts and humanities whose training requires them to approach texts multidimensionally, exploring contradictions and ambiguities."[41] Ruthven is not the only one to make this argument. Former Indonesian president and accomplished Islamic scholar in his own right, Abdurrahman (Gus Dur) Wahid, in a 2002 speech in Seoul, made a similar observation about the concretist orientation of many young Indonesian Muslims educated in technical disciplines in the West:

> Because they have not been trained in the rich disciplines of Islamic scholarship, they tend to bring to their reflection on their faith the same sort of simple modeling and formulistic thinking that they have learnt as students of engineering or other applied sciences.

Consequently, Gus Dur observed, they take a

> more or less literalistic approach to the textual sources of Islam . . . [and] use these texts in a reductionistic fashion without being able to undertake, or even appreciate, the subtly nuanced task of interpretation required of them if they are to understand how documents from the 7th to 8th centuries, from the tribal Arab society among the desert sands, are to be applied correctly to the very different world that we live in today.

It is significant that Gus Dur warned that if such well-educated but concretist and technically minded Muslims are not instructed "to approach their faith with the intellectual sophistication that the demands of the modern world require of them," then when they encounter "alienation, loneliness and the search for identity" abroad, they will be vulnerable to the "formalistic understanding of Islamic law" that breeds "violent radical-ism." He lamented in this respect that "precious few young Muslims from developing nations have the privilege of undertaking liberal arts courses in Western universities."[42] Khalid Duran, echoing both Gus Dur as well as the logic of the scholarly distance hypothesis, believes that "having an educa-tion in literature or politics or sociology seems to inoculate you against the appeals of fundamentalism."[43]

Concretist Cognitive Styles, Fundamentalist Mentalities, and Binary Worldviews

Gus Dur's comment about the relationship between a "formalistic understanding of Islamic law" and "violent radicalism" is pregnant with significance. Precisely because uncertainty is "deeply unsatisfactory to the fundamentalist [concretist] psyche,"[44] once such an individual discovers a religious or ideological system that satisfies his search for meaning, he would be limbicly disposed to tolerate "no ambiguities, no equivocations, no reservations, and no criticism."[45] Any perceived threat to his closely held belief system might even provoke aggression.[46] Thus, psychologists like J. Harold Ellens consider what he calls "fundamentalism"—in our terms, concretism—as a form of "psychopathology," defined as "a rigid structural-ist approach that has an obsessive-compulsive flavor to it."[47] This "obses-sive-compulsive" quality of a concretist cognitive style has the potential to in turn produce what critical theorist Stuart Sim calls the "fundamentalist mentality." An individual possessing a fundamentalist mentality not only displays the "desire for certainty" but also actively seeks "the power to en-force that certainty over others."[48]

This intrinsic rejectionist attitude toward difference, in the final analy-sis, makes the concretist-minded religious fundamentalist such a potential cause for concern, because by definition he would be limbicly hardwired to be, in Leon Festinger's terms, a *transformationist*. He simply cannot live and let live in matters of faith; he can only rest easy when the outside world is synchronized with his conception of the perfect society. In other words, he would feel compelled to define truth for everyone else around him as well.

This intrinsic desire to impose a favored vision of a perfect society on others, Sim explains, shows that "religious fundamentalism" is "more to do with power than spiritual matters," and "power is a political rather than a spiritual issue." In essence, the fundamentalist mantra—which has at its core the concretist cognitive style—is about "control, control, control."[49] Political scientist R. Hrair Dekmejian elucidates the links be-tween a concretist cognitive style, a fundamentalist desire for "epistemic" control, and intolerance toward difference in his description of the "*mutaasib*, or Muslim fundamentalist fanatic." Dekmejian argues that the *mutaasib* tends to be characterized by "rigid beliefs, intolerance toward unbelievers, preoccupation with power," and last but not least, a "vision of an evil world."[50] Dekmejian points out that such a "close-minded, rigid-thinking dogmatist" is "susceptible to a variety of rigid, and potentially destructive, ideologies."[51]

The route to such "potentially destructive ideologies" runs from an ambiguity-intolerant concretist cognitive style, through a power-seeking fundamentalist mentality, and ultimately to a rigidly held binary worldview. John E. Mack defines a worldview as "an organizing principle or philosophy" that is similar to an ideology, but "broader in scope," and a sort of "mental template into which we try to fit events."[52] Jemaah Islamiyah spiritual leader Abu Bakar Bashir's binary worldview in this respect is of interest. He once declared during a sermon:

> God has divided humanity into two parts, namely the followers of God and those who follow Satan. . . . God's group are those who follow Islam, those who are prepared to follow his laws and struggle for the implementation of *shariah* [Islamic] law. . . . Meanwhile what is meant by Satan's group are those people who oppose God's law, who . . . throw obstacles in the path of the implementation of God's law. [53]

Bashir was emphatic in declaring that there was no hope of conciliation between true Muslims who believed in the complete implementation of Islamic law and those that opposed this:

> We would rather die than follow that which you worship. We reject all of your beliefs, we reject all of your ideologies, we reject all of your teachings on social issues, economics or beliefs. *Between you and us there will forever be a ravine of hate and we will be enemies until you follow God's law* [emphasis added]. [54]

In sum, within non-Western, collectivist societies experiencing social dislocation due to accelerated globalization, religious radicalism may well result from a psychological pathway linking a concretist cognitive style, a fundamentalist mentality, and a binary worldview. Moreover, secular technical education, even higher education, may not only fail to mitigate but also even inadvertently *consolidate and reinforce* such a pathway. The impact of more narrowly focused religious education must now be analyzed against this wider sociocultural backdrop for its contribution to the religious radicalization process.

Ethnocentrism, Religion, and Radicalism

"The human mind," according to social psychologists, "groups people, as well as objects, into categories" that enable individuals to "simplify the present and predict the future more effectively."[55] The same social psychologists admit that it is also "a small step from categorization" to "stereotyping and favoritism for one's group." This ingroup bias exists because individuals define themselves partly by their group membership. Membership in a high-prestige group meets basic psychological needs such as "belongingness, distinctiveness," and "respect."[56] This is especially true for individuals with deep "affiliative needs" and an "as-yet incomplete sense of individual identity" that generates an intense need to belong. This impels them to "submerge their own identities into the group," so that a kind of "group mind" emerges.[57] Nevertheless, "taken to extremes," stereotyping of outsiders, fostered by the establishment of a "group mind" by charismatic religious leaders, for example, can foster dangerous prejudice.[58] What is more, religion can be exploited to legitimize the group mind and reinforce this prejudice against outsiders. Paul N. Anderson's comments shed light on the implications of Bashir's worldview cited earlier:

> An important aspect of religious power is that it creates an "us."
> It solidifies group identity and appeals to religious certainty,
> eternal consequences, and principled loyalties. [But] Yahweh's
> warfare against tribal adversaries in Hebrew Scripture, the de-
> humanization of infidels in the Koran, and the temporal and
> eternal warnings against the unfaithful in Christian Scripture
> function to create an us-versus-them mentality common to
> prejudice and violence. In that sense, the organizing power of
> religion to create intra-group solidarity becomes a devastating
> contributor to inter-group opposition. [59]

In short, when "everyday bias" is "supported and legitimated by religion," the "passions of ordinary malcontents" can be "intensified and focused."[60] Religious education in this respect can be exploited by radicals to ensure that concretist cognitive styles, fundamentalist mentalities, and binary worldviews are "intensified and focused," paving the way for the onset of radicalism and possibly even terrorism. This is readily illustrated in the case of *Pondok Pesantren al Mukmin*, the Indonesian religious boarding school founded in Solo, Central Java, in 1971 by Bashir and his late associate, Abdullah Sungkar.

In Indonesia today, there are two main forms of Islamic religious schools. The *madrassa* is an Islamic day school, while the *pesantren* is a boarding school. Indonesian *madrassas* provide primary, lower secondary, and upper secondary education. The majority of *madrassa*s are privately run, but some are regulated by the Indonesian Ministry of Religious Affairs. Whether privately or state-run, all *madrassa*s, under the Educational Law of 1989, are required to teach the national curriculum devised by the Ministries of Education and Religious Affairs.[61] This curriculum consists of 70 percent general subjects and 30 percent religious subjects.[62] While state *madrassa*s and private *madrassa*s run by progressive Islamic teachers adhere to the liberal educational thrust of the national curriculum, some private *madrassa*s do teach a more "radical educational agenda."[63] In 2001, more than 5.5 million primary, lower, and upper secondary students were enrolled in more than 35,000 private and state-run *madrassa*s.[64] *Madrassa*s are less expensive than public secondary schools and provide basic education in rural and lower-income urban areas.[65]

Pesantrens, on the other hand, teach at the secondary level only and function outside the state *madrassa* and public school system. In 2001, an estimated 2.7 million students were enrolled in 11,312 *pesantrens*.[66] Dating back to the late 19th century and the arrival of Islamic modernist currents from Cairo, the typical Indonesian *pesantren* exists "as a community with a compound, mosque and boarding system where students and teachers eat, sleep, learn, and generally interact throughout the day."[67] The generally cloistered *pesantren* environment is pregnant with significance.

Pondok Pesantren al Mukmin has sought to combine the best aspects of two well-known *pesantrens*, the modernist *Gontor* (where Bashir has studied) with its excellent Arabic training, and the hard-line *Persis* (Islamic Union) *pesantren* in Bangil, which remains noted for its teaching of *shariah*.[68] There has, however, been a hidden and more insidious agenda as well. In 2000, Abu Bakar Bashir spoke about the strategic importance of religious boarding schools in particular in strengthening the capacity of the *umma* to defend itself against the "enemies of Islam." He averred that "religious boarding schools are the bulwarks of Islam," and that "graduates of *pesantren*" must "truly become preachers and mujahideen." Harking back to the "learned men in the early days of Islam," Bashir opined that aside from "acting as scholars, missionaries, and moral teachers, they were also mujahideen who were always prepared to go to war and didn't just sit back in their mosques or schools giving lessons."[69] Bashir's comments show that in his mind, the true Muslim must always be prepared to wage both *dakwah* and jihad in the quest to set up a *Daulah Islamiyah*. His remarks set the context for a closer analysis of how religious education in al Mukmin helps fosters radicalism.

Al Mukmin usually draws students from 12 to 18 years of age, from West Java, Sumatra, Lombok, Central Java, West Irian, Sulawesi, Kalimantan, Singapore, Malaysia, and even Australia.[70] In terms of numbers, al Mukmin enrolls at any time about 2,000 students, including 800 girls.[71] The curriculum emphasizes both secular (mathematics, physics, English, business skills, and computers) and religious subjects (*fiqh* [Islamic jurisprudence], Arabic, and *aqidah*, or faith). Arabic, Bahasa Indonesia, and English are spoken in al Mukmin, but most students speak Arabic. During the long school day, which lasts from 3:00 AM to 10:00 PM, students pray, read the Koran, attend classes, and take part in sports or physical activity such as martial arts, soccer, badminton, mountaineering, and even long marches.[72] Since this sounds like a description of a regular Indonesian *pesantren*, it may well be asked: in what way does education at al Mukmin foster radicalism?

The answer is that radicalized binary worldviews are cultivated not so much through didactic means via the formal curriculum as through the semi-formal, "general culture" of the institution.[73] According to al Mukmin alumni, the boarding school nature of the *pesantren* expedites virtual "24-hour monitoring" of students by teachers and senior students in all spheres of activity: lessons, language, sports, cleaning, and so forth. This close contact ensures that the "emotional bond between teachers and students is very strong."[74] For instance, journalist Noor Huda Ismail, who attended al Mukmin from 1984 to 1990, between the ages of 12 to 17, used to share a "dingy student dormitory together with 20 other students and a volunteer resident assistant named Fadlullah Hasan" who was 3 years his senior and had "a perpetual blue bruise on his forehead from bowing his head to the floor as the result of his five prayers per day." After daily morning prayers at the adjacent mosque, Hasan would lead the boys in reading the Koran and urge them to "study and proselytize Islam." Hasan and Noor eventually developed a "tight bond."[75] Noor later recounted how such close personal ties between teachers and students helped "intensify and focus" embryonic concretist cognitive styles and binary worldviews. For example, Koran reading classes were conducted in groups of 20 students of 12 to 13 years in age, who were taught the "correct" interpretation of passages by a senior student, usually 16 years old, who had himself been taught in the same way.[76] In addition, al Mukmin organized frequent public-speaking sessions on Thursday nights, and the "most popular topic" was "the threats facing Islam," such as "Global Jewish power and Indonesia's Christian-controlled economy,"[77] as well as "jihad."[78]

Other ways in which al Mukmin students were drilled into the Wahhabi ideological storyline of "a malicious Crusader-Jewish alliance striving to eliminate Islam from all the continents" were through *halaqah* or small-group discussions involving students and a teacher, as well as one-way lectures, or *tausiyah*, conducted by *ustaz* (teachers). In addition, students themselves were required to engage in *dakwah*, or proselytization, exercises of their own, going out of al Mukmin to speak within nearby Islamic circles. Ismail also recounted how, for instance, during *halaqah* sessions, the *ustaz* would ask students what they intended to do on graduation, and when the latter replied that they may go into business, the *ustaz* would subtly plant the idea that perhaps participating in jihad to defend their oppressed Muslim brethren would be a better option. Other subtle indoctrination measures were used as well: during arduous 6-day marches from Solo to Surabaya, and martial arts training, the students would be urged by teachers to "be strong" and overcome fear and weakness, as Islam needed to be defended from its enemies.[79] Additional insidious elements discreetly programmed into the general culture of al Mukmin also helped "intensify and focus" binary worldviews and Wahhabi ideological perspectives. These included in-house martial music such as "Nasyid," an Arabic song about jihad,[80] as well as posters and signs proclaiming messages like "Jihad, Why Not?" and "No Prestige without Jihad" pasted "on walls, lockers, and walkways leading to classrooms."[81] Other graffiti spotted by visiting journalists evinced the simmering radicalism being bred within the school. These included messages such as "Bush and Sharon, if you like dead, come to here," and, less elegantly, "Bush is f*cked."[82] Visiting journalist Tracy Dahlby inadvertently shed additional light on the highly xenophobic culture of the *pesantren* simply by glancing at students' sandals:

> When we reached the front steps of the school and I bent down to remove my shoes as custom required, I couldn't help but notice that the dozens or so pairs of cheap plastic sandals scattered around the base of the stairs all had interesting little pictures or symbols of some kind etched in ballpoint pen on their insteps. When I took a closer look, however, my heart gave a thump—the little symbols were in fact crude renditions of the Holy Cross and the Star of David.[83]

Dahlby's guide explained: "So students can always step on them."[84]

The well-known scholar of comparative religion, Charles Kimball, has noted that problems arise within a religious constituency when "charismatic leadership" and an "unwavering commitment to compelling ideas and teachings" intersect with the "impulse to withdraw from society."[85] In like vein, Jonathan Drummond argues that physical withdrawal enables religious leaders to promote "alternative news sources," and "closed religious/ritual systems," to "pull one away from competing social networks and constructions of reality."[86] Certainly, al Mukmin's management appears to have appreciated the need to insulate the flock from the external environment.

Noor Huda Ismail observed that students were required to obey their teachers at all times and were not permitted direct personal contact with the outside world. Television, radio, magazines, and the Internet were all off-limits, as they were seen as vehicles of Westernization. Similarly, smoking, alcohol, jeans, baseball caps, and contact with females were all prohibited. Infractions of these rules would result in the offending student having his hair shaven and having to express regret for his act publicly.[87] Singaporean journalists corroborated Noor's comments, as they discovered that al Mukmin students were warned not to talk to strangers and were punished if they did.[88] In addition, in line with Drummond's argument, following the August 2003 J.W. Marriott JI attack in Jakarta, a pamphlet entitled "Marriott Conspiracy Theory," which blamed "Israeli and U.S. intelligence agents" for the incident, was circulating among the al Mukmin fraternity.[89] Al Mukmin, in sum, quite apart from intensifying and focusing concretist cognitive styles, power-oriented fundamentalist mental orientations, and binary worldviews, was seeking to complete the radicalization project by fostering nothing less than an alternate reality informed by the destructive al Qaedaist storyline.

Providing Education for De-Radicalization

We have argued that within non-Western, collectivist, ambiguity-intolerant societies undergoing rapid sociocultural changes with the onset of globalization and rapid urbanization, there are many individuals who are compelled to handle the cognitive dissonance generated by the collision of secular capitalist modernity and traditional value systems and structures. While some individuals are intrinsically *intuitive* and are generally able to cope creatively with such dissonance through social, economic, political, moral, and attitudinal adaptation, there are others, displaying what we have termed *concretist* cognitive styles, who are more solution- than problem-oriented and who seek, above all, answers in the midst of existential uncertainty. Especially within collectivist, high power-distance societies, including many Muslim countries, such concretists tend to gravitate toward charismatic religious clerics, for instance, who are able to articulate the clear and unambiguous answers they seek. Once these concretists find a religious or ideological system that meets their felt needs at a profound level, moreover, they tend, for psychobiological reasons, to be limbically committed to these belief systems, and may under certain circumstances even be prone to violence in defense of these ideas.

We also saw that it is a small step from concretist cognitive styles to power-seeking fundamentalist mentalities, as social networks of concretists, inspired and guided by charismatic religious clerics, seek to transform the wider society in accordance with what they hold to be "correct" religiously justified lines. When such attempts at societal transformation are thwarted by wider social and religious forces or a secular state, the result often is a rigid binary worldview dividing the world sharply into a "good" realm populated by the concretists and the "evil" realm dominated by the unbelievers. At this juncture, radicalization—defined as the desire on the part of the concretist-minded religious fundamentalists to affect the profound transformation of society from the roots up—sets in. They may either do so peaceably, through mass civil society organizations and political parties such as the Egyptian Muslim Brotherhood or Pakistani Jemaat-i-Islami, or more drastically, through violence, such as Egyptian Islamic Jihad or Southeast Asia's Jemaah Islamiyah. At this point, an ideology of resistance against either the "near enemy" or, as in the case of al Qaedaism, the "far enemy" of the "malicious Crusader-Jewish Alliance," is articulated to mobilize either political or violent dissent against the existing *jahili* political order and the international interests that prop up that order.[90]

What is to be done? Some analysts have called for improving the capacity of non-Western, especially Muslim, governments to provide better quality and more affordable secular public education, so that Muslim parents need not send their children to low-cost private Islamic schools. This suggestion, however, ignores the fact that one of the attractions of religious education for Muslim parents everywhere, apart from its low cost relative to secular public education, is the former's emphasis on moral values for "life's hard slog."[91] The real need, therefore, is to improve both secular public and private Islamic education. In this connection, the proposed Targeting Terrorists More Effectively Act of 2005, which states that it should be U.S. policy to raise "$7 to $10 billion annually to fund education programs in Islamic countries," is a step in the right direction. The International Youth Opportunity Fund, currently designed to provide funding aid to improve public education in the Middle East, is something that can and should be extended to other parts of the Muslim world as well.[92]

The question is how these funds should be spent. Within non-Western countries at the broader, societal realm, an all-important need remains to mitigate the social and cognitive implications of collectivist, high power-distance, and ambiguity-intolerant mass orientations. Simply put, people need to think more for themselves and not intellectually subcontract to religious or other ideologues the admittedly difficult philosophical problem of meshing traditions with secular, capitalist modernity. This is, of course, easier said than done, as the old Milgram experiments demonstrate that the urge to obey authority is a very strong one in all societies.[93] As the brutal examples of Rwanda, Yugoslavia, and the old Soviet Union remind us, the so-called power of the situation can well transform otherwise ordinary people into savage mobs blindly following the hate-filled agenda of ethnic entrepreneurs. Nevertheless, the argument being developed here is that the ability to critically analyze social life is a skill that should be inculcated from an early age. This is not to suggest that educational reform would be able to successfully transform deeply ingrained cognitive styles in toto. The idea, however, is to mitigate their worst effects. While intuitives can benefit much from the intellectual discipline and drive for the "truth" of the concretists, the concretists have much to learn from the intuitives' ability to cope with the amount of ambiguity necessary to modern life.

As far as the Muslim world is concerned, voices have already been raised in support of developing critical thinking skills. Roy Mottahedeh, for instance, argues strongly for a liberal arts emphasis in tertiary education, arguing that the "graduates of such an expanded liberal arts education system would be forces for economic development."[94] He adds that such education should be in the vernacular, so as to "reach the underprivileged, create the textbooks and even the language of discourse, and allow a discourse that draws on the cultures of these countries." To this end he goes so far as to call for an ambitious new "Fulbright Plan" to establish "well-funded liberal arts institutions" teaching in vernacular languages and offering bachelor's degrees in "Cairo, Karachi, and kindred places" throughout the Muslim world.[95] This is not to assert that science and technology education should be underemphasized, as these remain important drivers of industrialization, economic expansion, and job creation, especially in view of the so-called youth bulge affecting many Muslim countries. As Mottahedeh observes, critical thinking and writing should be the norm in "both the human and scientific spheres." This harkens back to the scholarly distance hypothesis of Beit-Hallahmi and Argyle. The key is to produce graduates in collectivist societies who have been trained to apply critical analysis to *both* the natural and the social worlds. Ameliorating the worst effects of the concretist cognitive style would go a long way toward establishing the intellectual preconditions for "the eventual emergence of a politics at once authentically Islamist yet also authentically liberal and democratic," and ultimately, a "Muslim Reformation."[96]

To expedite a Muslim Reformation, moreover, requires reform within the more narrowly defined realm of Islamic education worldwide. In this respect, former Thai Foreign Minister Surin Pitsuwan, a devout Muslim, laments that the original spirit of inquiry, which led Arab Muslim intellectuals of the past to attain great heights of achievement in science, philosophy, and the arts, has long been absent from Islamic education in general. Rather, the general principle in too many religious schools appears to be "memorization, stop thinking, stop rationalizing,"[97] a view that certainly seems to hold in the example of al Mukmin discussed earlier. Even at university level, autodidactic or monodimensional readings of Scripture—consistent with the concretist cognitive style—appear the norm, especially in secular, technical university campus environments. To prevent the development of tunnel vision among young Muslim undergraduates in the hard sciences and engineering, the latter should be encouraged to enroll for properly audited courses that would help them develop sophisticated methodologies for interpreting Islamic law. They should also be exposed to works by Islamic scholars like Averroes (Ibn Rushd) and Avicenna (Ibn Sina) that examine how Islam can engage with a real world environment in which "sexual equality, human rights, and the development of democracy" are burning issues of the day.[98]

Similarly, contemporary works by scholars such as Indonesia's Nurcholish Majid and Iran's Abdulkarim Soroush could also be studied at university level, as they are "trying to extract the prophetic truths from the Koran to show the inherent compatibility of modern-day concerns with the sacred texts."[99] The overarching idea, over time, is to develop well-balanced Muslim university graduates everywhere who are able to articulate for themselves what Rachid Ghannoushi once called a "realistic fundamentalism" or *usuliyah waqiyah*, rather than a rigid, doctrinaire Islam imported from 7th-century Arabia and unresponsive to the complexities of 21st-century, globalized Indonesia.[100] With a properly designed Islamic educational curriculum through cross-faculty cooperation between secular and Islamic tertiary institutions, concretist, monodimensional readings of Scripture would have a good chance of being replaced by more sophisticated and nuanced analysis. For instance, some devout Javanese Muslims have always felt that the preoccupation of Islamic fundamentalists with *shariah* was "an odd goal for a true Muslim to aspire to." The *shariah* is not the end, but only the way to the true goal: *hakikat*, or self-mastery, "Islam's highest level."[101]

Tertiary Islamic education aside, there is also considerable scope for reform of primary and secondary Islamic education, as Pitsuwan's remarks cited earlier attest. First, there is a real need to broaden if not eliminate the binary worldviews promoted by specific constituencies of hate such as al Mukmin. In this connection, Farid Ma'ruf, a senior instructor/professor at al Mukmin, once asked rhetorically:

> There is one community. Then there are some members of that community who have done something wrong. Is that community also at fault? [102]

This essay answers *yes*, not because this constituency explicitly advocates violence against outsiders, but because it promotes a worldview or mental template that under certain circumstances may lead certain alumni to embrace violence. Hence what is needed, as al Mukmin alumnus Noor Huda Ismail argues, is greater institutionalized exposure of the members of cloistered constituencies of hate such as al Mukmin to *difference*. This injunction translates into exposure to different interpretations of key concepts such as jihad by visiting *ustaz* from other *aliran* (ideological streams); more interfaith dialogues; dialogues with alumni who have become successful in the secular world; and greater contact with and more access to information about the outside world.[103] The overarching concern at the level of dealing with specific, physically isolated religious schools, especially boarding schools, would be to open up the vistas of its members by humanizing the "Other." When non-Muslims are seen more as fellow human beings than as "disembodied" abstractions, the potential for radicalism and ultimately terrorism is decreased.[104] Charles Kimball correctly argues that at the heart of healthy religion is the willingness of teachers and followers to ask questions and to challenge dogma. Claims of absolute truth and blind obedience are two signs of corrupted religion.[105]

It should be emphasized that progress in the educational sphere cannot be divorced from concrete policy elsewhere. Precisely because radical Islamist ideologies seek to exploit failures on the part of Muslim governments to provide security, welfare, and justice, Western-led programs to improve the overall capacity of these governments for effective governance to alleviate poverty, generate economic growth, and eliminate corruption in the justice system would go a long way toward reducing the "political oxygen" that radical Islamist ideologues exploit to strengthen the virulent binary worldviews they seek to propagate.

Finally, improving the image of the United States around the Muslim world cannot be ignored. Part of the problem encumbering progressive Muslim scholars as they seek to delegitimize the virulent ideologies and binary worldviews of radical Islamists is that U.S. policy toward the Muslim world—with which the progressives are often associated in wider Muslim opinion—often appears anti-Muslim. Quite apart from stepped-up public diplomacy showcasing the ways the United States has sought to help the global *umma*, such as the interventions in Kuwait (1990), Bosnia (1995), and Kosovo (1999) to aid oppressed Muslims, care must be taken to ensure that stark errors in U.S. policy, strategy, and tactics are minimized. In this regard, the notorious and extremely damaging 2004 Abu Ghraib prison scandal in Iraq, and the allegations of desecration of the Koran by military interrogators at Guantanamo Bay, Cuba, all helped radical Islamists everywhere reinforce the worldviews that encourage radicalism. In sum, better education can only be a necessary, but by no means sufficient, antidote to Islamist radicalism.

Notes

[1] Fred Kaplan, "Rumsfeld's Pentagon Papers," *Slate*, October 23, 2003, available at <slate.msn.com/id/2090250>.

[2] Most notably Tahir Andrabi et al., "Religious School Enrollment in Pakistan: A Look at the Data," World Bank Policy Research Working Paper No. 3521 (Washington, DC: The World Bank, March 2005).

[3] Christopher M. Blanchard, "Islamic Religious Schools: *Madrassas*: Background," Congressional Research Service Report for Congress, February 10, 2005, 5.

[4] *Geography of the Muslim World*, Grade 8 (1994).

[5] Lawal defines *power-distance* as "the extent to which a society accepts unequal distribution of power," *uncertainty avoidance* as "the extent to which a society feels threatened by uncertainty and ambiguity," and *individualism/collectivism* as "the extent to which dominant values in society emphasize assertiveness and material acquisition." Olufemi A. Lawal, "Social-Psychological Considerations in the Emergence and Growth of Terrorism," in Chris E. Stout, *The Psychology of Terrorism*, vol. 4: *Programs and Practices in Response and Prevention* (London and Westport, CT: Praeger, 2002), 26–27. Lawal draws these typologies from Geert Hofstede, *Culture's Consequences: International Differences in Work-Related Values* (Beverly Hills, CA: Sage Publications, 1984), 65–148.

[6] Lawal, "Socio-Psychological Considerations," in Stout, *The Psychology of Terrorism*, vol. 4, 27.

[7] Ibid.

[8] Ibid.

[9] Ibid.

[10] Ibid., 12.

[11] Michael J. Stevens, "The Unanticipated Consequences of Globalization: Contextualizing Terrorism," in Chris E. Stout, *The Psychology of Terrorism*, vol. 3: *Theoretical Understandings and Perspectives* (Westport, CT: Praeger, 2002), 37–38.

[12] Ibid., 38.

[13] Ibid., 39.

[14] Charles Selengut, *Sacred Fury* (Walnut Creek, CA: Altamira Press, 2003), 157–158.

[15] Stevens, "Unanticipated Consequences," in Stout, vol. 3, 40.

[16] Selengut, 158.

[17] Ronald Johnson, "Psychoreligious Roots of Violence: The Search for the Concrete in a World of Abstractions," in J. Harold Ellens, *The Destructive Power of Religion*, vol. 4: *Contemporary Views on Spirituality and Violence* (Westport, CT: Praeger Publishers, 2004), 200–202. Johnson draws these typologies from C. G. Jung, *Psychological Types* (Princeton, NJ: Princeton University Press, 1971).

[18] Jessica Stern, *Terror in the Name of God: Why Religious Militants Kill* (New York: HarperCollins, 2003), 69.

[19] Johnson, "Psychoreligious Roots," in Ellens, 207.

[20] Benjamin Beit-Hallahmi and Michael Argyle, *The Psychology of Religious Behavior, Belief, and Experience* (London and New York: Routledge, 1997), 115.

[21] *Singapore White Paper: The Jemaah Islamiyah Arrests and the Threat of Terrorism* (Singapore: Ministry of Home Affairs, January 7, 2003), 17.

[22] Johnson, "Psychoreligious Roots of Violence," in Ellens, 195; J. Harold Ellens, "Fundamentalism, Orthodoxy, and Violence," in Ellens, 124.

[23] Rush W. Dozier, Jr., *Why We Hate: Understanding, Curbing, and Eliminating Hate in Ourselves and Our World* (New York: Contemporary Books, 2002), 6.

[24] Ibid., 5–8.

[25] Ibid., 11.

[26] Ibid., 12.

[27] Ted G. Goertzel, "Terrorist Beliefs and Terrorist Lives," in Chris E. Stout, *The Psychology of Terrorism*, vol. 1: *A Public Understanding* (Westport, CT: Praeger, 2002), 98.

[28] Ellens, "Fundamentalism, Orthodoxy, and Violence," in Ellens, 120.

[29] Daniel Pipes, *Militant Islam Reaches America* (New York: W.W. Norton, 2002), 56.

[30] Malise Ruthven, A *Fury for God: The Islamist Attack on America* (London and New York: Granta, 2002), 217.

[31] "Indonesian Linked to Manila, Jakarta Bombings," Laksamana.Net, July 6, 2002, available at <laksamana.net/vnews.cfm?ncat=22&news_id=3127>.

[32] Michael Day and David Bamber, "Universities Spy for MI5 on Foreign Students," News.telegraph.co.uk, August 28, 2004, available at <telegraph.co.uk/news/main.jhtml?xml=/news/2004/03/21/nspy21.xml&sSheet=/news/2004/03/21/ixnewstop.html>.

[33] Maria Ressa, "Al Qaeda Operative Sought Anthrax," CNN, October 10, 2003, available at <cnn.com/2003/WORLD/asiapcf/southeast/10/10alqaeda.anthrax>.

[34] Dr. Azahari Husin was killed in November 2005.

[35] "Azahari: Professor, Bomb-Maker and Fanatic," Channelnewsasia.com (Singapore), September 10, 2004, available at <channelnewsasia.com/stories/afp_asiapacific/view/105933/1/.html>; Dan Murphy, "Leaderless, Terror Group Still Potent," *Christian Science Monitor*, August 18, 2003.

[36] Ibid.

[37] Beit-Hallahmi and Argyle, 181.

[38] Ibid., 182.

[39] See Steven Emerson, *American Jihad: The Terrorists Living Among Us* (New York: The Free Press, 2002), 172.

[40] Ibid., 173.

[41] Ruthven, 103.

[42] Abdurrahman Wahid, "Best Way to Fight Islamic Extremism," *The Sunday Times* (Singapore), April 14, 2002.

[43] Emerson, 173.

[44] Ibid.

[45] Moojan Momen, "Fundamentalism and Liberalism: Towards an Understanding of the Dichotomy," *Bahai Studies Review* 2, no. 1 (1992).

[46] Steve S. Olweean, "Psychological Concepts of the 'Other': Embracing the Compass of the Self," in Stout, vol. 1, 116.

[47] Ellens, "Fundamentalism, Orthodoxy, and Violence," in Ellens, 120.

[48] Stuart Sim, *Fundamentalist World: The New Dark Age of Dogma* (Cambridge: Icon Books, 2004), 29.

[49] Ibid., 100.

[50] Cited in Neil J. Kressel, *Mass Hate: The Global Rise of Genocide and Terror* (New York: Westview, 2002), 199.

[51] Ibid., 199, 211.

[52] John E. Mack, "Looking Beyond Terrorism: Transcending the Mind of Enmity," in Stout, vol. 1, 176. I would also like to acknowledge my appreciation of the insights into Indonesian radical Islamist worldviews of my colleague Faizah Samat of the International Center for Political Violence and Terrorism Research within the Institute of Defence and Strategic Studies.

[53] Cited in Sally Neighbour, *In the Shadow of Swords* (Sydney: HarperCollins Publishers, 2004), 1.

[54] Ibid., 2.

[55] Kressel, 211.

[56] Michael J. Stevens, "Unanticipated Consequences," in Stout, vol. 3, 44.

[57] Jerrold M. Post, "Terrorist Psycho-Logic: Terrorist Behavior as a Product of Psychological Forces," in Walter Reich, *Origins of Terrorism: Psychologies, Ideologies, Theologies, States of Mind* (Washington, DC: Woodrow Wilson Center Press, 1998), 33.

[58] Kressel, 211.

[59] Paul N. Anderson, "Religion and Violence: From Pawn to Scapegoat," in J. Harold Ellens, *The Destructive Power of Religion: Violence in Judaism, Christianity and Islam*, vol. 2: *Religion, Psychology, and Violence* (London and Westport, CT: Praeger, 2004), 270–271.

[60] Willard Gaylin, *Hatred: The Psychological Descent Into Violence* (New York: Public Affairs, 2003), 244.

[61] Azyumardi Azra, "Bali and Southeast Asian Islam," in Kumar Ramakrishna and See Seng Tan, *After Bali: The Threat of Terrorism in Southeast Asia* (Singapore and River Edge, NJ: World Scientific Publishing Company, 2003), 42.

[62] Martin Van Bruinessen, "'Traditionalist' and 'Islamist' *Pesantren* in Contemporary Indonesia."

[63] Mochtar Buchori, "RI's 'Madrasah' Producing Techno-Illiterates," *Yaleglobal* On line, July 3, 2002, available at <yaleglobal.yale.edu/display.article?id=194>.

[64] Usmar Anza, "Islamic Education: A Brief History of *Madrassas* with Comments on Curricula and Current Pedagogical Practices," unpublished paper, March 2003, 10.

[65] Ibid.

[66] Ibid.

[67] Ibid.

[68] Van Bruinessen.

[69] Cited in Neighbour, *In the Shadow of Swords*, 14–15.

[70] Noor Huda Ismail, presentation on *Pondok Pesantren Al-Mukmin* to Institute of Defence and Strategic Studies (IDSS), Nanyang Technological University, Singapore, April 8, 2005.

[71] Tracy Dahlby, *Allah's Torch: A Report From Behind the Scenes in Asia's War on Terror* (New York: William Morrow & Co., 2005), 230.

[72] Noor Huda Ismail.

[73] The phrase is Martin van Bruinessen's.

[74] Noor Huda Ismail.

[75] Noor Huda Ismail, "Ngruki: It is a Terrorism School?" Part 1, *The Jakarta Post*, March 15, 2005.

[76] Noor Huda Ismail, IDSS talk.

[77] Noor Huda Ismail, "Ngruki," Part 1.

[78] Noor Huda Ismail, IDSS talk.

[79] Ibid.

[80] Noor Huda Ismail, "Ngruki," Part 1.

[81] Zalman Mohamed Yusof and Mohammad Ishak, "Inside a JI School," *The New Paper on Sunday* (Singapore), January 4, 2004.

[82] Neighbour, 6.

[83] Dahlby, 229.

[84] Ibid.

[85] Charles Kimball, *When Religion Becomes Evil* (New York: HarperCollins, 2003), 74.

[86] Jonathan T. Drummond, "From the Northwest Imperative to Global Jihad: Social Psychological Aspects of the Construction of the Enemy, Political Violence and Terror," in Stout, vol. 1, 76.

[87] Noor Huda Ismail, IDSS talk.

[88] Yusof and Ishak.

[89] Timothy Mapes, "Indonesian School Gives High Marks to Students Embracing Intolerance," *Asian Wall Street Journal*, September 2, 2003.

[90] The concept of *jahiliyya* can be understood as "a condition of ignorance and unbelief." John L. Esposito, *Unholy War: Terror in the Name of Islam* (New York: Oxford University Press, 2002), 30.

[91] Dahlby, 231–232.

[92] Blanchard, 6.

[93] For details of these famous experiments proving that ordinary people are well capable of engaging in antisocial behavior as long as they feel that their actions are legitimized by a perceived higher authority, refer to Stanley Milgram, *Obedience to Authority: An Experimental View* (London: Tavistock Publications, 1974).

⁹⁴ Roy Mottahedeh, "Help Get Education Running Again," *The International Herald Tribune Online*, February 13, 2002, available at <iht.com/articles/47879.html>.

⁹⁵ Ibid.

⁹⁶ Graham E. Fuller, "The Future of Political Islam," *Foreign Affairs* 81, no. 2 (March/April 2002), 59.

⁹⁷ Surin Pitsuwan, "Strategic Challenges Facing Islam in Southeast Asia," lecture delivered at a forum organized by the Institute of Defence and Strategic Studies and the Centre for Contemporary Islamic Studies, Singapore, November 5, 2001.

⁹⁸ Mohamed Charfi, "Reaching the Next Muslim Generation," *The New York Times*, March 12, 2002, available at <nytimes.com/2002/03/12/opinion/12CHAR.html>.

⁹⁹ Karim Raslan, "Now a Historic Chance to Welcome Muslims into the System," *The International Herald Tribune Online*, November 27, 2001, available at <iht.com/articles/40072.html>.

¹⁰⁰ John L. Esposito and John O. Voll, *Makers of Contemporary Islam* (New York: Oxford University Press, 2001), 108.

¹⁰¹ Dahlby, 265.

¹⁰² Maria Ressa, "Jihad Rules in Islamic School," CNN.com, February 26, 2004.

¹⁰³ Noor Huda Ismail, IDSS talk.

¹⁰⁴ J. Harold Ellens, "Revenge, Justice, and Hope: Laura Blumenfeld's Journey," in Ellens, vol. 4, 227–235.

¹⁰⁵ Kimball, 41–99.

Chapter Seven

Sacred Values and the Limits of Rational Choice: Conflicting Cultural Frameworks in the Struggle Against Terrorism

Scott Atran

Generating a worldwide consensus against terrorism, and thus turning the tide of global support (especially in the Muslim world) for violent actions against the United States and its allies, requires a profound understanding of different cultural points of view. If we recognize that the struggle is not merely about control of Afghanistan or Iraq, but rather about meaningful cooperation with future generations of Muslims emerging from the massive transnational political awakening prompted by easy access to global media, particularly the Internet, it is obvious that a deeper understanding of the attitudes and beliefs of these people is essential to success. Moreover, given that much of the world's Muslim population is engaged in a quest for meaning, stability, and hope for achievement in an increasingly mobile and rootless world that levels history and flattens culture in the name of universal access to economic participation and progress, we must also understand not only what the cultural values of Muslims are, but also what they are becoming. We need to reassess the motivations and objectives of jihadis—America's most implacable foes—but also our society's own political and popular motivations and objectives in meeting the threat.

Writing in the last century, when the great debates between secular ideologies seemed to drive world politics, French resistance leader, stateman, and man of letters André Malraux said: "The next century will either be religious or it won't *be*." Malraux's insight into what politicians and pundits—and especially scholars—were missing was an important one. For decades, the only attention given to ideas in analysis of the Middle East was to the Western *isms*: colonialism, nationalism, socialism, communism, democratic liberalism, and so forth. In Southeast Asia, Muslims who identified themselves as such were labeled by scholars as "statistical" or "nominal" Muslims. Many in the academic establishment completely missed the boat, particularly those engaged in postmodernist and postcolonial critical studies. Part of the reason may have been intellectual fashion, but probably more significant was a failure to appreciate the power of religious faith, which has always colored how most people in nearly all societies believe that they ought to act toward others.

The power of faith to provide people a sense of community and direction is something the current U.S. administration, like much of the American public, appears to take to heart at home but not to appreciate fully when it is manifested abroad. While many recognize that preempting and preventing terrorism require understanding the conditions and the enlistment processes[1] that inspire people to give their lives in the name of a greater cause, the approaches employed to analyze options for countering these forces often assume that adversaries model the world on the basis of rational choices that are commensurable across cultures. Such assumptions prevail in risk assessment and modeling by foreign aid and international development projects run by institutions such as the World Bank and nongovernmental organizations, and by U.S. diplomatic, military, and intelligence services.

While the political and economic conditions that are the basis for such assessments are important, understanding that people of varying cultures may respond to identical conditions in different ways is even more important. Recent work in psychology, anthropology, religious studies, and political science relating to social conflicts shows that culturally distinct value frameworks constrain preferences and choices in ways not readily translatable between cultures. Planning and acting in ignorance or disregard of different value frameworks may exacerbate conflict, with grievous loss of national treasure and lives.

The promise of redeeming real or imagined historical grievances through a religious (or transcendent ideological) mission that empowers the militarily weak with unexpected force against enemies materially much stronger is one with age-old appeal. This was true for the Jewish Zealots who sacrificed themselves to kill Romans two millennia ago, and interviews with terrorists and those who inspire and care for them indicate it is just as true for Muslim jihadists today. Individuals who join the jihad, especially would-be martyrs (suicide bombers), are often motivated by small-group dynamics and noninstrumental values—values that trump rational self-interest because they are seen not as means to an end but as having intrinsic worth. Challenges to such values lead to moral outrage and often to what outsiders consider an "irrational" need for vengeance.

The aim of this chapter is to offer a better understanding of the role of sacred values (noninstrumental, moral, or protected values) and the limits of rational choice in maintaining and helping to resolve seemingly intractable cultural and political conflicts. Sacred values appear to involve behavior that seems motivated "independently of its prospect of success," often involving ethical or religious beliefs. Such values are not sensitive to standard calculations regarding cost and benefit, to quantity, to tradeoffs across moral categories (for example, family versus God), or to commensuration between different cultural frames. This means that traditional calculations of how to defeat or deter an enemy—for example, by providing material incentives to defect or threatening massive retaliation against supporting populations—might not succeed. For negotiators, policymakers, and others who must interact with unfamiliar cultures, it is important to understand sacred values to know which social transgressions and offers for tradeoffs are likely to remain morally taboo.

Theoretical Background: Sacred Values in Religiously Inspired Decisions and Actions

At the same time that Americans, inspired by Benjamin Franklin's credo that "rebellion to tyrants is obedience to God," were rising against England, the English historian Edward Gibbon was writing *The Decline and Fall of the Roman Empire*, attributing Rome's collapse to religious infection by Christianity.[2] Ever since, most politicians and ordinary people have continued to praise God, while most scientists and secularly minded scholars have continued to bemoan religion's baneful influence and predict its demise. If anything, religious fervor is increasing across the world, including in the United States, the world's most economically powerful and scientifically advanced society. An underlying reason is that science treats humans and their intentions only as incidental elements in the universe, whereas in religion, they are central. That is why Thomas Jefferson's impersonal deist God and the French Revolution's neutral deity fell by the wayside, and why as much as half the population in the ostensibly godless Soviet Union professed religious belief. Religion endures and thrives because it addresses people's deepest emotional yearnings and society's foundational moral needs. No society has ever endured more than a few generations without a moral foundation that is considered to be true without question but which is nevertheless not rationally scrutable.

In a competition for moral allegiance, secular ideologies are at a disadvantage—particularly one such as post-Enlightenment liberalism, which contends that new moral discoveries are constantly being made. If some better ideology is likely to be available in the future, backward induction argues that there is no compelling reason other than self-interested convenience to accept the current ideology. And if people come to believe that all apparent commitment is self-interested convenience or, even worse, manipulation for the interest of others, then commitment withers and dies. By contrast, religion passionately rouses hearts and minds to break out of this viciously rational cycle of self-interest and to adopt group interests that can benefit individuals only in the long run. In the narrowest case, a married couple bound in devotion to one another more easily overcomes personal ups and downs than a couple whose marriage is a matter of material convenience. In the broadest case, mutual faith in an omniscient and omnipotent agent, such as the supreme deity of the Abrahamic religions, mitigates the mentality of "every man for himself."

Religious behavior often seems to be motivated by sacred values, which incorporate moral and ethical beliefs that may motivate action "independently of its prospect of success." Max Weber, a leading scholar and founder of modern sociology and political economics, distinguished the noninstrumental "value rationality" of religions and transcendent political ideologies from the "instrumental rationality" of Realpolitik and the marketplace.[3] Instrumental rationality involves strict cost-benefit calculations regarding goals; ones that are too costly to achieve are adjusted or abandoned. By contrast, as Immanuel Kant explained, virtuous religious behavior (an example of a sacred value) is its own reward. Indeed, any attempt to justify virtuous behavior based on utility nullifies its moral worth.[4]

High-cost personal sacrifices to (non-kin) others in society typically seem to be motivated by, and framed in terms of, such noninstrumental values. This includes jihadi conceptions of martyrdom, which involve a moral commitment to kill infidels for the sake of God. One review finds that "only a minority of human violence can be understood as rational, instrumental behavior aimed at securing or protecting material rewards."[5] Historically, violence motivated by religious values tends to underpin the most intractable and enduring conflicts within and between cultures[6] and civilizations.[7]

Political scientists and economists acknowledge the role of religious values in coordinating groups for economic, social, and political activities, and in providing people with the immunity that goes with action in large numbers.[8] From a rational choice perspective, such values operate instrumentally to form convergent trust among masses of people with disparate interests and preferences,[9] thus reducing "transaction costs" that would otherwise be needed to mobilize them.[10] Others grant the instrumental value of "ethnicity" and values rooted in other ascriptive (birth-based) identities such as religion and language but question why ethnicity would be the basis for mobilization at all.[11] And why does the mobilization of these values energize the most enduring and intractable conflicts between groups? The fact that noninstrumental values are such powerful motivators to conflict suggests that they possess inherent qualities that instrumental values lack, such as passion and obligation. It also suggests that these two sorts of values can interact in intricate ways.

Sacred Values and the Logic of Terrorism

Identifying sacred values in different cultures and how they compete for people's affections is a first step in learning how to prevent differences between those values from spiraling into mortal conflict between societies. All religions and many quasireligious ideologies that make claims about the laws of history or universal missions to reform humanity are based on sacred values, which are linked to emotions that underpin feelings of cultural identity and trust.[12] These emotion-laden sentiments are amplified into moral obligations to strike out against perceived opponents no matter what the cost when conditions of relative deprivation reach a point at which some group members see no acceptable alternative within their society's framework of sacred values.

Such sentiments are characteristic of emotionally driven commitments, such as heartfelt romantic love and uncontrollable vengeance, which are apparently arational and may have emerged through natural selection to override rational calculations when confronted with seemingly insurmountable obstacles to the attainment of deep-seated needs.[13] In religiously inspired terrorism, these sentiments are manipulated by organizational leaders, recruiters, and trainers, mostly for the organization's benefit at the expense of the individual. In times of crisis, every society routinely calls upon some of its own people to sacrifice their lives for the general good of the community. One important difference is that for militant jihadis, crisis is constant, and extreme sacrifice is necessary as long as there are nonbelievers (*kuffar*) in the world.

In addition to being an expression of the atavistic cultural elements just described, global jihadism is a thoroughly modern movement filling the political void in Islamic communities left in the wake of discredited Western ideologies coopted by corrupt local governments. The fact that jihadism is to some extent a countermovement to the view expressed in the *National Security Strategy of the United States* that liberal democracy is the "single sustainable model of national development right and true for every person, in every society" does not make its appeals to Muslim history and calls for the revival of the caliphate any less heartfelt.[14] At the same time, jihadism's apocalyptic yearnings and born-again vision of personal salvation through radical action are absent from traditional Islamic exegesis and, indeed, perhaps as much may be learned about such apocalyptic yearnings from the New Testament's Book of Revelations as from the Koran.[15] Nor does Islam per se or "Muslim civilization" have anything in particular to do with terrorism—no more than some impossibly timeless or context-free notion of Christianity, Judaism, Hinduism, or Buddhism can be held responsible for the millions of deaths that have occurred in the name of these religious traditions.[16]

Jihadi leaders and ideologues, beginning with bin Laden himself, have used the edited snippets and soundbites favored by today's mass media with consummate skill, not as a factual description of the way the world actually is or was, or even as a reflection of the ideologues' own mores, but as a means of motivating potential followers to violent action. In the jihadi-friendly media, local and historically nuanced interpretations of religious canon have been flattened and homogenized across the Muslim world and beyond, in ways that have nothing to do with actual Islamic tradition but everything to do with a polar reaction to perceived injustice in the prevailing unipolar world. At the same time, the historical narrative, however stilted or fictitious, translates personal and local ties within and across small groups into a profound connection with the wider Muslim community (*umma*). In the competition for people's allegiance between those who would level history in order to open a global economic playing field and those who would tap people's personal experiences and deeply emotive ancestral narratives in the name of access to a purportedly just world, it is not at all clear that the message of moderation and modernity wins.

Yet it is nonsense to claim that al Qaeda and its sympathizers have no morality and simply want to annihilate Western civilization. In general, charges of nihilism against an adversary usually reflect willful ignorance regarding the adversary's moral framework. At every turn, Osama bin Laden has sought moral justification and sanction for al Qaeda's actions and demands.[17] This includes his invocation of a fatwa published in May 2003 by the radical Saudi cleric Hamid bin Al-Fahd permitting the use of nuclear weapons to inflict millions of casualties upon Americans unless the United States changes its foreign policy in the Middle East and elsewhere in the Muslim world.[18] One important post-9/11 development is that al Qaeda splinter groups no longer consider themselves to be territorially rooted in supporting populations. Thus, unconstrained by concrete concerns for what will happen to any population that supports them, deracinated jihadis can seriously consider any manner of attack, including one leading to fulfillment of Hamid bin Al-Fahd's apocalyptic vision.[19]

By helping to provide political and economic opportunity, honest and efficient social and economic policies may help prevent some people from beginning the downward spiral toward conflict between incommensurable moral views of the world. But for some, once that spiral starts, the task becomes much more difficult. Once sacred values come into play, negotiated tradeoffs based on balancing costs and benefits become taboo, just as selling off one's child or selling out one's country is taboo, no matter the payoff. In these cases, offers of compromise or exchange are met with moral outrage. Counting on military pressure, the imposition of democratic institutions, the economic power of globalization, or the Western media's powers of persuasion to get others to give up such sacred values is a vain hope. Policymakers from nations that fight sacred terror and hope to defeat it need to reach people before they get to the point at which commitment becomes absolute and nonnegotiable.

Perhaps equally as important as identifying positive steps that may reduce the likelihood of invocation of sacred values in this conflict of worldviews is understanding what actions increase the probability of a confrontation between sacred values. Recent psychological research concerning the similar concepts of protected values and taboo tradeoffs provides useful insights.in this regard. [20] Psychologist Phil Tetlock and his colleagues define a *protected value* as "any value that a moral community implicitly or explicitly treats as possessing infinite or transcendental significance that precludes comparisons, tradeoffs . . . with bounded or secular values."[21] Despite more than a decade of research on protected values and decisionmaking, however, knowledge of their influence is quite limited. What is clear is that sacred or protected values have a privileged link to moral outrage and other emotions, especially when a person holding a sacred value is offered a secular value or tradeoff such as selling one's child. The strong negative reaction to a 2003 proposal by the Defense Advanced Research Projects Agency to set up a futures trading market to predict terrorist attacks is another case in point.[22]

Instrumental decisionmaking involves strict cost-benefit calculations regarding goals and the willingness to abandon or adjust them if costs for realizing them are too high. One claim is that protected (sacred) values are associated with deontological criteria—that is, they are matters of moral obligation whose importance cannot be measured by consequentialist rules such as weighing benefits against costs or linking means to ends. People whose sacred values are at stake often say that they have a moral obligation to act, independent of the likelihood of success, "because I couldn't live with myself if I didn't." But there is little analysis of the mental accounting involved in quantity insensitivity or the stability of values across decision frames.[23] For example, a medical decision framed as a matter of life or death may be insensitive to cost, but one framed in terms of a marginal increase in prospects for survival may not be.[24] Researchers have found protected values to be associated with the elimination of otherwise robust framing effects, such as favoring choices framed as gains over those framed as losses.[25] Beyond this, there is little consensus. Moreover, analyses that have been carried out primarily have used "standard" laboratory populations of university students in fictional scenarios—a practice that sometimes produces results that do not readily generalize to other populations and methods,[26] no matter how statistically reliable the results seem to be.[27]

Some tentative new studies coupled with analysis of world events in which people with sacred values engage in self-sacrifice ranging from acts of heroism to suicide terrorism underline the importance of morally motivated decisionmaking.[28] But significant empirical and theoretical challenges remain. For example, people who ostensibly hold sacred values sometimes seem to treat them as having infinite utility (for example, in refusing to consider tradeoffs). Because infinite utility is incompatible with any sort of "preference schedule" (mathematically, one cannot compute expected utilities, which are weighted averages, when one of the terms is infinite), people who believe their sacred values are of such absolute importance should theoretically spend literally all their time and effort protecting and promoting them. Yet this does not happen.[29]

Thus, some have suggested that such values are only pseudosacred;[30] others have noted that people may engage in indirect tradeoffs despite the sacredness of the values involved.[31] One may be tempted to think of sacred values as self-serving posturing, but the reality of acts such as suicide bombings or a Buddhist monk's self-immolation undermines this stance.[32] Moreover, it may be that sacred values necessary to an individual's identity take on truly absolute value only when value-related identity seems gravely threatened (for example, via humiliation), just as food may take on absolute value only when sustenance for life is threatened.

Although the field of judgment and decisionmaking has made enormous progress,[33] much more is known about various facets of economic decisionmaking than about morally motivated decisionmaking. In particular, there is little knowledge or study of so-called sacred or protected values—that is, values that a moral community implicitly or explicitly treats as possessing transcendental significance that precludes comparisons, tradeoffs, or any other mingling with bounded or secular values. The scant research suggests that standard political and economic proposals (such as a democratic vote in favor of majority interests with just material compensation for the minority) rarely succeed in resolving conflicts over sacred values.

For example, a research team led by Jeremy Ginges recently conducted surveys of 601 Israeli settlers and 535 Palestinian refugees in the West Bank and Gaza on the relationship between essential or sacred values and support for political violence or peace. It found that emotional outrage and support for violent opposition to compromise over sacred values are not mitigated by offering instrumental incentives to compromise but are decreased when the adversary makes instrumentally irrelevant compromises over their own sacred values.

In the representative survey of Jewish settlers conducted in August 2005, days before Israel's withdrawal from Gaza, the team randomly presented participants with one of several hypothetical peace deals. All involved Israeli withdrawal from 99 percent of the West Bank and Gaza in exchange for peace. For the 46 percent of participants who believed the "Greater Land of Israel" was a sacred value, this was a "taboo" tradeoff. Some deals involved an added instrumental incentive, such as money ("taboo plus"), while in other deals Palestinians also made a "taboo" tradeoff over one of their own sacred values in a manner that added no instrumental value to Israel (contextually "tragic"). From a rational perspective, the "taboo plus" deal is improved relative to the "taboo" deal, and thus violent opposition to the "taboo plus" deal should be weaker. However, the team observed the following order of support for violence: "taboo plus" is preferred to "taboo," which in turn is preferred to "tragic" (see figure 7–1A); those evaluating the "tragic" deal showed less support for violent opposition than the other two conditions. An analysis of intensity of emotional outrage again found that "taboo plus" provoked greater outrage than "taboo," which provoked greater outrage than "tragic" (see figure 7–1C); those evaluating the "tragic" deal were least likely to feel angry or disgusted.

These results were replicated in a representative survey of Palestinians in Gaza and the West Bank conducted in late December 2005, one month before Hamas was elected to power. In this experiment, hypothetical peace deals all violated the Palestinian "right of return," a key issue in the conflict.[34] For the 80 percent of participants who believed this was a sacred value, we once more observed that those evaluating a "taboo plus" deal showed the highest support for violent opposition, while those evaluating a "tragic" deal showed the lowest support (see figure 7–1B). Further, the same order was found for two measures ostensibly unrelated to the experiment belief that Islam condones suicide attacks and reports of joy at hearing of a suicide attack; compared to refugees who had earlier evaluated a "taboo" or "taboo plus" deal, those who had evaluated a "tragic" deal believed less that Islam condoned suicide attacks and were less likely to report feelings of joy at hearing of a suicide attack (see figure 7–1D).[35] In neither the settler nor the refugee study did participants responding to the "tragic" deals regard these deals as more implementable than participants evaluating "taboo" or "taboo plus" deals.

Thus, for both the Israeli settler and Palestinian refugee populations, participants in the "taboo plus" condition (which offered the instrumental incentive of a tangible improvement in living conditions) showed greater hostility to the tradeoff than those in the "taboo" condition (which offered no incentive), who in turn showed greater hostility to the tradeoff than participants in the "tragic" condition, in which the one side is merely required to recognize the other side's sacred value. This result is precisely the opposite

Figure 7–1. **Population's Predicted Use of Violence to Oppose Actions Considered Taboo**

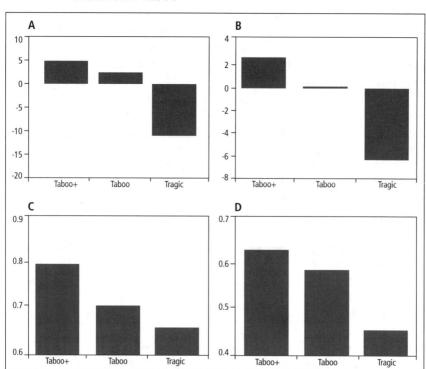

Figure represents percentage of population predicted to use violence to oppose a peace deal perceived to violate a sacred value ("taboo" condition), the taboo deal plus an added instrumental incentive ("taboo plus"), or the taboo deal plus a sacred value concession without instrumental value, from the adversary ("tragic") for (A) Israeli settlers (linear trend $F[1,195] = 5.698$, $P = .018$) and (B) Palestinian refugees ($F[1, 384] = 7.201$, $P = .008$). Parallel results obtained for emotional reactions by (C) settlers reporting anger or disgust at an Israeli leader who would agree to the tradeoff being evaluated ($F[1, 260] = 4.436$, $P = .036$), and (D) refugees reporting joy at hearing of a suicide bombing according to the type of tradeoff being evaluated ($F[1, 418] = 7.48$, $P = .007$). The trend of emotional intensity and support for violence in each case, "taboo plus" > "taboo" > "tragic," could not be predicted by an instrumental rationality account of human behavior.

of what one would expect if calculations were based on straightforward notions of economic or political utility.[36]

These experiments reveal that in political disputes where sources of conflict are cultural, such as the Israeli-Palestinian conflict or emerging clashes between the Muslim and Judeo-Christian world, violent opposition to compromise solutions may be exacerbated rather than decreased by insisting on instrumentally driven tradeoffs, while noninstrumental compromises, which might seem merely symbolic to outsiders, may actually reduce support for violence.

It would seem reasonable to expect the same pattern of behavior in religiously motivated terrorists. Most terrorists who have been studied, including would-be or captured suicide bombers, fail to show any psychopathology or sociopathy and are generally at least as educated and economically well off as their surrounding populations.[37] Such findings are often taken to support the idea that terrorist action, including self-destruction, derives from rational decisions to optimize strategies for attaining sociopolitical goals:[38] the religious "bargain" of mostly young men dying for a promising afterlife;[39] ultimate sacrifice as maximizing the goal of improving lives of family or compatriots, which offsets the "opportunity cost" of an educated life lost prematurely;[40] or "trading life" for a social identity that is affirmed in death but devalued by continued living.[41]

These speculations are plausible theoretically, but no study involving structured interviews or experiments with religious suicide terrorists has ever put them to the empirical test. Rather than obeying a utilitarian "logic of rational consequence," these actors perhaps more closely follow a similar "logic of moral appropriateness"[42] to that evinced by the Israeli settlers and Palestinian refugees. For example, in recent interviews, a number of self-identified recruits for martyr attack from the Hamas Bloc at al-Najah University in Nablus (which provides more suicide bombers than any other demographic group of Palestinians) as well as a number of active fighters in Indonesia from Jemaah Islamiya (JI), al Qaeda's main ally in southeast Asia, who trained in Afghanistan, the southern Philippines, Sulawesi, and the Mollucas, were asked such questions as: "What if your family were to be killed in retaliation for your action?" or "What if your father were dying and your mother found out your plans for a martyrdom attack and asked you to delay until the family could get back on its feet?" To a person, they answered along lines that there is duty to family, but duty to God cannot be postponed. When asked what if their action resulted in no one's death but their own, the typical response was, "God will love you just the same." When these same questions were posed to the alleged emir of Jemaah Islamiya, Abu Bakr Ba'asyir, in Jakarta's Cipinang prison in August 2005, he responded that martyrdom for the sake of jihad is the ultimate *fardh 'ain*, an inescapable individual obligation that trumps all others, including four of the conventional five pillars of Islam (prayer, Ramadan fast, alms, and pilgrimage; only the fifth pillar, profession of faith in God and the Prophet, remains on a par with jihad). What matters for him, as for most would-be martyrs and their sponsors who were interviewed, is the martyr's intention and commitment to God, so that blowing up only oneself has the same value and reward regardless of whether any of the enemy are killed in the process.[43]

Such answers are typical of confrontations over sacred values, which are not sensitive to standard calculations regarding cost and benefit, quantity, tradeoffs across moral categories, or commensuration between different cultural frames.[44] This means that traditional calculations of how to defeat or deter an enemy, such as by providing material incentives to defect or threatening massive retaliation against supporting populations, might not succeed.

While this may be an accurate description of the value motivation that drives people to become suicide terrorists or to support terrorism, the organizations that actually direct suicide terrorism are motivated by instrumental rationality to fight the policies they abhor. Al Qaeda deputy Dr. Ayman al-Zawahiri argues in his testament, *Knights under the Prophet's Banner*, that "the method of martyrdom operations [i]s the most successful way of inflicting damage against the opponent and the least costly to the mujahidin in casualties." Jihadi leaders also point to the sacrifice of their "best and brightest" as proof of the movement's commitment to the Muslim community, which increases the organization's political market share. Furthermore, the decision of the terrorist organization to encourage suicide attacks may be driven by a military-technological calculus. In September 2004, Sheikh Hamed al-Betawi, a spiritual leader of Hamas, told me, "Our people do not own airplanes and tanks, only human bombs. Those who undertake martyrdom actions are not hopeless or poor, but are the best of our people, educated, successful. They are intelligent, advanced combat techniques for fighting enemy occupation." Most of the would-be suicide bombers interviewed also say that if a roadside bomb can produce the same damage (that is, without causing the deaths of any members of the group), then the roadside bomb is preferable.[45]

In sum, would-be martyrs and their sponsors appear to use instrumental reasoning when focusing on the consequences of their actions. Interviewees would usually agree to the substitution of a roadside bombing that would not kill the bomber for a suicide bombing that would, and they would also agree to delay a roadside bombing to fulfill a commitment to one of the sacred pillars of Islam, such as making a first pilgrimage to Mecca. But when the choice before them highlights clashing values, then deontological (moral) considerations seem to trump consequentialist (utilitarian) ones. For example, our interviewees also say it is wrong to delay a suicide operation for a first pilgrimage or simply to prevent lethal retaliation against the bomber's family. From an instrumental perspective, roadside bombing is preferable to suicide bombing, and pilgrimage is preferable to either. However, from a moral perspective, suicide bombing was preferable to pilgrimage. This resulting "nontransitivity" in reasoning seems inconsistent with standard notions of "rationality" that drive most current political and economic theorizing.

In addition, inverse consequentialist reasoning is apparent in populations sympathetic to suicide bombings. That is, the greater certain kinds of instrumental incentive to undertake a suicide bombing (for example, the greater the quantity of money offered the martyr's family for their child's martyrdom action) are, the less those incentives are morally tolerable and the more likely they are to be disincentives (see figure 7–2). Of course, one can always recast noninstrumental values in instrumental terms, just as one can always frame any perceptual or conceptual relationship in terms of "similarity," but the issue is whether, in doing so, explanatory power to predict further judgments and decisions is helped or hindered.

Promoting Democracy: The Impact of Sacred Values

Social psychologists cite robust experimental evidence that a realist bias is commonly held by most people in whatever culture, including leaders: most people tend to believe that their behavior speaks for itself, that they see the world objectively, and that only other people are biased and misconstrue events.[46] Moreover, individuals tend to misperceive differences

Figure 7–2. **Palestinian Judgments of Acceptability for a Family to Request Compensation (in Dinars) for a Son's Martyrdom Operation**

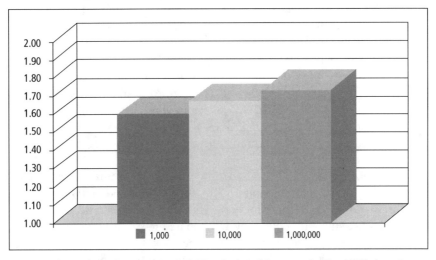

Between-subjects design for a representative West Bank and Gaza sample (N = 1267) shows inverse instrumentality (linear trend, p = .01). 65 percent of respondents "strongly support" suicide bombing; 50 percent associate it most strongly with "joy" ("pride" = 12 percent, other emotions < 10 percent). Y-axis: 1 = "acceptable"; 2 = "unacceptable"

between group norms as more extreme than they really are. The resulting misunderstandings—encouraged by religious and ideological propaganda—lead antagonistic groups to interpret each other's views of events, such as terrorism or freedom fighting, as wrong, radical, and/or irrational. Mutual demonization and warfare readily ensue. The problem is to stop this spiral from escalating in opposing camps.

The current U.S. national security strategy, including its overarching strategy for a successful pursuit of the war on terror, is based on the assumption that promotion of democracy ultimately promotes peace and stability in the world and protects the United States. In the long run, this may prove true. But just as our discussion of the impact of sacred values on individual behavior would lead us to expect, history has uniformly and mercilessly shown that precipitous or unyielding attempts to impose outside beliefs on a foreign society, or to act as if members of that foreign society really wanted to believe and act as the outsiders do, lead to strategic failure.

The error of assuming that others will or want to believe and act as we do leads to the fallacy of assuming that the spread of democracy among all peoples and nations is an inexorable natural process. In fact, there is no more reason to believe this now than there was at the end of World War I, when the United States, Western Europe, and the League of Nations originally proposed a similar vision for Iraq, the Middle East, and the rest of the world. Democratic freedoms are not natural or inevitable parts of the human condition. They are not universal, timeless, or absolute; even freedom of thought and expression has public limits that are continually being recalibrated through political negotiation. They are instead a reflection of the values of the communities in which democracies arise and flourish. Democracy grows painstakingly through the dedication of an increasingly educated citizenry steeped in a sense of national unity and committed to the defense of differences of interest and opinion. At best, a democratic transformation of the Middle East will take many years, perhaps generations. It may never come about; or if it does, it can still fail, as it did in France and Mexico in the 1800s, Germany and Spain in the 1930s, and Iran and Guatemala in the 1950s.

The objection may be raised that surveys of Islamic opinion consistently show that many people in the Middle East and elsewhere in the Muslim world do yearn for democratic choice. But there are no polls or any other evidence suggesting that they are prepared to subordinate the interests of their own ethnic group or religion to the greater common interest of an entire country, a pattern of behavior that has heretofore been essential for successful democracy at a national level. The current international system of nation-states, enshrined in the United Nations charter, was established by Europeans (and derivatives) that had already developed firm national identities by the time the United Nations was created. Even those countries that did not enjoy democratic governance between the end of World War II and the late 1980s possessed strong senses of national identity and solidarity. Thus, it may not be possible to extrapolate the successful democratic transitions of countries in South America, Eastern Europe, and East Asia—all of which had clear national identities—to Middle Eastern countries that neither possess such identities nor the other factors, such as a robust middle class, that political scientists have shown to be linked to successful democratic development.

In Indonesia, for example, the entrenchment of democracy has, if anything, weakened the country's willingness to fight terrorism. Militant jihadi groups as well as mainstream Islamic parties that seek to transform Indonesia into a state ruled by sharia were banned from serious public politics until the downfall of Suharto's dictatorship in 1998, but their acquiescence or support is now critical to a government in which no party controls more than 25 percent of parliament. President Yudyhono, whose own party has just 8 percent of parliament, says he cannot submit legislation proscribing Jemaah Islamiya because of insufficient "proof" that the organization even exists. The speaker of Indonesia's parliament, along with many of the country's Muslim leaders, has even visited JI's leader, Abu Bakr Bashir, in jail to show solidarity with this "victim" of U.S. and Australian pressure and interference—all this after JI operatives plotted to assassinate the previous president, Megawati Sukarnoputri. Indonesian intelligence has also authenticated a 1998 letter to regional jihadi directors in which Bashir declared he was acting on Osama bin Laden's behalf to advance "the Muslim world's global jihad" against "the Jews and Christians [who] will never be satisfied until they see you follow their way of worship."

It cannot possibly be in the Indonesian government's interest to continue to shelter an organization with such violent intentions, but the country's officials may have concluded that it is even riskier to support American policies by taking action against JI. According to the latest survey conducted by the Pew Global Attitudes Project, Indonesian views of the United States, which were largely favorable before the invasion of Iraq, plummeted to 15 percent favorable right after. In Pew's June 2005 survey, 80 percent of Indonesians actually expressed fear that the United States would attack their country.

All that said, the credibility of what the United States sets forth as its own sacred values leaves it no option but to continue to promote democratic choice. It should do so even if it means accepting governments hostile to U.S. interests, provided such governments do not support violence against the United States or its allies. But it must not attempt to impose democracy, which may simply backfire or, worse, intensify the spirit of protecting indigenous values. In any case, simply providing an institutional framework for democracy, such as a constitution and courts, may be meaningless if the concept is not organically based in local society, history, and culture. Fostering the creation of a large and stable middle class is probably necessary, though not sufficient. Opening up economic opportunity will help but, again, not if the path to economic improvement is widely perceived as undermining moral values and inciting a clash between traditional and modern cultures.

The Importance of Small Group Dynamics

Especially after 9/11, nationalist Islamist movements from Morocco to Indonesia, which had jealously guarded their independence, spiritually united under the al Qaeda logo. Intense public targeting and discussion of al Qaeda encouraged homegrown groups only tenuously connected with bin Laden, if at all, to claim responsibility for attacks in al Qaeda's name so they would be taken more seriously by friend and foe alike. Abu Mus'ab Al-Zarqawi's Iraq-based jihadi group, whose violently anti-Shi'ite policy was never at the top of bin Laden's agenda,[47] is a good example.

But the terrorist actions that are often attributed to al Qaeda are now chiefly executed by self-forming cells of friends that swarm for attack and then disappear or disperse to form new swarms. Independent studies by the Nixon Center's Robert Leiken[48] and by Marc Sageman[49] show that over 80 percent of known jihadis currently live in diaspora communities, which are often marginalized from the host society. As with the decentralized anarchist movement (including suicide attackers) that terrorized the world a century ago, killing U.S. President William McKinley and the Archduke of Austria to spark World War I, most jihadis follow whomever they like more than they follow orders from an impersonal command hierarchy. Their hard-to-penetrate social networks consist of about 70 percent friends and 20 percent family.

Living mostly in the diaspora, unconcerned by retaliation against the populations of the countries in which they live, jihadis who are frequently middle class, secularly well educated but often "born-again" radical Islamists (including converts from Christianity) embrace apocalyptic visions for humanity's violent salvation. Interviews with culturally uprooted and politically restless youth elicit expressions of a stunningly simplified and decontextualized embrace of martyrdom for the sake of global jihad as life's noblest cause. For the most part, these young people are completely sincere and, increasingly, many are as willing and eager to die as they are to kill. Not only in Muslim countries, but in nearly every Western European city, bright and idealistic Muslim youth, even more than the intellectually marginalized and dispossessed, take in the jihadi story. They are the ones who most keenly feel their swelling, media-fed aspirations lanced by the impoverished reality of the neighborhoods in which their people live—as that reality is simplified through the imagery of global jihad.

Seeking a sense of community and a deeper meaning in life, small groups of friends and family from the same area bond as they surf Islamist Web sites to find inspiration and direction from al Qaeda's message. In 5 years, the number of Web sites carrying Islamist messages has increased from under 20 to over 3,000,[50] with about 70 avowedly militant sites collectively forming a virtual jihadi university.[51] Thus, an October 2005 posting by Ahmad Al-Wathiq bi-Llah, "Deputy General Emir" of the Al-Zarqawi–affiliated Global Islamic Media Front, reissued a 2003 announcement for the "Al-Qaeda University of Jihad Studies . . . a tangible reality for the enemies of the Nation and the Faith; a decentralized university without geographical borders, present in every place."[52] Graduates, he explains, pass through "faculties" that advance the cause of a global caliphate through morale boosting and bombings, and specialize in "electronic jihad, media jihad, spiritual and financial jihad." Inspiration can be found in the recent online musings of Abu Mus'ab Al-Suri, the new global jihadi Web figure and principal theoretician of "leaderless jihad."[53]

Veteran jihadis may sometimes help trigger the newer groups into action, although even information for the sort of do-it-yourself explosives used in Madrid and London is available on the Internet.[54] And as in the case of the Madrid train bombers, the death or capture of all plotters need not affect the ability of other groups to organize and stay motivated. Thus, the December 2003 Internet tract that foreshadowed Madrid, "Iraqi Jihad, Hopes and Risks," inspired attacks that would force Spain's withdrawal from Iraq, which the plotters hoped would in turn generate "huge pressure on the British presence, which Tony Blair could not overcome."[55] But Britain did not follow suit, so a mix of homegrown talent (three cricket friends of Pakistani origin, one married, one in college, one "born again," later joined by a convert from Christianity) fused by foreign-born incitement apparently decided they would bomb London to press the matter. Web sites such as the Global Islamic Media Front that host these tracts increasingly control the distribution of knowledge and resources as physical agents like bin Laden once did. (Moreover, they can be modeled and monitored as such.) Although Web sites are assuming central actor, hub, and bridge positions in the network, the network itself is shifting profoundly to an acephalic "leaderless resistance."

Most jihadi cells have only a few members. The preferred size of these bands of brothers of fictive kin, who are as willing to die for one another as a parent is for a child or one sibling for another, is 8 members (about the number of intimate friendships that people across the world tend to develop between the ages of 15 and 30; before then, primary relations are mostly with immediate kin and neighbors, and after, few enduring new relationships tend to form other than with one's own affines, such as family by marriage). Although the members of each cell usually show remarkable in-group homogeneity (age, place of origin, residence, educational background, socio-economic status, and so on), there is little homogeneity across the jihadi diaspora. This renders attempts at profiling practically worthless. Cells are often spontaneously formed and self-mobilizing, with few direct physical contacts to other cells. But radicalization usually requires input from, and interaction with, the larger jihadi community. The Internet is taking over from the hands-on gurus of global jihad in radicalizing groups of friends into pseudo-families within which each member will give his life for the others.[56] Without the Internet, the extreme fragmenting and decentralization of the jihadi movement into a functioning global network might not be possible. But despite the different modern dimensions of time and space characteristic of this information age, from the perspective of anthropology, there is much about terrorism that resembles the patterns of aggression found among hunter-gatherers and other chiefless tribes—particularly spiraling wars of revenge based on codes of intercommunity reciprocity and retaliation—more than it does the warfare of hierarchical societies.[57]

From the perspective of psychology, we are unlikely ever to be able to prevent terrorist attacks by trying to profile terrorists; they are not different enough from everyone else in the source population to make them remarkable. Insights into homegrown jihadi attacks will have to come from understanding group dynamics, not individual psychology. Small group dynamics can trump individual personality to produce horrific behavior in ordinary people, not only in terrorists but in those who fight them.[58] Social psychologists have investigated the "fundamental attribution error," a tendency for people to explain behavior in terms of individual personality traits, even when significant situational factors in the larger society are at work. U.S. Government and media characterizations of Middle East suicide bombers as cowardly homicidal lunatics may suffer from a fundamental attribution error: no instance of religious or political suicide terrorism has ever been known to stem from the lone actions of a cowering or unstable bomber. Rather, they stem from the same kind of group dynamics elucidated by psychologist Stanley Milgram's experimental demonstration of philosopher Hannah Arendt's thesis of the "banality of evil," using ordinary Americans.[59]

After the Nazi atrocities of World War II, Milgram wanted to find out whether ordinary Americans would also readily obey destructive orders under the right circumstances. For his experiments, Milgram recruited a number of college-educated adults, supposedly to help others learn better.

When the "learner," hidden by a screen, failed to memorize arbitrary word pairs fast enough, the "helper" was instructed to administer an electric shock, and to increase the voltage with each erroneous answer. (In fact, the learners were actually actors who deliberately got the answers wrong, and, unbeknownst to the helpers, no electrical shock was actually being applied.) Most helpers complied with instructions to give what would have been potentially lethal shocks (labeled as 450 volts) despite the learners' screams and pleas. Although this experiment specifically showed how situations can be staged to elicit blind obedience to authority, a more general lesson is that manipulation of context can trump individual personality and psychology to generate apparently extreme behaviors in ordinary people. In another classic experiment from over 30 years ago, the "Stanford Prison Experiment," normal college-age men were assigned to be guards or prisoners; the "guards" quickly became sadistic, engaging in what psychologist Philip Zimbardo called "pornographic and degrading abuse of the prisoners."

If joining the jihad is crucially (though not exclusively) an institution-level phenomenon, finding the right mix of pressure and inducements to get the communities themselves to abandon support for institutions that recruit suicide attackers may be essential to preventing individuals from being recruited. One hypothetical way to achieve that goal would be for antiterrorist forces to damage the community's social and political fabric so severely that any support by the local population or authorities for sponsors of terrorist attacks collapses, as happened regarding the kamikaze as a byproduct of the nuclear destruction of Hiroshima and Nagasaki. In today's world, such an approach would not only be morally unjustifiable, it would also be impractical given the dispersed and distributed organization of terrorist institutions among distant populations that collectively number in the hundreds of millions.[60] Even in more localized settings, such as the Israeli-Palestinian conflict, coercive policies alone may not achieve lasting relief from attack and can exacerbate the problem over time.

For example, in a representative survey of 1,260 Palestinians from the West Bank and Gaza carried out by the Palestinian Center for Policy and Survey Research in December 2005–January 2006, the following questions were asked:

■ What is the position of Islam in your opinion regarding the bomber who carries out the bombing attack (martyrdom attacks to some, suicide attacks to others) killing himself with the aim of killing his enemies as some Palestinians do? Does Islam allow such action?

■ If a chosen martyr's father became ill and his family asked him to take care of his father, would it be acceptable to delay the action indefinitely?

■ Would it be acceptable to permanently forego martyrdom if there were a significantly high chance that the chosen martyr's family would be killed in retaliation?

■ And what if the bombing attack led to the destruction of olive trees and the bombing of his hometown and school and the death of the students? Would it be acceptable to forego the attack in this case?

Seventy-two percent of respondents said "yes" to the first question, and 77 percent of those who responded "no" to it also responded "yes" to the second question. But 43 percent of respondents who answered in the affirmative to the first question responded "no" to the third and fourth ones, whereas 72 percent of those who responded "no" to the first responded "yes" to the third and fourth questions. In other words, Palestinians who support suicide bombing are less likely to support abandoning extreme violence to save a whole family or village from destruction at enemy hands than merely to help out a family member. These results suggest that those who have become radicalized to jihad (as measured by support for suicide actions) respond to both instrumental sticks (enemy counterviolence) and carrots (recall the results for Palestinian refugees on "taboo plus" tradeoffs) with even greater support for violence. Note also, however, that in our interviews with actual members of action groups (for example, Hamas and JI leaders and militants belonging to "martyr groups"), there was overwhelming refusal to consider abandoning a suicide attack either to prevent lethal retaliation against the family or to help out a sick father. This suggests that those who have joined groups committed to acting in support of radical jihad may reject all tradeoffs.

On the inducement side, social psychology research indicates that people who identify with one side in a struggle use conflicting information from the other side to reinforce their sense of antagonism. Thus, trying to persuade Muslims who are hostile to the United States to cease their support for terrorism simply by bombarding them with what they will interpret as self-serving information may only increase their hostility. On the other hand, other research suggests that most people in any group actually have more moderate views than what they consider their group norm to be. Inciting and empowering moderates within the Islamic community to confront inadequacies and inconsistencies in the community's knowledge (of others as good or evil), values (respect for life), and behavior (support for killing),[61] can produce emotional dissatisfaction among other members of the community, leading to lasting change in the group norms and enhanced influence on the part of the more moderate elements.[62] Funding for civic education and debate might help with this process, as might interfaith confidence-building through intercommunity interaction initiatives.

The insights provided by examining terrorist organizations in the context of small group dynamics also suggest that efforts could be made to foster alternative peer groups for these "cultural orphans" in cities and cyberspace, peer groups that would be as committed and compassionate toward their own members as are terror groups, but in life-enhancing ways, as well as being committed and compassionate to others outside the group. Accomplishing this in the context of cyberspace will require careful monitoring of, rather than simply taking down, existing jihadi Web sites. What is needed is subtle exploitation of opportunities to create chat rooms as well as physical support groups that advance causes that can play to sentiments sympathetic to jihadi rhetoric in a constructive way, such as providing faith-based social services.

Behavior and attitudes in the Muslim world could also be affected by directly addressing and lessening the sources of grievance and humiliation, especially in Palestine, where images of daily violence have made the confrontation with Israel the global focus of Muslim attention. No evidence, historical or otherwise, indicates that popular support for terrorism will evaporate without a visible process toward achieving at least some fundamental goals that the terrorists and their supporting communities share. Of course, this does not mean negotiating overall goals, such as al Qaeda's quest to replace the Western-inspired system of nation-states with a global caliphate, first in Muslim lands and then everywhere. Unlike other groups, al Qaeda publicizes no specific demands after martyr actions. As with an avenging army, it seeks no compromise. But most people who currently sympathize with al Qaeda's goals do have specific tangible demands for which they might be prepared to negotiate.

Conclusion: Using the Soft and Transformative Power of Sacred Values

What lessons does an understanding of sacred values hold for combating the new wave of sacred terror that is expanding across the globe?

First, the sacred values of others, no matter how alien they may seem, must not be ignored or disregarded. Such values provide the moral foundations of society and determine cultural identity, which is often the core of an individual's own identity—who that person believes himself or herself to be. The perceived violation of core cultural values is usually deeply felt as a personal humiliation, even if the person is only a witness to an injured party who may live thousands of miles away, such as an Indonesian who is provoked to anger by observing events in Palestine on television or over the Internet.

Holy wars depend first and foremost on deep pools of such perceived humiliation, not on military occupation per se, argues Harvard political scientist Jessica Stern, who talks to terrorists and those who sponsor them.[63]

Especially in Arab societies, where the culture of honor applies to the humblest family as it once applied to the noblest families of the American south,[64] the abuse of elders in front of their children, whether in the form of verbal insults at roadblocks or strip searches, indelibly stains the memory of any community member who witnesses such events. What may be considered standard police practice in the United States or Europe may warrant undying calls for revenge when carried out in another society, especially when the practice involves outsiders humiliating members of the community. The power of cultural humiliation to motivate intense hostility is illustrated by the extreme example of the torture committed by American solders at Abu Ghraib prison. That the U.S. Government initially responded to the news of the misconduct with denials rather than apologies has arguably served the jihadi cause even more than the invasion of Iraq itself. As far away as the jungles of Sulawesi in Indonesia, people sincerely express their determination to fight Americans to the death because "what they have done to Muslims they would not do even to animals."

Our insistence that such transgressions do not represent true American ideals is meaningless to foreign audiences. As a rule, intentions and thoughts do not translate well across cultures; people generally pay much more attention to consequences and behavior. For example, who in America really cares what motivated the 9/11 bombers? Who in Iraq, or elsewhere in the Muslim world, really cares if coalition forces actually intended to kill innocent civilians? It would not be a great sacrifice of American prestige to reverse course and show more than token accountability—perhaps even suffer a little loss of face—over events such as those at Abu Ghraib, thereby acknowledging the validity of other people's sacred values even as we highlight the redemptive qualities of our own society's sacred values of justice and equality before the law.

A second lesson is to not try to undermine the values that inspire people to radical action directly and not attempt to substitute our own preferred values by forceful imposition or through propaganda. Experiments in cognitive and social psychology repeatedly show that such tactics usually only incite further moral outrage and extreme behavior.[65] Rather, the aim should be to show how deeply held sacred values can be channeled into less belligerent paths. What has struck me in my interviews with mujahideen who have rejected suicide bombing is that they remain very committed to Salafi principles. Indeed, even their religious militancy remains steady and deep. Instead, those who seem to succeed best in convincing their brethren to forsake wanton killing of civilians do so by promoting alternative interpretations of Islamic principles that need not directly oppose Salafi teachings.

A good example is the recent book by Nasir Abas, *Unveiling Jemaah Islamiyah*.[66] Abas, one of Jemaah Islamiya's top leaders, trained the Bali bombers Ali Imron and Imam Samudra. Much of the book is a rebuttal to Samudra's own published apology for terrorism and what Abas believes to be a tendentious use of the Koran and Hadith to justify suicide bombing and violence against fellow Muslims and civilians. "Not one verse in the Koran contains an order for Muslims to make war on people of another religion," Abas writes, "or that killing women, children and civilians can ever be proper, just or balanced. [The contrary belief] has only created discord in the Muslim community and has led non-Muslims to regard Islam as sadistic and cruel." He reasons that the best way to turn altruistic suicide bombers, who believe that what they are doing is sacred, away from violence may be by promoting competing sacred values. Jemaah Islamiya, like many of the militant Salafi groups sympathetic to al Qaeda, is riddled with internal divisions over the wisdom of killing fellow Muslims and civilians, and sincere alternative appeals to sacred values could widen these fissures to the point of undermining consensus for violent jihad. America and its allies should quietly encourage this process, while being careful not to strangle it in a public embrace.

A third lesson is to stress the compatibilities between the sacred values of different cultures and to promote them for the common good rather than merely for self, or even joint, interests. Our respective religions tell us that the highest form of help is given without demands for reciprocity or returns. Muslims and Jews even use essentially the same word for such freely given alms: *sadaqah* (Arabic) or *tsadaqah* (Hebrew). This was the essence of America's hugely successful Marshall Plan. Such assistance is also wise from a strategic perspective, for in the competition for moral allegiance, trust vanishes and cooperation is undermined if people learn that another's commitment to them is mostly a matter of convenience or, even worse, manipulation for the interests of others. Especially in times of vulnerability and stress, social deception and defection in the pursuit of self-preservation are more likely to occur, as the great Arab historian Ibn Khaldûn noted long ago.[67] Noninstrumental or "sacred" values can passionately rouse hearts and minds to break out of this rational cycle of self-interest and to adopt group interests that may benefit all in the long run. The jihadis understand the power of such values in motivating people to act beyond their own self-interest. Let us also learn what these values are and speak to them, or help those better able than ourselves to do so. That may be the most effective and enduring way to wean hearts and minds away from terrorizing others.

Notes

¹ Direct recruitment plays only a minor role in the global jihadi expansion. Membership increases largely through enlistment (that is, self-recruitment). Even in al Qaeda's heyday, before 9/11, would-be jihadis came knocking at al Qaeda's door, rather than the other way around; al Qaeda accepted less than 20 percent for significant operations.

² Edward Gibbon, *Decline and Fall of the Roman Empire* (London: International Book Co., 1845, originally published 1776–1788).

³ Max Weber, *Economy and Society*, vol. 1 (Berkeley: University of California Press, 1978), 24.

⁴ Immanuel Kant, *Critique of Practical Reason* (Cambridge: Cambridge University Press, 1997, originally published in 1788).

⁵ Roy F. Baumeister, Laura Smart, and Joseph M. Boden, "Relation of Threatened Egotism to Violence and Aggression," *Psychological Review* 103, no. 5 (1996).

⁶ Gordon W. Allport, *The Nature of Prejudice* (Cambridge, MA: Harvard University Press, 1956).

⁷ Samuel P. Huntington, *The Clash of Civilizations* (New York: Simon and Schuster, 1997).

⁸ Thomas C. Schelling, *The Strategy of Conflict* (New York: Oxford University Press, 1963).

⁹ Russell Hardin, *One for All: The Logic of Group Conflict* (Princeton: Princeton University Press, 1995).

¹⁰ Francis Fukuyama, *Trust* (New York: Free Press, 1995).

¹¹ Ashutosh Varshney, "Nationalism, Ethnic Conflict, and Rationality," *Perspectives on Politics* 1, no. 85 (2003).

¹² Scott Atran, *In Gods We Trust: The Evolutionary Landscape of Religion* (New York: Oxford University Press, 2002).

¹³ Robert H. Frank, *Passions Within Reason: The Strategic Role of the Emotions* (New York: Norton, 1988).

¹⁴ George W. Bush, introduction to *National Security Strategy of the United States* (Washington, DC: The White House, September 2003).

¹⁵ For an extreme example of convergence, compare Ayman Al-Zawahiri's *Knights Under the Prophet's Banner* (trans. Al-Sharq Al-Awsat, London, December 2, 2001, available at <fas.org/irp/world/para/ayman_bk.html>) and the works of White Supremacist ideologue William Pierce: for example, *The Turner Diaries* (Washington, DC: National Alliance, 1978), which ends with the hero plowing his jet into the Pentagon on a successful suicide mission; also see Pierce's analysis of the 9/11 attacks as being carried out for the right reasons by the wrong people, *Free Speech* 7, November 2001, available at <natvan.com/free-speech/fs0111c.html>. Since the closing of the Aryan Nation compound in Idaho and several recent leadership changes, these people have begun calling their new mission Aryan Jihad: "Before opening up a bit to other races that oppose Judaism, it is necessary that 'the System' be disrupted and broken down. This is the same 'System' that not only oppresses Aryans but is also responsible for oppressing all persons of whatever race or nationality who oppose the erroneous, Judaic-based authority which is the premise for System-rule." Available at <aryan-nations.org/about.htm>.

¹⁶ Arguments by outsiders that militant Islam can be undermined by showing it does not reflect the religion's "truth" or "essence" are likewise vacuous, for there is no "essence" or fixed content to *any* religion: Scott Atran and Ara Norenzayan, "Religion's Evolutionary Landscape: Counterintuition, Commitment, Compassion, Communion," *Behavioral and Brain Sciences* 27, 713 (2004). Nevertheless, debates among Muslims about, for example, whether killing children is acceptable are critical to how their religion will be interpreted and applied.

¹⁷ Michael Scheuer, *Imperial Hubris* (Dulles, VA: Potomac Books, 2004).

¹⁸ Reuven Paz, "The First Islamist *Fatwah* on the Use of Weapons of Mass Destruction," *PRISM Special Dispatches on Global Jihad* 1, no. 1, May 2003; available at <e-prism.org>.

¹⁹ For example, although Egyptian Islamic Jihad (EIJ) and Egyptian Islamic Group (EIG) have common roots in Egyptian society, one crucial difference between them is that the EIJ leadership under Al-Zawahiri left Egypt to join bin Laden in Afghanistan, whereas EIG remained behind in Upper Egypt (Said). The hostile reaction of Saidis to the 1997 EIG massacre of 58 tourists at the Temple of Queen Hatshepsut in Luxor, and to interference by outside jihadis and loss of trade, effectively ended EIG's ability to mount military operations. By contrast, Al-Zawahiri

continues to urge jihadis everywhere to inflict the greatest possible damage and cause the maximum casualties on the West, no matter how much time and effort these operations take, and regardless of the immediate consequences.

[20] Alan Page Fiske and Philip E. Tetlock, "Taboo Tradeoffs: Reactions to Transactions that Transgress the Spheres of Justice,"*Political Psychology* 18, no. 255 (1997).

[21] Philip E. Tetlock, "Coping with Trade-offs: Psychological Constraints and Political Implications," in *Political Reasoning and Choice*, ed. Arthur Lupia, Matthew D. McCubbins, and Samuel L. Popkin (Berkeley, CA: University of California Press, 2000).

[22] Douglas Medin et al., "The Semantic Side of Decision Making," *Psychonomic Bulletin and Review* 6, no. 562 (1999).

[23] Baruch Fischoff, Paul Slovic, and Sarah Lichtenstein, "Knowing What You Want: Measuring Labile Variables," in *Cognitive Processes in Choice and Decision Behavior*, ed. T.S. Wallstein (Hillsdale, NJ: Erlbaum, 1980).

[24] Amos Tversky, Paul Slovic, and Shmuel Sattath, "Contingent Weighting in Judgment and Choice," *Psychological Review* 95, no. 371 (1988).

[25] Carmen Tanner and Douglas Medin, "Protected Values: No Omission Bias and No Framing Effects," *Psychonomic Bulletin & Review* 11, 185 (2004).

[26] Joseph Henrich et al., "In Search of *Homo economicus*: Behavioral Experiments in 15 Small-Scale Societies," *American Economic Review* 91, no. 73 (2001).

[27] Douglas Medin and Scott Atran, "The Native Mind," *Psychological Review* 111, no. 960 (2004).

[28] Linda J. Skitka and Elizabeth Mullen, "The Dark Side of Moral Conviction," *Analyses of Social Issues and Public Policy* 2, no. 35 (2002); Scott Atran, "Mishandling Suicide Terrorism," *The Washington Quarterly* (Summer 2004).

[29] Jonathan D. Baron and Mark Spranca, "Protected Values," *Organizational Behavior and Human Decision Processes* 70, no. 1 (1997).

[30] Jonathan D. Baron and Sarah Leshner, "How Serious Are Expressions of Protected Values?" *Journal of Experimental Psychology: Applied* 6, no. 183 (2000).

[31] Philip E. Tetlock, "Thinking the Unthinkable: Sacred Values and Taboo Cognitions," *Trends in Cognitive Sciences* 7, no. 320 (2003).

[32] Diego Gambetta, *Making Sense of Suicide Missions* (New York: Oxford University Press, 2005).

[33] For a review, see Daniel Kahneman, "Maps of Bounded Rationality: Psychology for Behavioral Economics," *American Economic Review* 93, no. 1449 (2003).

[34] Jacob Shamir and Khalil Shikaki, "Public Opinion in the Israeli-Palestinian Two-Level Game," *Journal of Peace Research* 42, no. 311 (2005).

[35] For joy as a neurophysiological correlate of revenge, see Dominique J.-F. de Quervain et al., "The Neural Basis of Altruistic Punishment," *Science* 305, no. 1254 (2004).

[36] One alternative interpretation of the data is to argue that the Palestinian "sacred value" tradeoffs in the tragic condition signaled greater willingness to compromise on their part. If that were the case, the "tragic" condition might be superior *instrumentally* to the other two conditions because participants could find it easier to believe that the peace deal would be peacefully and successfully implemented. To test this interpretation, participants were asked whether they believed that the deal they had been presented with would be "peacefully and successfully implemented." Responses were scored 1 for "yes," 0.5 for "not sure," and 0 for "no." The data showed that this alternative interpretation did not hold.

[37] See Alan Krueger and Jitka Malecková, "Seeking the Roots of Terror," *Chronicle of Higher Education* (June, 6, 2003), available at <chronicle.com/free/v49/i39/39b01001.htm>; Scott Atran, "Genesis of Suicide Terrorism," *Science* 299, no. 1534 (2003); Marc Sageman, *Understanding Terror Networks* (Philadelphia: University of Pennsylvania Press, 2004); Ariel Merari, "Social, Organization, and Psychological Factors in Suicide Terrorism," in *Root Causes of Suicide Terrorism*, ed. Tore Bjorgo (New York: Routledge, forthcoming).

[38] See Robert Pape, *Dying to Win: The Strategic Logic of Suicide Terrorism* (New York: Random House, 2005); Mia Bloom, *Dying to Kill* (New York: Columbia University Press, 2005); Julian Madsen, "The Rationale of Suicide Attack," *Risq*, September 2004, available at <risq. org/modules.php?name=News&file=print&sid=367>.

[39] Rodney Stark, *The Rise of Christianity* (Princeton: Princeton University Press, 2000).

[40] See Jean-Paul Azzam, "Suicide-Bombing as Intergenerational Investment," *Public Choice* (forthcoming); Gary S. Becker, "Crime and Punishment: An Economic Approach," *Journal of Political Economy* 76, no. 169 (1968).

[41] See Mark Harrison, "An Economist Looks at Suicide Terrorism," in *Terrorism: Challenge for the 21st Century? Understandings and Responses*, ed. Christopher Ankersen (London: Polity Press, forthcoming); George A. Akerloff and Rachel Kranton, "Economics and Identity," *The Quarterly Journal of Economics* 115, no. 715 (2000).

[42] Bruce Hoffman and Gordon H. McCormick, "Terrorism, Signaling, and Suicide Attack," *Studies in Conflict & Terrorism* 27, no. 243 (2004).

[43] Scott Atran, "The Emir," *Spotlight on Terrorism* (Jamestown Foundation), September 15, 2005, available at <jamestown.org/terrorism/news/article.php?articleid=2369782>.

[44] Granted, instrumental cost-benefit calculations often prevail within a moral frame. Most would-be martyrs and jihadi religious leaders interviewed by the author also say that if a roadside bomb can produce the same damage without causing the deaths of any members of the group, then it is preferable.

[45] Scott Atran and Jessica Stern, "Small Groups Find Fatal Purpose through the Web," *Nature* 436, no. 620 (2005). For a sample set of questions and responses, see Atran, "The Emir."

[46] Lee Ross and Constance Stillinger, "Psychological Factors in Conflict Resolution," *Negotiation Journal* 7, no. 389 (1991).

[47] For example, Ali Mohamed, in his plea hearing in New York on October 20, 2000, described the meeting he set up between bin Laden and the Shi'ite chief of Hizbollah, at which it was agreed that Hizbollah would provide explosives training. See transcript of pre-sentence hearing, October 18, 2001, available at <cryptome.org/usa-v-ubl-78.htm>. Bin Laden also praised the Shi'ite group Saudi Hizbollah for the 1996 Khobar Towers suicide bombing of U.S. military housing.

[48] Robert S. Leiken, "Bearers of Global Jihad? Immigration and National Security after 9/11," March 25, 2004, available at <nixoncenter.org/publications/monographs/Leiken_Bearers_of_Global_Jihad.pdf>.

[49] Sageman.

[50] Luis Miguel Ariza, "Virtual Jihad: The Internet as an Ideal Recruiting Tool," *Scientific American* (January 2006), available at <sciam.com/article.cfm?chanID=sa006&articleID=000B51 55-2077-13A8-9E4D83414B7F0101&pageNumber=1&catID=4>.

[51] According to the European Interactive Advertising Association, the Internet increasingly represents the essential media for the 15 to 24 age group, which is "the holy grail" for most advertisers: "European Youth Ditching TV and Radio for Web," *European Tech Wire* (June 24, 2005), available at <europeantechwire.com/etw/2005/06/24/>. Personal bonds formed online without physical contact appear to generate solid reputations for trustworthiness and all the deep commitment that physical intimacy does, but it often occurs faster and over a wider set of personal relations: Paul Resnick, Richard Zeckhauser, "Trust Among Strangers in Internet Interactions," in *Advances in Applied Microeconomics*, vol. 11, ed. Michael Baye (Amsterdam: Elsevier Science, 2002). A recent study of online dating by researchers at the University of Bath indicates that the Internet allows men to manifest emotions that cement durable relationships in ways more easily than from face-to-face contact: "Internet Dating Much More Successful than Thought," online press release, University of Bath, February 2005, available at <eurekalert.org/pub_releases/2005-02/uob-idm021305.php>. The Web also lets women enter into chat rooms with men who would otherwise shun female contact, and it empowers a minority of two in dialogue with the sentiment that they can span the world.

[52] Al-Farouq jihadi forum, October 7, 2005, available at <Al-farouq.com/vb/>.

[53] The phrase *leaderless jihad* was aptly coined by Marc Sageman to refer to recent developments in the global Salafi movement, exemplified by Mustafa Setmariam Nasar (also known as Abu Mus'ab Al-Suri). A veteran of the Soviet-Afghan war, al-Suri had lived and married in Spain and later went to England, where he edited *Al-Ansar* for the Algerian *Groupe Islamique Armée* (GIA). After the falling out between GIA and bin Laden, in 1997 Al-Suri joined bin Laden in Afghanistan and began lecturing in mujahideen training camps on leaderless resistance. His collected works were published online in early 2005 in a 1,600-page manifesto, *Da'wah lil-Muqawamah Al-Islamiyyah Al-'Alamiyyah* (*A Call for the Islamic Global Resistance*), available at <fsboa.com/vw/index.php?subject=7&rec=27&tit=tit&pa=0>. There are striking similarities to

the original treatise on "Leaderless Resistance," written in 1983 by Louis Beam, former Aryan Nations ambassador and Texas Ku Klux Klan leader; available at <reactor-core.org/leaderless-resistance.html>. Leaderless resistance rejects traditional pyramidal organization in favor of a collectivity of ideologically motivated cells with no apparent leader. Cells act on their own initiative and based on their own interpretation of ideology to carry out attacks or foment violence against the American government (also Jews, blacks, and other non-white Christians, supposedly in accordance with the Book of Revelation 12:10). The aim is to protect the wider movement from destruction through decapitation, and by absolving it of responsibility for the actions of member cells. Beam's brief tract became the new bible of the cyber-based White Pride Movement that extends across the Americas, Europe, and into South Africa, and its philosophy of plausible deniability has become the legal foundation for numerous radical and militant Internet Web sites that host extreme *better* ideas and plans.

[54] Raymond Bonner, Don Van Natta, and Stephen Grey, "Investigators So Far Find Little Foreign Involvement," *The New York Times*, July 31, 2005.

[55] Scott Atran, "The Jihadi Mutation," *Terrorism Monitor* (Jamestown Foundation), March 25, 2004, available at <jamestown.org/publications_details.php?volume_id=400&issue_id=2929&article_id=23646>.

[56] Jihadi Web sites are sound and light shows that capture attention with religious narratives set to music of gruesome images of infidels killing and humiliating Muslims followed by cathartic images of martyrdom actions. As advertisers and cognitive psychologists are well aware, such vivid effects reliably increase the audience's emotional support for, and trust in, the message conveyed.

[57] Jared Diamond, *Guns, Germs, and Steel* (New York: Norton, 1997), 277–278.

[58] Philip Zimbardo, "The Stanford Prison Experiment," available at <prisonexp.org/>.

[59] Stanley Milgram, *Obedience to Authority* (New York: Harper & Row, 1974).

[60] Robert Axelrod and William D. Hamilton, "Evolution of Cooperation," *Science* 211, no. 1390 (1981).

[61] Max H. Bazerman and Margaret A. Neale, *Negotiating Rationally* (New York: Free Press, 1991).

[62] Alice Eagly and Shelley Chaiken, *The Psychology of Attitudes* (Fort Worth, TX: Harcourt Brace, 1993).

[63] Jessica Stern, "Beneath Bombast and Bombs, a Cauldron of Humiliation," *The Los Angeles Times*, June 6, 2004.

[64] Richard E. Nisbett and Dov Cohen, *The Culture of Honor: Psychology of Violence in the South* (Boulder, CO: Westview Press, 1996); J. G. Peristiani (ed.), *Honor and Shame: The Values of Mediterranean Society* (Chicago: University of Chicago Press, 1966).

[65] One reason pro-American news and broadcasts worked in Eastern Europe to undermine communism was that the great majority of Eastern Europeans never wanted to be communists, and there were also varying degrees of familiarity with democratic processes before imposition of communist rule. But most Muslims are more attuned to messages that will first and foremost help them become *better* Muslims.

[66] Nasir Abas, *Membongkar Jamaah Islamiyah* (Jakarta: Grafindo Khazanah Ilmu, 2005).

[67] Ibn Khaldûn, *The Muqaddimah*, 3 vols. (London: Routledge & Kegan Paul, 1958, originally composed in the 14th century).

Chapter Eight

Restoring America's Good Name: Improving Strategic Communications with the Islamic World

Peter W. Singer and Hady Amr

The United States needs to shift its priorities and programming dramatically to enhance and improve its efforts at public diplomacy and strategic communications with the Islamic world. Restoring trust in America's word and rebuilding the shattered foundations of understanding between the United States and the world's Muslim states and communities form a critical pillar of success in the war on terror and therefore must be a top priority for the current and future administrations. However, America's efforts at strategic communications since 9/11 have lacked an overarching, integrated strategy (in part because an overall national strategy that takes full account of the complexities involved in combating terrorism is still a work in progress). The result has been informational programming that has lacked priority or been misdirected; has not been sufficiently nuanced for dealing with diverse regional and issue areas; and has not reached out to the swing audiences needed to marginalize and root out violent extremists.

For its efforts at strategic communications to be effective, the U.S. Government must move beyond understanding the problem as simply a matter of better public relations. Shaping the views and attitudes that foreign populaces hold toward the United States and its policies requires more than just trying to reverse steep losses in some global popularity contest; it must be a continuing process that directly affects America's relationship with populations and civil societies around the world and with the groups and governments they influence. How America engages with the outside world, and with what elements in that world, helps determine the success or failure of U.S. foreign policy.

Although better strategic communications and public diplomacy cannot substitute for better policy, they can help America reconnect with moderate and reform-oriented Muslims who share an interest in transforming the region and fighting radical militants. Better strategic communications can even help engage the region's conservatives in the effort to defeat violent extremism. The goal of such a campaign is to marginalize the radical militants, reversing the present trend in which the U.S. voice is the one being marginalized. Moreover, with the spread of bin Ladenism having taken on the characteristics of a diffused, decentralized, transnational Islamist insurgency, special attention must be given to the interface between traditional means of public diplomacy and the role that the U.S. military can play in the effort.

The Missing Strategy

The deep and rapid deterioration of its image in the Islamic world is one of the greatest challenges the United States faces in conducting the war on terror. Polls in the Islamic world indicate that, despite slight improvements in the last 2 years, as much as 80 percent of the populace still has a negative view of the United States.[1] The erosion of the U.S. image in the region effectively denies American ideas and policies a fair hearing. In turn, the negative lens through which the United States is viewed means that its actions are often interpreted in a manner that reinforces the propaganda efforts of adversaries. Winning the war on terror depends substantially on winning the war of ideas; by most available metrics, however, the United States is not winning that war.

The challenges in this domain were laid out in a self-critical private memorandum issued by Secretary of Defense Donald Rumsfeld to his senior staff in 2003 and subsequently leaked to the media. The media focused on his admission of a "long, hard slog" being the state of affairs in Iraq, contrary to the overly optimistic predictions made earlier, but more significant were Rumsfeld's questions on whether we are "winning or losing the Global War on Terror." He described how his department had yet to enact a bold, measurable, or systematic plan to win the war on terror, despite being 2 years and 2 ground wars into the fight. Rumsfeld's memorandum described as most troubling the manifest absence of a strategy to deal with the severe antipathy toward the United States, observing that failure in this area effectively keeps a terrorist supply pipeline flowing:

> Does the U.S. need to fashion a broad, integrated plan to stop the next generation of terrorists? The U.S. is putting relatively little effort into a long-range plan, but we are putting a great deal of effort into trying to stop terrorists. The cost-benefit ratio is against us! Our cost is billions against the terrorists' costs of millions . . . Is our current situation such that "the harder we work, the behinder we get"?[2]

The significance of this missing strategy is heightened by the fact that Rumsfeld's memo did not yield immediate results. It took more than a year before the Department of Defense (DOD) was able to establish the *National Military Strategic Plan for the War on Terrorism* that would link overall strategic thinking to the forces that must implement it. More importantly, as long as it took, DOD was still making more progress than the rest of the U.S. Government. As of mid-2006, although the latest *National Security Strategy of the United States* cites winning the war of ideas as the key to long-term success in the war on terror, a detailed strategic plan that brings together the overall strategy and facilitates integrated, interagency strategic planning and execution remained lacking.[3]

Many thinkers term the situation facing the United States not as a set of discrete attacks and conflicts, but rather as a long-term conflict, akin to the Cold War, much of it taking place in the realm of ideas, but still with a decidedly tangible security aspect.[4] If this comparison is valid, then measured according to a Cold War timeline, the state of development of our strategy is circa 1946, as we still struggle to answer the fundamental questions of who and what we are facing in this conflict and what the nature of our long-term response should be.

The role of communications in this strategy is critical to overall national security now and will remain so in decades to come, especially because much of the threat seems to be coming from terrorists acting in an apparently decentralized, self-inspired fashion. However, our present security concerns extend beyond the militants in Iraq or terrorists inspired by al Qaeda to a longer term issue of grand strategy that may be feeding a wider threat of tomorrow. The United States—and the world—may be standing on the brink of emerging fault lines, or a "clash of civilizations" as Samuel Huntington has warned.[5] The widely held view in the Muslim world that describes the war on terror as a "war on Islam" is perhaps most illustrative of this problem. The deepening divide between the United States and the world's Muslim states and communities is a critical impediment to success in goals ranging from running down terrorist groups, their leaders, and supporters, to expanding human development and freedom, the absence of which steers the next generation of recruits to radicalism. Failure in this effort will not only damage America's standing in the long term, and therefore its ability to lead effectively, but also widen the scope of those who would seek to harm the United States in the coming decades.

Why Our Communication Matters

Striving to be a respected and moral world leader has been central to the goals of U.S. foreign policy over the last 50 years. Other schools of foreign policy thinking also recognize the importance in maintaining global esteem. For example, even an observer who sees the U.S. role in the world as an imperial one can admit that the most enduring empires have led by persuasion, respect, and the force of ideas, not just by imposing their will by the power of military force. Or, if one takes a values-based assessment in connecting American morals to its foreign policy, few Americans would take pride in being hated, preferring to see the United States respected as a world leader.

An important distinction must be made between public affairs on the one hand and public diplomacy and strategic communications on the other. In the international context, public affairs is "the provision of information to the public, press, and other institutions concerning the goals, policies, and activities of the U.S. Government."[6] It is basically reactive, typified by the image of a spokesperson answering media questions or coordinating "messages for the day." By contrast, public diplomacy is proactive, long-term outreach toward other states and their people, aimed at building understanding of and support for U.S. policies. As long defined by the United States Information Agency (now part of the Department of State), public diplomacy is those activities that seek "to promote the national interest and the national security of the United States through understanding, informing and influencing foreign publics and broadening dialogue between American citizens and institutions and their counterparts abroad."[7] A classic case from the Cold War was the effort to engage European leaders and publics on the decision to locate intermediate range missiles within Europe (a decision that, over time, moved from being viewed as provocative to being understood as matching and balancing Soviet deployments). In an ideal world, these activities are part of an overall program of strategic communications, which undertakes a comprehensive set of outreach mechanisms aimed at long-term goals of transforming beliefs and attitudes, so as to create an environment more conducive to policy success.[8]

Such programming can never be effective when tasked with communicating bad policies, but even good policies can be hamstrung by an inept public diplomacy effort. These activities shape the context in which American policy operates, and thus can either be an aid, a hindrance, or of no effect at all. More importantly, public diplomacy is a major tool through which the United States can harness what Joseph Nye, former dean of Harvard University's Kennedy School of Government, has described as one of America's greatest assets and a cornerstone of American influence across the globe: its influence through "soft power."[9] Soft power is "the ability to get what you want by attracting and persuading others to adopt your goals." It is the most efficient and effective means of power, as it does not require the use of force or huge financial expenditures to achieve or sustain policy goals.

Foreign good will has a direct value to the pursuit of our own national security, something that the crafters of our Cold War strategy—particularly as exemplified in the design of such programs as the Marshall Plan, Voice of America, and the Peace Corps—understood. Good will creates reservoirs of understanding and appreciation of mutual interests that allow alliances to endure beyond temporary disputes. Most importantly, good will saves the U.S. Government from fighting a series of uphill battles, contrary to our professed respect for democracy, to persuade allied or client governments to align themselves with us against the democratically expressed opinion of their general public. The very real policy blowback from failing in such matters was illustrated during the lead-up to the 2003 Iraq war. The Turkish public's distrust of American intent prevented the United States from opening a true second front in the war and resulted in delays in troop levels early in the occupation that may have been crucial in permitting the incipient insurgency to take root.[10]

Obstacles to Communication

We now face a communications challenge that dwarfs any in U.S. history, at a time when our reserve of soft power has dwindled precipitously. Unlike prior ebbs and flows of U.S. standing in the world, the present situation may be evolving into something more intrinsic. As detailed in the previous chapters, relations between the world's sole superpower and one of the world's largest and most strategically located religious communities—approximately 1.4 billion Muslims—stand at issue for the long term, with potentially disastrous consequences for both.

While the past several years have been marked by American military success in overthrowing autocratic, oppressive regimes in Afghanistan and Iraq, they have also seen political and diplomatic failure, exemplified by the deepening tensions between the United States and the wider Islamic world, including Muslim communities in Europe and Southeast Asia. As discussed in chapters 2 and 3, polls across the Islamic world suggest a steep decline in esteem for the United States in general, and for U.S. foreign policy in particular.[11]

Some in the American body politic have argued that such trends should be ignored, or even that they are a source of pride.[12] Such thinking is shortsighted and dangerous (and ignores the lessons not only of history but also of strategists ranging from Machiavelli to Mao). Until the chasm between the United States and the global Islamic community is bridged, it will continue to thwart our attempts to secure the homeland and prevent the success of our foreign policy. At the same time, local attitudes toward us and our adversaries are key factors as to whether violent radical movements flourish. Indeed, terrorist groups have often been highly responsive to local opinion at the tactical level; the frequent changes by Hamas in its operations and tactics are illustrative.

Geopolitics is not a popularity contest, but it is dangerous to disregard international public opinion to such a degree as to assist indirectly in the recruitment and growth of radical groups through either behavior that inspires anti-American hatred (such as the Abu Ghraib prison scandal) or the absence of a cohesive public diplomacy strategy and apparatus. In the wake of the 9/11 attacks and the terrorists' self-evident violation of all moral and religious codes of conduct, the United States should have been able to isolate al Qaeda from the broader Islamic public and thus cut it off from the support and recruiting structures that would allow it to thrive. Instead, we have become isolated and conversely have seen bin Laden and al Qaeda rise in stature.

The present situation is troubling. While the United States and its allies have seized some al Qaeda lieutenants and assets, the movement remains vibrant and its senior leadership largely intact. More critical, though, is that its popularity is greater than ever, its ability to recruit individuals and affiliate organizations to its agenda is unbroken, and its ideology is spreading across a global network from Algeria and Belgium to Indonesia and Iraq. Of greatest concern is its evolution into a wider, decentralized movement, which appears to have maintained its potential to strike at American citizens and interests both at home and abroad. As the Madrid and London attacks reveal, its capabilities may even be growing, and we may be witnessing the transformation of the threat of al Qaeda to the threat of al Qaedaism.[13]

This evolution of the primary threat from a specific organization into a networked ideology is important. The attacks from Bali to Morocco to Madrid to London all reveal that the threat has evolved from being highly centralized to becoming self-organized, self-inspired, and cellular. That is, instead of an attack of the type that occurred on September 11, which was tightly orchestrated from camps in Afghanistan and took as long as 5 years to conceptualize, we are seeing the proliferation of self-forming cells, inspired by al Qaedaism, but composed of small groups of friends and family that are difficult to infiltrate and only loosely linked with the organization itself. Such groups' attacks may not be as spectacular as those of 9/11, but they can be just as disturbing to the target populations and are even cheaper than the notably inexpensive 9/11 operation. (The explosives used in the July 7, 2005, London subway bombings could be purchased for around $10,000 on the black market.) The hallmark of such net-centric groups is that the sum of their threat is greater than their constituent parts.

It is important to note, however, that the war of ideas in this global insurgency is not a battle already lost. Attitudes within Muslim communities indicate many nuances and subtle bright spots. For example, while anti-Americanism has surged in the last few years, the United States stands in an interesting position of being hated not because of its values, but rather because of the perception of how Americans conduct themselves. While there is great anger with U.S. policies, esteem for American values of freedom and democracy, as well as for American education and technology, remains relatively high.[14] At the same time, fears about the repercussions of Islamic extremism and frustration with the tactics of violent radicals are on the upswing in many Muslim states.[15] This subtle turn clearly cannot be viewed as a success for which any American government agency can take credit, as most analysts feel the source of this turn is "primarily the actions of the terrorists themselves." [16] Nevertheless, a nascent backlash among Muslims against extremist ideology and tactics could indicate openings to both improve respect for the United States and defuse tacit support for radical militants.

Thus, as we look to our strategy for the future, the lessons gained by the bipartisan 9/11 Commission (chaired by former New Jersey Governor Thomas Kean and former Indiana Congressman Lee Hamilton) are instructive. In discussing what could be done in the future to prevent similar acts of terrorism, one of the three key focus areas the commission identified was to "prevent the continued growth of Islamic terrorism," specifically through efforts to "communicate and defend American ideals in the Islamic world through much stronger public diplomacy to reach more people including students and leaders outside government." The report went on to say, "Our efforts here should be as strong as they were in combating closed societies during the Cold War."[17] Likewise, in the 2005 *National Military Strategic Plan for the War on Terrorism*, one of the three pillars of action (lines of operation) that DOD commanders are directed to pursue is "countering ideological support for terrorism."

To accomplish these objectives, a far more strategic approach to communication is necessary as part of U.S. policy toward the Islamic world. The United States must complement its programs of antiterrorism and engagement with a public diplomacy and strategic communications effort that demonstrates its commitment to the values of democracy and human rights and support for the forces of progress in the Islamic world, all with the goal of undermining the factors that aid radicalism. An integrative strategy that weaves communications into the policymaking process will make U.S. efforts more effective by standardizing messages, maximizing interagency coordination, and generating genuine dialogue between the United States and civil society in the Islamic world.

What Have We Done?

In a January 2005 interview prior to his second inauguration, President Bush acknowledged that declining U.S. popularity in the Islamic world would be one of his greatest challenges in the subsequent 4 years. However, as he depicted it, the problem was merely one of poor public relations: "The propagandists have done a better job of depicting America as a hateful place, a place wanting to impose our form of thought and our religion on people. We're behind when it comes to selling our own story and telling the people the truth about America."[18]

This dual response illustrated the problems U.S. strategic communications have faced since 9/11, and why efforts so far have been largely unsuccessful. The evidence of unprecedented levels of anti-American sentiments in the Islamic world is undeniable and has therefore pushed the issue of public diplomacy to the top of the agenda. Restoring the world's trust in America's word and rebuilding the shattered foundations of understanding between the United States and the world's Muslim states and communities are critical pillars to success in the war on terror and therefore must be a top priority for the current and future administrations.

U.S. efforts at strategic communications since 9/11 have too often been understood in the context of public relations. More importantly, when it comes to actual programming and implementation, they have not been sufficiently rooted within an overarching, integrated strategy. In part, this reflects the relatively minor role to which the problem of strategic communications was relegated in the February 2003 *National Strategy for Combating Terrorism*, a conceptual shortfall that is only now being addressed in a systematic way. The result has been public diplomacy and related programming that has lacked priority or been misdirected; has not been sufficiently nuanced in dealing with diverse regional and issue areas; and has not reached out to the major swing audiences needed to marginalize and root out violent extremists.

The rapid turn against America in the region is striking. Two of our closest regional allies made this point in April 2004: Egyptian President Hosni Mubarak said that there was more hatred of America today in the Arab world than ever before, and King Abdullah II of Jordan warned that U.S.-Arab relations were the worst he had ever seen them in his lifetime, and he abruptly canceled a meeting with Bush that month.[19] A legion of independent public voices has echoed these sentiments. A wide array of public opinion surveys confirms a similar pattern across the Arab and Islamic world: a dramatic rise in anti-American sentiments and loss of the confidence of mainstream Muslims in a period in which their actions and views are of great importance to our national and security interests.

Association with America was once seen positively in many respects; it is now largely viewed negatively and can be an economic and political liability. While the statistics are highly illustrative, anecdotes can be even more telling. A leading Kuwait-based conglomerate formed in the 1960s adopted the name "Americana"—a thinly veiled attempt to leverage the positive image of the United States in the region. The company is now, however, stuck with the name, and recently began an advertising campaign designed to disassociate itself from the United States: "Americana: 100% Arab." Similarly, the fast-food giant McDonald's ran a campaign in the Arab world pledging a percentage of each sale to Palestinian charities. But perhaps more illustrative is the cultural vibe that permeates relations. For example, the most popular movie in Egypt at the time of writing is "The Night Baghdad Fell," which describes an American invasion of Egypt, the destruction of Cairo, and a faux Condoleezza Rice in a sex scene, while in Turkey the most popular film is "Valley of the Wolves," which fantasizes about Turkish troops wreaking revenge on Americans troops, who have just shot up a wedding and bombed a mosque (the prime minister's wife even attended its premiere).

These trends were reinforced by the stories of abuses at Abu Ghraib and other prisons in the U.S. detention system, which presented the worst face of America to the world. Such mistakes were not just contrary to codes of conduct, but also had a reverberative effect by reinforcing the propaganda put out by radicals; indeed, the fact that these incidents were proven true provided fuel to radical attempts to sell claims of even worse abuses so as to bolster their narrative of a conspiratorial and inherently anti-Muslim United States.[20] Moreover, not only have the abuses tarnished the image of the United States, they also have made life more difficult for local moderates and reformists who used to look to the United States for support. For example, the governments of Indonesia, Libya, Sudan, and even Israel have all cited the Abu Ghraib abuses as an excuse for their own questionable human rights practices.

Challenges and Inconsistencies

The present challenge is to bridge the gap between rhetoric and reality that has characterized policy toward the broader Islamic world, especially in the strategic communications sector. Senior officials have frequently spoken of the need for democracy and reform across the Arab world and for public diplomacy to overcome rising anti-Americanism. However, there has been a repeated failure to deal with these issues on a dedicated basis and adequately fund public diplomacy programming. The priority of the issue has not been matched by actual strategy development and implementation.

Efforts to respond to spiraling anti-Americanism have been half-hearted at best. The bipartisan Advisory Commission on Public Diplomacy issued a sweeping indictment of the decline in American public diplomacy capabilities and offered a range of practical steps that could be taken. Rather than seizing the opportunity, the Bush administration declined to request sufficient additional funding and has shown little interest in implementing the commission's recommendations. Congressman Frank Wolf (R–VA), who called for the advisory commission, has described the administration's response as "lackluster" and "disappointing."[21]

Funding is perhaps the easiest of the multiple metrics that exist for measures of activity and attention. Public diplomacy had already suffered from steep budget cuts in the 1990s, and since 9/11, many of the remaining options to ensure that America's voice is heard within the region (including American institutes, student visas, and exchange programs) have been severely curtailed. The Advisory Commission on Public Diplomacy argued that an effective strategy would require a massive increase in the funding and staffing of programs on the ground throughout the region. Instead, these programs have languished. Despite bipartisan support, spending on public diplomacy programs remains deeply underfunded, especially in comparison to the scale of the challenge. Overall public diplomacy funding in fiscal year 2004 was $539 million, of which only about 27 percent was dedicated toward the Muslim world, primarily through cultural and education outreach.[22] This share of funding is not remotely consistent with the centrality of global Islamic communities to the key national security issue facing America today.

Another measure of seriousness is bureaucratic attention. Faced with evidence of America's collapsing image abroad, President Bush created the position of Under Secretary of State for Public Diplomacy. However, the publicity that was given to the establishment of the position was not matched by a serious commitment to filling and supporting it. When Under Secretary Charlotte Beers resigned in March 2003, the position was left unfilled for 9 months—during the Iraq war and its aftermath, the single most important period for U.S. public diplomacy since the days immediately following 9/11. Beers' eventual successor, Ambassador Margaret Tutwiler, resigned the post after less than 6 months on the job. As a result, for most of the Bush administration's first term, no one was clearly and consistently responsible for crafting America's public diplomacy strategy. Nearly a year after Tutwiler's resignation, the President announced that his former campaign adviser, Karen Hughes, would be taking over the position. The President's naming of a personal confidant illustrated the importance of the position to the U.S. Government, but even so, another 4 ½ months elapsed from the time Hughes's nomination was announced until confirmation hearings were held. The very act was the message; Hughes was expert neither in the issues nor public diplomacy, and indeed had no experience in international affairs at all. But her nomination was meant as a demonstrable signal that the problem had been accepted as real and significant.

Now that Hughes is in place, the true test will not be the actual appointment, but the level of activity (both here and abroad) carried out by the appointee and her office, and the amount of support that the programming she seeks to put together gets from the leadership structure. Since her appointment, Hughes has traveled to a number of Muslim countries including Egypt, Indonesia, Malaysia, Pakistan, Qatar, Saudi Arabia, and Turkey, but often for only a few days at a time. She played a leading role in arranging for the United States Institute of Peace Muslim World Advisory Board, composed mostly of American-Muslims, to meet with Secretary of State Condoleezza Rice and others within the administration. She has also sought to expand programming and has requested more extensive reviews and evaluation of programming underway. Despite the improvement over the previous 5 years, there is still far to go in terms of effectiveness and impact.

Missed Opportunities

Outside of planned programming, the United States has frequently failed to take advantage of opportunities that presented themselves and has shown little interest in actual dialogue and engagement with moderate Muslims. For example, when a summit of over 150 top U.S. and Muslim world leaders and opinion-shapers—including leading business executives, civil society activists, government ministers, and news editors from more than 35 countries—met in Doha, Qatar, in January 2004, the United States was the only major government that did not send a senior political official. Moreover, even U.S. Central Command turned down an invitation to send an officer to speak to the group, despite the opportunity it presented to explain U.S. military operations in the region to key leaders whom the command had been unable to reach through its own briefings. The Bush administration was even criticized by the pro-Republican journal *Weekly Standard* for not seizing this opportunity.[23] Nonetheless, the episode was repeated the very next year, when a follow-up U.S.-Islamic world leader summit was held. Once again, not one currently serving senior leader from the American administration made the effort to speak to this influential audience from across the Muslim world. It was not until the 2006 forum that the United States sent Karen Hughes to speak at the opening event, serving on a panel with three Muslim foreign ministers.

The manner in which the United States engages and communicates is also important. In the Islamic world (and elsewhere), the United States is widely perceived as lecturing without listening, and often is viewed as arrogant and uninterested in the opinion of others. The administration's rhetoric is heard as lacking sympathy for Arab and Muslim concerns, leading to unintended misunderstandings. Even leaders within the U.S. policy structure note that America's voice has been unclear or muted at a time when dialogue and engagement with potentially friendly members of civil society in the Muslim world are a strategic necessity. For example, Christopher Ross, the State Department's special coordinator for public diplomacy in the Arab world, notes, "We must listen to the world as well as speak to it. The failure to listen and to provide more avenues for dialogue will only strengthen the stereotype of the United States as arrogant."[24]

While there was great fanfare about Karen Hughes' appointment, U.S. public diplomacy has remained in spin mode, treating public diplomacy like an extension of an election campaign. Hughes' limited forays have been rife with photo opportunities (a public diplomacy "success story" spun by the State Department was Hughes going to a cooking class in Germany), and staged meetings with prescreened groups of elites. Too often, even these have backfired, such as the infamous lecture given to rich Saudi women on their right to drive. Hughes' speeches in the region also stand as a guide on how not to communicate with the Muslim world, veering from pandering references that lack local cultural awareness to finger-wagging lectures. As one prominent American Muslim imam describes, "She seems to have taken on a very narrow mission of trying to convince people over there of how correct the administration is, no matter what people might think."[25] An evangelical Christian newsletter in the United States was even more blunt in its depiction of the speech she gave at the U.S.-Islamic World Forum in Qatar: "America's relationship with the Muslim world has hit rock bottom . . . and we have begun to dig."[26]

How the United States interacts with the new media rising in the Middle East is a tragic illustration of the shortcomings in our public diplomacy strategy. The breaking of state monopolies on the news, particularly by satellite news channels, has provided an opportunity to reach the general public with an immediacy not previously available. After 9/11, the Bush administration recognized the importance of such news media and made the point of sending officials to speak on al Jazeera to explain the administration's positions. This opportunity has, however, been insufficiently exploited. The administration's media outreach campaign lacked stamina and has since been essentially abandoned, thus yielding more air time to voices that condemn the United States and fuel the fires of conspiracy theory.

The administration has compounded its problems by frequently lashing out at the satellite news channels, al Arabiya and al Jazeera, that are most popular among Arabs (al Jazeera has some 35 million viewers, while al Arabiya has some 20 million).[27] It has declared these stations as major problems for U.S. efforts in Iraq and for the war on terrorism and has pressured the Qatari government to compel al Jazeera to make editorial changes. The efforts have backfired, as the channels now identify themselves as being locked in a public conflict with the United States (gaining further viewers), while the pressure tactics pursued by the United States have undermined its own rhetoric in support of a freer press in the Arab world.

While the content on Arabic-language satellite news channels is often genuinely troubling, these channels are not the cause of American problems in Iraq and the region. Experts and public opinion polls agree that the expression of anti-American opinions on the Arab satellite media is more than anything a reflection of existing Arab sentiments.[28] In fact, while al Jazeera is often singled out by the Bush administration for fostering anti-Americanism, it was long seen in the Arab world as being too pro-Israeli and pro-American, because it was the first international Arab station in the region to regularly bring on Israeli guests and cover the Israeli parliament. In any case, polling has shown that there is no evidence that frequent viewers of Arabic satellite news channels like al Jazeera are any more likely to have negative perceptions of U.S. foreign policy than others.[29]

The Bush administration's public criticism of Arabic satellite news channels and its attempts to pressure these stations to make editorial changes have only exacerbated the U.S. image problem in the Middle East. America appears hypocritical when it speaks of the merits of freedom of the press while it asks friendly governments in the region to influence the editorial content of the satellite news channels. The United States should endorse and encourage a free and professional media, even when it is the target of criticism from such media.

This does not mean that the United States should tolerate hateful speech or the distribution of lies in the Arab media; in fact, it should be more consistent and focused in combating inaccuracy and incitement. The failure of senior U.S. leaders to cite specific footage and broadcast dates in lieu of broad claims undermines the accusations. For example, at a 2005 summit of defense ministers in Southeast Asia, Secretary Donald Rumsfeld accused al Jazeera of airing videos of terrorists beheading hostages, which the station claims it had never done. The truth is clearly one or the other, and specificity would prove the point. Similarly, the administration has been injudicious in its use of labels such as "incitement," often reacting to a report broadcast read on al Jazeera more vociferously than a very similar report broadcast on one of the region's state television networks. This inconsistency has eroded the perceived legitimacy of U.S. criticisms. In short, the United States has neither been able to distinguish between hate speech and political opposition in its outreach to those who channel the news and influence opinions, nor to make clear to Arab journalists and editors the importance of this distinction.

In one distinct area of activity in strategic communications, the United States has invested significant sums in creating American government–backed media outlets, al Hurra television and Radio Sawa. This largely misguided effort was undertaken contrary to the advice of the Advisory Commission on Public Diplomacy. Besides taking the bulk of new funding in the public diplomacy domain, these stations have reinforced the view of many in the region that the United States is interested not in free media but only in pro-American media. More importantly, there is no evidence that the two outlets—which were never shown to be linked to the sources from which people get their news anyway—have altered people's beliefs on the ground or even that they have swayed the information market in any way. Al Arabiya and al Jazeera remain the most viewed news channels. Surveys in Saudi Arabia found that while al Jazeera and al Arabiya are regularly watched by 82 percent and 75 percent of households (as in the United States, households watch multiple channels regularly), only 16 percent regularly watch al Hurra. In the United Arab Emirates, only 11 percent of young nationals regularly watch al Hurra, as compared to 52 percent for al Jazeera. Only in Iraq is al Jazeera not in first place; al Iraqiya, watched by 74 percent of respondents, has the best broadcast footprint. Al Hurra, hampered by the fact that only 4 percent of those polled in Iraq consider it trustworthy, comes in at 6 percent.[30]

Moreover, al Hurra and Radio Sawa may have had another little-noted effect. Because of al Hurra's U.S. Government affiliation, American officials might be more likely to grant an interview to it rather than another outlet. Thus, the stations have further drawn American officials away from appearances on Arabic-language stations that have larger audiences. The end result is that U.S. Government–operated news outlets in the Arab world take up a considerable portion of the allocations for public diplomacy yet have yielded few significant positive results. Given the mediocre payoff, the failure to make similar efforts toward the far greater number of Muslims who live outside the Arab world may reflect a lack of nuance in U.S. efforts, but at the same time, may be for the best.

Another serious shortcoming in U.S. strategic communication efforts is the failure to engage the core swing audiences that are the most critical for defeating radicalism. The political spectrum across the Muslim world is quite diverse. In addition to varying regional contexts and concerns (for example, while the Israeli-Palestinian conflict overshadows any discussion of political reform in the Arab world, Indonesians care more about U.S. policy on Aceh than they do about Palestine), widely differing interest groups and demographic sectors exist within each area of the Muslim world. These include regime retainers, including members of the army and the bureaucracy; secular reformers, the liberal and leftists groups most oriented to Western modes but typically lacking local power and credibility; gradualist mainstreamers, typically the largest set of the professional and business class who are generally disposed to gradually amending the status quo; Islamist social conservatives, who carry the widest support and seek a far greater role for Islam in society (and thus are disposed toward both democratic reform and anti-Americanism); radical Islamists (who advocate a regime overturn and the implementation of full sharia); and, ultimately, militant activists and terrorists themselves (those who undertake or provide active support to violent action).

Engagement with the Islamic World

Such divisions cannot be described perfectly, but the important point is that market segmentation exists within the populations to which the United States needs to speak in the Muslim world. As an illustration, the rough rubric used by the Defense Science Board Task Force on Strategic Communication broke society in the Islamic world into five segments relevant to public diplomacy:

- Group 1: regime retainers, including members of the army and the bureaucracy
- Group 2: professional and business class
- Group 3: workers and small business owners
- Group 4: establishment, nonmilitant Islamic activists
- Group 5: militant radicals.

Within each group are members with often divergent interests and perceptions of the world, and for each group, the optimal means of communications are different as well. [31]

All of these segments of the Islamic world, with the exception of militant radicals, need to be engaged, but in different ways. Thus, using the Defense Science Board typology, the core of any U.S. public diplomacy strategy must be efforts to engage groups 2, 3, and 4, who comprise what would be called the "swing voters" in American parlance in any effort to defeat radical forces. This means outreach toward not only moderate, often secular, reformers, but also conservatives and nonmilitant Islamists, who form the majority of society and carry far greater local credibility than most Western-oriented reformers. Indeed, the conservative segments of society are quite significant. In Jordan, Egypt, and the Occupied Palestinian Territories, about two-thirds of Muslims feel that society should be governed only by Islamic law, while in Lebanon and Syria, the figure was one-third. Positive engagement with moderate reformers is key to building a successful coalition for progress, but outreach to conservatives is necessary to curb militant inroads into their ranks.

U.S. strategic communications have often failed to appreciate the diversity of opinion within and between countries and, worse, have held both reformers and conservatives at arms' length. While reaching out to like-minded reformers is simply a matter of increased support and attention, the critical challenge is how the United States will deal with the rising power and popularity of Islamist groups. As Shibley Telhami writes,

> The reality shown by Hamas's victory in the Palestinian elections is this: If fully free elections were held today in the rest of the Arab world, Islamist parties would win in most states. Even with intensive international efforts to support civil society and nongovernmental organizations (NGOs), elections in 5 years would probably yield the same results. The notion, popular in Washington over the past few years, that American programs and efforts can help build a third alternative to both current governments and Islamists is simply a delusion.

These groups not only are far more influential than any other constituencies in local civil society, but they also share a world view that is often at odds with U.S. policies and values. However, the groups may be thought of as akin to the socialist parties and labor unions of post–World War II Europe. The United States certainly may not be able to persuade them to push for American policies overnight, but it can and should engage and communicate with them in an effort to prevent their cooption by the other side.

To date, the United States has steered clear of the tough challenges involved in engaging such groups and frequently has made the fundamental mistake of assuming that any Islamist group is inherently violent and al Qaeda–oriented. Failing to appreciate the diversity of groups and ideologies in the Muslim world could have the same strategic consequences that the lumping together of the Red Menace did in the early Cold War; the mistaken assumption that the Soviets, Red China, and anticolonial nationalists were all the same groups pursuing the same interests was not fully disentangled until President Richard Nixon's trip to China. At the same time, comparing the limited amount of activity in this sector to the scale of the efforts that surrounded the Marshall Plan would almost be insulting.

In sum, if the present trend continues, the Muslim world will view the United States primarily through a lens that distortedly emphasizes the perceived American threat. The context for American foreign policy will be made more challenging, and the ranks of Muslim extremists will grow. If the proposed solution is only better public relations efforts to help "sell" America, and the problems of priority, focus, and nuance are not dealt with, then the terrible dynamic presently set in place will worsen.

Recommendations for Success: Reversing the Trend

By failing to pursue effective public diplomacy, the United States largely has conceded the war of ideas in the Islamic world to the radicals. To win this war, the administration must recognize the importance of America's voice and good standing as elements of its power and influence in the world. A major, integrative initiative in public diplomacy and strategic communications is needed to bridge the divide between the United States and Muslim states and communities (ranging from Algeria to Indonesia, and including Muslim minority communities extending from Europe to India).

Strategic communications activities and the war of ideas are essential to winning the conflict we presently are fighting. The global war on terror is not a traditional military conflict of set-piece battles, but rather is a series of small wars and insurgencies in places ranging from Iraq and Afghanistan to Pakistan, Egypt, and even England, where the United States must sway a broader population from hostility to support if it wants to oust terror cells and shut down recruiting pipelines. As the foreword to a proposed revision of the famous U.S. Marine Corps Small Wars Manual (which sought to update it for the 21st century and the global war on terror) notes, "Small wars are battles of ideas and battles for the perceptions and attitudes of target populations."[32] Within these wars, nonkinetic tools (as opposed to fielded weaponry) make up "the fire and maneuvers of small wars. They frequently are the main effort simply because of the criticality of the functions they perform."[33]

Engendering better relations with the Islamic world strengthens U.S. national security, but it requires more than Federal pocket change. The President must designate the task as an issue of the highest national security importance. It should also be integrated into the policymaking apparatus; public diplomacy officials cannot simply be seen as a clean-up crew. The tactics in the new approach should be innovative, and, at the same time, the campaign as a whole must be self-critical, regularly evaluating its own performance, and ready and able to change accordingly.

Five broad principles must guide the strategy to influence foreign publics and, as the official definition of public diplomacy puts it, to "broaden dialogue between American citizens and institutions and their counterparts abroad":

■ There must be an integrated approach among the various U.S.

Government agencies so as to maximize efforts and resources and speak with a credible voice.

■ The effort must be conceptualized as a dialogue, maximizing jointness of projects and participation with foreign constituencies.

■ The United States must reach out to the diverse set of regional players and constituencies, including conservatives, rather than "preaching to the choir."

■ Strategies and programs must be nimble and responsive.

■ The investment in the programming should reflect its strategic priority.

Integrate the Effort to Maximize the Effect

An integrative communications strategy is required, both across our agencies and across the divide between the United States and the region, so that the U.S. voice is amplified and resonates.

Within the executive branch, far better coordination is needed. The administration should seriously consider a range of organizational options. At the high end of these would be a formal Public Diplomacy Coordinating Structure, as proposed by the Council on Foreign Relations' independent task force on public diplomacy. This structure, similar and parallel to the National Security Council (NSC), would coordinate more cohesive public diplomacy activities across Federal agencies. At the low end would be the expansion in responsibilities of the Deputy Assistant to the President and Deputy National Security Advisor for Strategic Communications and Global Outreach to include coordinating the range of interagency public diplomacy activities. (In the past, the position followed a very public affairs–type outreach, coordinating "messages of the day," but a comprehensive and long-term strategy is needed.) This position could then serve as the umbrella for subordinate regional coordinators who would synchronize U.S. Government public diplomacy, public affairs, and information operation activities for each region, helping to bring together the various State, Defense, and Central Intelligence Agency efforts. The intent of such structural change must be not only to provide better visibility for the issue at the White House level, but also to ensure that lessons learned through dialogue in public diplomacy inform the foreign policymaking apparatus. In terms of viability and workability, the latter proposal is the quicker and easier to implement and thus should be enacted in the short term, but bureaucratic exploration can be made of the broader structure.

Two-Way Communications Open Doors

A successful public diplomacy strategy must aim to both inform and actively engage important communities in the world and shape the context in which they experience "America." When facing an uphill battle in which the United States is looked upon with bias, establishing credibility and demonstrating respect for the other side will be key. "Dialogue," as King Abdallah of Jordan said at the 2003 World Economic Forum, is "the key to the door." When the United States plans its public diplomacy activities without its allies in foreign constituencies, it misses an opportunity to strengthen the effectiveness of its programming investments.

Thus, as listening begets listening, it will prove more effective to plan joint programming, in which citizens and officials from the United States and Muslim countries participate in both the activities and as the target audiences, where possible and appropriate. The principle of dialogue and the maximization of jointness in planning and execution of programming seek to accomplish two tasks:

- By involving and thus integrating the audience into the exercise, the message is far more likely to be understood and accepted positively.

- Feedback loops will be created that better inform policymakers (and offer metrics), as well as improve the public diplomacy efforts that follow.

To yield maximum effectiveness and create a self-sustaining program, coordination of such efforts with local institutions and organizations will be useful. These groups should be identified by local U.S. Embassies, which will have a sense of their credibility. The U.S. Government must be sensitive to the particular security and political backlash challenges that such groups will face. At all times, the United States must seek to be an enabler, not a driver; it must be willing to take a back seat in the short term when it comes to setting mandates or getting credit, in order to yield the maximum long-term consequences.

Engage the Full Spectrum

A shift needed in strategic thinking is the realization that much as the military attempts to shape battlefields on which it operates, the U.S. Government can and should attempt to shape the political environment in which it functions. Compared to traditional diplomacy, which focuses only on dialogue between governments in pursuit of their respective national interests, public diplomacy is the business of communicating with nonstate, civil society actors and the general public. The goal is to interact with and build support for two proximate reasons. First, they have an ability to influence our national security and prosperity directly either as allies or adversaries in the effort to strengthen American security. Second, civil society actors are able to influence our national security and prosperity indirectly through their influence on their own governments' actions. In the long term, such efforts should support the structures and institutions needed within the wider Muslim world to weather future political, social, and economic challenges, recognizing that failure to do so will reinforce the frustration and anger that feed radical groups.

While moderates and reformers represent America's natural core allies in the region, extra steps should be taken to include social conservatives as we engage in dialogue across the Islamic world. Conservatives are the swing voters in this critical effort. They may seem to represent the most convenient potential allies for the radical militant extremists, but in fact they must play a crucial role if al Qaeda and other radicals are to be marginalized. Our adversaries realize this and, indeed, when al Qaeda releases video or audio tapes, they clearly are trying their hardest to sway the conservative segment of society. America needs to respond if it hopes to ever neutralize this segment of society as a potential support group for the radical militant extremists. Excluding nonmilitant conservatives from the process will only alienate them further; skillfully including them in dialogue, alongside moderates and reformers, will reduce the likelihood of their being recruited by radical militants for either direct or rhetorical support, and even strengthen the efforts of our reformist allies. We should be prepared to enter into dialogue with any group that is willing to both renounce violence and respect a diversity of views. When we lump such groups together with radicals and refuse to engage with them because of Islamist ideology, we then aid our true foes.

Read, React, and Change

On the ground, especially in predominantly Muslim regions, public diplomacy efforts should be more responsive to local developments. Like a U.S. political campaign, changes in public opinion should be tracked on a regular basis, and strategy and tactics should adapt accordingly, as close as possible to real time. Additionally, the nature of on-the-ground public diplomacy should shift away from unilateral proclamations toward dialogue, which will further mutual understanding and increase public confidence in the bona fides of American public diplomacy activities.

Match Programming to Importance of Task

Overall funding levels for public diplomacy are minimal, with $539 million budgeted for public diplomacy in fiscal year 2004, of which 27 percent (about $150 million) was spent in the Muslim world.[34] This is a negligible amount for something that has been identified by the new *National Military Strategic Plan for the War on Terrorism* (not to mention various other bipartisan reports) as an essential element for success. If strategic communications has been declared a core tool, the budget should reflect it. Comparing expenditures on strategic communications with spending on the other two strategic pillars (homeland security and operations to attack terrorist networks) would be somewhat simplistic, but it is nevertheless obvious that what we are spending on strategic communications does not match the priority that our evolving strategy supposedly places on it. Developing truly effective programming would require a significant budget recalculation, potentially of an order of magnitude.

At the same time, agencies engaged in various international activities and outreach (from the State Department to the National Institutes of Health) should be required to ensure that the percentage of their outreach programming toward the Islamic world reflects the present strategic importance of this region. Bureaucratic inertia extending beyond the executive branch has stalled the focus of many programs on Cold War or post-Soviet needs. For instance, the Congressional Fellows program brings in 50 young leaders each year to spend 10 months working in Congressional offices. In 2003, only 1 of the 50 was from the Islamic world (Egypt).[35]

Specific Initiatives to Strengthen U.S.-Muslim Relationships

The success of any program will rely on a centralized vision and strategy matched with localized and agency-specific implementation. The development of these strategic goals and programs should be carried out at the senior levels of the National Security Council and appropriate Executive agencies, with input from other interested parties, including legislative bodies, universities, think tanks, and friends in the Islamic world. Advice solicited from bipartisan boards of experts should be built into policy, rather than cast aside, as happened with reports ranging from the Congressional commission to the Council on Foreign Relations report. In order to ensure both high-level support and the durability of the strategy, the ultimate findings should be embodied in a National Security Presidential Directive that would identify our strategic agenda for building positive relations with Muslim countries and movements through strategic communications.

With the strategic goals established, policymakers could then develop a more systematic approach to ascertain how far short the United States falls from this target state and what is required to attain it. This analytical and planning process will also elaborate tangible courses of action in the most important issue areas (for example, alleviating the intensity of anti-Americanism in certain core states and increasing levels of cooperation on antiterrorist activity). In other words, the objective is not only a methodological approach to evaluating our successes and failures, but also a guide to steer the right course in the future.

Restoring America's credibility and rebuilding the shattered foundations of trust must be top priorities. Because both style and substance matter, changing the style of communication with the Islamic world is key.

Many Muslims say they feel that senior American officials use an arrogant and patronizing style and tone of communication; taking greater care in this area could have an immediate impact. As an example, the empathic and measured tone that Secretary of State Rice took after the alleged Koran desecration incident in 2005 was an example that should be repeated. U.S. leaders also need to adopt a less confrontational and hostile attitude toward the Arab media, seeking over time to bolster its professionalism rather than constantly castigating it for perceived bias. Staffing the office of the under secretary for public diplomacy and better integrating it with the range of U.S. Government programming is a clear need. The appointment of Karen Hughes to lead the public diplomacy effort may have given the post the recognition that is required. But the test will be what happens next. The effort will need a full rethinking of roles, strategy, and expansion of budget to begin to surmount the challenges it faces.

Finally, Presidential effort is needed to ensure the resources necessary to establish a significant American presence on the ground to reach out directly to civil society and individual Arabs and Muslims. As the Defense Science Board wrote on the need to upgrade strategic communication in 2004, "only White House leadership . . . can bring about the sweeping reforms that are required," also noting that "nothing shapes U.S. policies and global perceptions . . . more than the President's statements."[36]

An overall strategy must also be creative and open to new initiatives. Several specific efforts that merit deeper exploration and potential implementation are discussed below. While implementing these recommendations, the five core principles noted earlier need to be embraced.

Create and Deploy America's Voice Corps

Perhaps the most shocking finding in the Advisory Commission on Public Diplomacy report was that the State Department had only five Arabic speakers capable of appearing on Arabic-language television on behalf of the U.S. Government. Presidential support is needed for the rapid recruitment and training of at least 200 fully fluent Arabic speakers trained in public diplomacy skills—about 10 per Arab country. A cadre of fluent speakers could establish a regular and productive presence in the Arab media as well as in two-way dialogue on the ground with members of civil society. Ideally, America's Voice Corps would develop appealing and popular personalities who would become prized guests for Arabic-language talk show hosts. It is important to remember that most Arabs are Muslim, but most Muslims are not Arab. As a result, it is equally important to train speakers in the other languages used. Speakers of Bahasa Melayu, Bahasa Indonesia, Persian, Urdu, and Turkish number over 500 million and reside in strategically important countries such as Indonesia, Iran, Malaysia, Pakistan, and Turkey.

Establish American Centers in Cities

After World War II, the United States launched dozens of "America Houses" in town centers across Germany as focal points to build democracy and foster a German bond with America. After 40 years under American stewardship, many of these centers were transformed from American entities into German NGOs called German-American institutes.[37]

A war of ideas that may last for generations in countries with large populations under the age of 25 must target the countries' youth. The frustration that Muslim youth feel with the status quo could be harnessed into a progressive demand for reform; the United States must play a role in developing and articulating a real alternative to offer this next generation.

To that end, a revitalization of American youth centers and libraries throughout the region is needed. A goal that reflects the Marshall Plan–like significance of the task at hand would be establishing at least one public American center in every major city in the Muslim world. A similar approach today, creating Indonesian-American, Iraqi-American, or Moroccan-American institutes in major cities across the Muslim world, would both foster a more local sense of ownership and reduce security concerns. They should be staffed in part by members of the America's Voice Corps, and should be a major distribution point for translated works from the American Knowledge Library Initiative (discussed below).

These American centers should offer state-of-the-art English-language training programs, seminars, discussions, and a wide selection of current periodicals, newspapers, and literature. They should also offer free Internet access and moderated programs that promote direct exchange with Americans through the use of modern information technology. American centers should not just provide a window into American life, but also enable open, critical dialogue on issues of local and international concern, helping to spur the values of political discourse.

An objection may be raised that the security situation in the Islamic world is simply too volatile—that any center providing such easy access to locals would be a target for terrorists. Some of them undoubtedly would be targeted; sometimes we would lose our investment and, more importantly, people might lose their lives. This is a reality in all international programming today. But if we are serious about engaging the terrorists on their turf instead of ours, we must calculate the losses to be incurred in using this weapon in the battle of ideas against those we would incur if we fail to do so. Additionally, the concept of jointness in activities and programming would give a sense of local ownership, meaning that the attacks would be interpreted as attacks not merely on American interests, but also on local interests and citizens, potentially backfiring on the terrorists.

Implement the American Knowledge Library Initiative

The Advisory Commission on Public Diplomacy pointed out the dearth of Arabic translations of major works of American literature and political theory. While certain U.S. Embassies do undertake translations of books into Arabic, the scale is minuscule compared to the need. The absence of widely available translations means that many Arabs are cut off from direct contact with American history, political ideas, literature, and science. A project to translate 1,000 books a year would soon make such works widely and inexpensively available. Partnerships with Arabic publishers (such as through a consortium of Arab and American publishers with the Government contributing to start-up costs such as payment of rights and translation costs) could aid public acceptance in the region and enable us to leverage existing distribution channels and marketing capacities. The American Centers proposed earlier could also aid in the effort by hosting book groups and discussions of the translated works. Again, the same point concerning the vast number of non–Arabic-speaking Muslims also applies to this translation effort.

Create a Nonpartisan Center for Strategic Communication

A positive step to energize action would be the creation of a center for strategic communication, as endorsed by the Defense Science Review Board. One concept is a hybrid organization, modeled after the RAND Corporation, established as a tax-exempt foundation with private citizens, government, NGO, and business leaders on its board of directors. The center would be established for three purposes: to develop self-initiated public diplomacy and communications programs; to provide analysis to decisionmakers; and to be contracted by the Government to implement public programs where appropriate. Creating distance in the relationship between the U.S. Government and the public diplomacy programs—similar to that offered by the National Endowment for Democracy—could strengthen the credibility of the center with those suspicious of U.S. Government motives. The Center would be independent, but, at the same time, the NSC Deputy National Security Advisor for Strategic Communication and Strategic Communication Committee members should provide program direction.

The Center should also be governed by an independent board appointed by Congress with the Deputy National Security Advisor as an ex officio member of the board, which in turn would appoint the Center's director. As part of its program implementation, the Center should have a budget allocation for two key areas outside of normal operations and programs. The first would be an initiative for intensively gathering public opinion data in a systematic fashion (rather than relying as at present on the changing universe of public organization polls, which often ask different questions of different populations in different years). This effort would not generate data for data's sake, but rather allow rigorous program monitoring and evaluation. At the same time, the center should have a modest budget for research and development. This would allow experimentation to be made with programming to see what works before full deployment, rather than developing huge public diplomacy programs and becoming invested in them bureaucratically only to discover after the fact they are not useful.

Privatize al Hurra and Radio Sawa

The overt association with the U.S. Government of the two principal U.S. broadcast media operating in the Arab-speaking world effectively delegitimizes them in the eyes of most Arabs. Moreover, challenging the practice of government control of media in the Arab world is difficult when the U.S. Government is running and funding its own media. The United States has invested significantly in creating state-of-the-art facilities for these stations; now is the time to let them compete in the Arab media environment on their own. America should have a voice in the region, but this voice will best be heard if people understand whether it is coming from a government or a private source, rather than the perception inspired by the current muddled arrangement. As endorsed by the Defense Science Board, more collaboration is needed with the private sector, which often is a more credible messenger than the U.S. Government itself, and the privatization of al Hurra and Radio Sawa is a good place to start.[38]

Create C-SPANs for the Islamic World

Credible sources of general, unfiltered information are sorely lacking in the Islamic world, even though there is a palpable appetite for them. For example, during the Abu Ghraib crisis, Arabic language news channels provided live coverage of U.S. Congressional hearings, and the public watched with great interest. Scenes of American policymakers and military leaders directly answering probing questions from the legislature and media presented a powerful example of democracy in action, a sharp contrast to authoritarian practices common in the region.

Seeking to tap this interest, al Jazeera recently launched a new channel, al Jazeera Live, which features coverage of events that are conducted in Arabic as well as of events translated into Arabic from the original languages. But the channel clearly has not saturated the marketplace for ideas and information in either the Middle East or beyond. There are multiple Cable-Satellite Public Affairs Networks (C-SPANs) and C-SPAN imitators within the United States, including local cable equivalents that cover state and municipal politics. Similarly, there can be multiple channels that provide live video of public affairs events across the Arab and Muslim world, ranging from legislatures to local events hosted by NGOs to book talks at the American Centers. By being unfiltered and, ideally, coordinated with local organizations, the channels will leap across the credibility gap that has undermined Sawa and al Hurra. Similar opportunities are available for public affairs channels that target the huge number of speakers of other Islamic world languages, such as Farsi, Urdu, Bahasa, and Turkish.

Reach Out to Civil Society

Public diplomacy in the Arab and Islamic world should be targeted directly toward civil society and wider public opinion. There is a powerful, if thus far narrow, constituency of moderates demanding internal reform; polling shows that media and business elites view the United States more positively than the general public. These people should be cultivated as potential allies. The United States should bring institutions of civil society into the reform process and give them the opportunity to express their own views to their own people. This would not only aid those fighting for internal change but also bolster our own standing. Such programs must be cognizant of the negative association that too close an alignment to the United States can sometimes bring to civil society leaders and ensure modesty in our claims; that is, the U.S. Government should portray itself as facilitating a long-term constructive discussion, rather than imposing its views and picking winners and losers in its outreach. Presidential leadership is needed to make a point of seeking dialogues with a wide range of voices in the region, including even those willing to criticize our policies in a constructive and tolerant manner (indeed, such meetings will carry a higher value-added). The United States must be seen as a positive agent of change rather than an impediment to it.

Bolster Exchange Programs

To improve relations, we must enlist all means in the toolbox and provide a role for every willing American. The administration should increase exchanges of youth and young professionals, offer incentives for cooperative business ventures, and facilitate cultural and artistic exchanges, cooperative media ventures, mutual education programs, investment in development, technology, and education initiatives in the Islamic world, and interfaith dialogue. Such endeavors need not be restricted to the physical realm; the media in the United States and the Islamic world—television, print, and Internet—can be used to multiply the effects of these exchanges. Not only should exchange programs like the Fulbright and Humphrey programs be expanded in size, but other types of virtual youth exchanges also need to be developed that harness the Internet and video-conferencing for multiplicative affects.

Akin to the Cold War programs that built up allies around the world, we must expand our people-to-people interaction with the Islamic world, not place more obstacles in its path. The current visa procedures often impose onerous requirements and delays, such that Washington is seen as humiliating Arabs and Muslims from abroad rather than welcoming them to visit the United States. These procedures negate efforts to reach out to people who could become ambassadors attesting to the reality of American good will. We need more efficient visa policies, especially for students where the goal is quick processing that weeds out dangerous elements, while providing a clear welcome to the majority. A premium should be placed on an increase in foreign exchange programs to bring Arabs and Muslims directly into contact with American society.[39]

Special attention must be given to integrating official visitor programs across agencies. Awkward episodes of one U.S. Government agency inviting visitors from the Islamic world only to have another mistakenly arrest them, and high-profile visa delays need to be avoided, not merely out of embarrassment, but as part of the overall effort at outreach. Examples of this include the case of Ejaz Haider, an editor of one of Pakistan's most moderate newspapers, who was arrested by the Department of Homeland Security agents on visa charges that later proved false. Indeed, Haider was actually in the United States at the direct invitation of the State Department. Those sympathetic to the United States could only conclude charitably that one American hand did not know what the other was doing; unsurprisingly, those less favorably inclined took a darker view and made sure to publicize their own conspiracy theories. Nor is this an isolated instance. Tariq Ramadan, a prominent European Muslim intellectual who had previously been to the United States to address U.S. Government audiences in Washington, had his visa withdrawn mere days before he was to begin a professorship at the University of Notre Dame, with no explanation offered.

Working in conjunction with the other agencies, Homeland Security must establish a systematized approach toward weighing the competing domestic imperatives of zero-tolerance admissions and the dire foreign policy need of maximum outreach toward critical states and communities. A particular need is to develop a rigorous and rapid ability to scrutinize individual, high-profile cases, such as well-known figures like Dr. Ramadan, from which a visa decision in either direction will bring great attention. In such cases, visa denials must be based truly on security issues and not simply because a pressure group does or does not like the views of a visitor.

When the United States is willing to host Muslim leaders with whom some groups may disagree, we get a chance not only to engage directly with them but also prove to the world that we are, as we claim, a tolerant and open society, confident in our beliefs and values in a way that other nations that resist open debate are not.

Harness Islamic Respect for U.S. Education, Science, and Technology

While positive attitudes toward the United States in general and U.S. foreign policy in particular hover in the single digits, U.S. science and technology and education are viewed as positive by 80 percent or more of the population. The implication here is that even in the countries with the most anti-American sentiments, the United States can lead with its most welcome and respected institutions to build direct inroads. But new policy efforts are needed. First, the post-9/11 environment reduced the flow of students from the Islamic world to the United States due to both visa restrictions and fears that the civil rights of Arabs and Muslims would be infringed in the United States. To remedy the situation, student visas must be processed quickly but thoroughly, and the United States needs to do more to convince Arabs and Muslims that they will be free from arbitrary government harassment while visiting. Second, U.S. universities (which polls show are greatly trusted and respected) should be encouraged and funded to create joint programs with universities in the Islamic world—to create American studies centers, for student video-conferencing, and to strengthen our own Islamic world studies centers through participation of students and teachers from the region. For example, for about $20 million per year, the United States could fund a handful of indigenous American studies centers at universities across the Islamic world in places like Jordan and Egypt where the regimes are friendly but anti-Americanism runs high among the population. Such centers should not be branded as flag-waving pro-American entities, but simply academic institutions where American culture, politics, and history are studied, the good together with the bad. Such efforts are likely to be successful and diffuse the appearance of U.S. intervention if the effort is jointly funded and planned with local government or business leaders.

Harness Arab-Americans and American Muslims as a Key Bridge

America must leverage the strength of its diversity. At a time when the U.S. Government lacks both credibility abroad and the local language speakers to represent our views, the distance between it and the domestic Arab and Muslim communities is stunning. For example, the State Department's office for public diplomacy did not include a single American Muslim on its staff until 2006. The same diversity problem is repeated across agencies. The Departments of Defense, Homeland Security, Justice, and State should all examine how they can better tap the strengths of these communities, both in programming and recruiting. The administration must move beyond symbolic respect for Muslim rituals, such as once a year convening *Iftar* dinners, to actual programming designed to demonstrate it in fact. For example, Arab Americans and American Muslims can help prepare and even accompany officials when they visit the region, just as political donors and corporate executives often join delegations.

Maximize Presidential Leadership in Public Diplomacy

Finally, Presidential leadership is absolutely vital for successful public diplomacy. The President himself must make it clear that Cabinet and sub-Cabinet level officials must consider America's standing in the world to be a priority for action. They not only should make the effort to conduct interviews with the foreign press on a regular basis, but they also should engage in genuine dialogue, even with those who hold negative views of the U.S. Government. In other words, public diplomacy must go beyond "preaching to the converted." Visits by senior U.S. officials to the region should include meetings with local students, civil society leaders, and reformers, and even conservative leaders who might be susceptible to the rhetoric of the militant radicals. Similar efforts should be made by Department of Defense civilian and military leaders operating at both the Pentagon and regional command level, following the Cold War model of a wide engagement strategy to expand and deepen relationships with U.S. allies and counterparts in what were then battleground states in the developing world.

The White House must play a key role in bringing attention to the major issues confronting the Islamic world and the West and in swaying popular views among Muslims. Given the importance of the war on terror and the risks of a greater rift between the United States and the Islamic world, the office should be utilized to the maximum extent possible in reaching out to news media in Muslim-majority countries. Likewise, efforts should be made to bring the President into personal contact with reform and civil society leaders, which will help bolster both parties' standing and understanding. In addition, the President should make time in his schedule for interviews with news media from the Muslim world. President Bush's May 2004 interview with al Arabiya was a good step in this direction, but it only occurred after a major scandal—revelations of the Abu Ghraib prison abuses—and similar interviews have not taken place in the 2 years since. Outreach to news media in the Muslim world must be proactive and sustained rather than merely reactive for damage control after terrible incidents. Nor should the President restrict himself to Arabic-language news outlets. There are other important outlets in the Muslim world, including the popular and independent GEO TV in Pakistan.

Furthermore, the President should use the bully pulpit to condemn hate speech, including by American policymakers themselves. Immediately after 9/11, the President visited the Islamic Center of Washington, the capital's leading mosque, to ensure that Americans and the world knew that the administration understood that Islam was not to blame for the attacks. Unfortunately, the clarity of this message has been lost. A series of anti-Muslim statements have since been made by policymakers and private organization leaders who have been either inside or associated with the administration.[40] Most of these comments have passed without consequences or condemnation. Bigotry in our midst is not just distasteful, it also directly undermines our security. We live in an era where the world constantly watches to see whether we actually live up to our ideals. At a time when many in the world expect the worst of us, such statements only support enemy propaganda. The President must publicly condemn such statements in specific, disassociate himself from their authors, and hold them liable. That would be a powerful demonstration of Presidential leadership and moral authority.

The Military Role

Often ignored in discussions of public diplomacy is the vital role that the military can play in helping to restore America's standing. Both diplomats and military leaders often have some discomfort with this concept, but the fundamental fact is that the military's role is to fight and win the Nation's wars. In the 21st century, as in the Cold War, not all wars are conventional. Thus, an important realization in the overall National Security Strategy (though not always carried over in implementation) is that the United States must shift from state-centric thinking and deal with the new challenges of a new century. Specific to the battle against terror, this will require a multifaceted strategy aimed at undermining the structures and support for networked nongovernmental organizations. Public diplomacy is not the primary role for the military, but assisting in efforts to meet this latest security challenge is necessary.

The doctrinal mandate for such action is eloquently laid out in the update to the Marine Corps Small Wars Manual, which seeks to provide guidance to officers facing the challenges of 21st-century wars and the global war on terror:

> The prevalence of new information technologies and the pervasive presence of modern media, require that we redouble our public diplomacy and educational efforts and begin focusing on

shaping the informational dimension of the battlespace. Because small wars are information wars, it is possible that successful shaping operations can be sufficient to accomplish the desired end-state and thus can become 'decisive' operations.[41]

Thus, as the military must begin to face the long-term challenge ahead of it in protecting American interests and security, discussions of transformation must be about more than precision strikes and gigabytes. Rather, the military structure must weigh needs and priorities in areas ranging from training to force structure. As an illustration, a great need remains for expertise in Arabic and other Muslim cultures and languages for Soldiers and intelligence analysts (with a significant portion of communications with local populations being mediated through contractors). This stands in contrast to the crash-course mentality that built up great levels of expertise in Slavic languages and cultures in the early years of the Cold War.

Much as Presidential leadership is needed to energize action across the U.S. Government, leadership within the Pentagon is also required. The questions of how the military can better support and integrate its own public diplomacy, public affairs, and information operations require senior leadership to pay heed to the issue. At the simplest level, it requires that leaders take seriously and implement the very advice they sought from their own advisors, such as the Defense Science Board. At the same time, the leadership must focus on how it can push for and support other agencies to fulfill their responsibilities in this area. Too frequently, Pentagon frustration with other agencies' foot-dragging (or its greater funding) leads it to undertake programming, with the thinking that "if others aren't going to do it, then we might as well."[42] This can-do attitude is highly laudable, but planners should be careful to ensure that it does not lead the military into areas that may not be the most appropriate in the long term.

Options for the Military

As with the general public diplomacy activities previously discussed, the military is uniquely suited for a number of activities and initiatives that can be explored for consideration. Some (but by no means all) programming concepts include:

Integrate activities into planning. A joke circulating within the military's public affairs field depicts their officers as fire extinguishers behind glass, to be broken out only after the emergency. This analogy is a bit extreme but does reflect one of the problems in the present institutionalization of public affairs/public diplomacy efforts by the military. Such programs are felt to be an afterthought to, rather than an inherent part of, warfighting.

This dynamic is worsened by the fact that minimal consideration is given to the target set (the audience), so that the audience considered in the planning may not be the right one. For example, a planner for Operation *Iraqi Freedom* discussed how the strategic audience he was most concerned with (the one whose interpretations were most sensitive in shaping limitations on military plans such as targeting airstrikes) was "Paris, Brussels, and Berlin."[43] When thinking about how foreign audiences might view U.S. military actions in the war on terror, the swing audience is different than the one we thought of during operations in the Balkans in the context of North Atlantic Treaty Organization (NATO) approval. Instead, the key audiences must be the populations of the Islamic world for whose "hearts and minds" we are in competition with al Qaeda and its affiliates, not Europeans residing in the capitals of NATO states *without* troops on the ground.

Senior leadership must recognize this gap and link such efforts into regional strategic planning (visualizing public diplomacy efforts as part of preventive diplomacy and deployments efforts) and most particularly in operation planning. For example, in the run-up to the Iraq war, the military did an excellent job of implementing and discussing with the (American and European) media and public the measures it would take to prevent civilian casualties in combat operations, to the extent that the United States put into place greater measures aimed at saving civilian lives than in any other war in history. But, as with much else, there was no planning in this domain for the postconflict phase. The result in Iraq was catastrophic. The regional interpretation of U.S. operations turned overnight from one of a quick victory and liberation to one of chaos and failure, based largely on the inability of the United States to protect the average Muslim civilian on the ground and a failure to adequately explain why. The problem was not just that the chaos happened, but also that the United States had neither a process to discuss its implications nor a contingency plan for how to deal with and mitigate the repercussions.

Senior leaders must also recognize that they play an important personal role in the overall strategic communications strategy and implementation. The local political context will shape interpretations of much of the audience in the Muslim world (most live in states where the military plays a dominant role), meaning that they will project their understanding of politics onto the United States. They will often disregard what is said or done by politicians or diplomats and instead focus most on what defense officials and military officers say and do. This puts a great burden of responsibility on senior defense leadership, which is often not understood.

For example, the aforementioned problem of postwar chaos was worsened by the failure of senior U.S. defense and military leaders to convey sympathy and concern for the well-being of the Iraqi people during this period, which in turn undercut any benefit from earlier efforts to show that the United States cared more for Iraqi civilians than did the Baathist regime.

The problem is often exacerbated by the temptation for senior officials conducting press conferences to utter catchy sound bites for the nightly news in the United States. This was perhaps best exemplified by the episode in which a senior official responded that "stuff happens" when asked about the hardship imposed on Iraqi civilians by the postwar violence, crime, and looting. More attention must be paid to the way such statements play out with regional audiences and thus backfire on U.S. troops in the short term and American prestige in the long term.[44]

Speak with the same message. As complex as the challenges are that the United States faces in the area of strategic communications and public diplomacy, they are only complicated further by the number of agencies and personnel operating in this sphere. These range from State Department public diplomacy efforts, U.S. Agency for International Development activities on the ground, Central Intelligence Agency information and psychological operations, military public affairs at the Pentagon, military information operations conducted at all levels from strategic to tactical, and the various other military activities that could be characterized as public diplomacy broadly defined, ranging from port visits and humanitarian relief efforts to personnel exchanges and training programs. However, bureaucratic firewalls and stovepipes often prevent unity of effort across agencies. Instead of the synergy that is necessary for these efforts to have maximum effect, we have a system that is barely coordinated. Indeed, in some conflict zones, the representatives of each of the agencies engaged in strategic communications have never even sat around the same table.[45] This underlines our previous points about how an overarching strategy is clearly needed, one that not only lays out what the goals and activities should be, but also clarifies responsibilities and deconflicts activities and messages.

Develop our own networks for net-centric warfare. Like all exchange programs with foreign audiences, foreign military training and exchanges should be seen as a critical opportunity to expand U.S. relationships and alliances and build networks of local allies. Despite the fact that association with the United States in the general social sphere is viewed negatively in the Muslim world today, association with the United States in the military sphere is still considered a positive career enhancer; those who participate in U.S. military programs typically advance to more senior levels. Therefore, the full value of such programs should be exploited so as to ensure that the United States develops close working relationships with the next generation of military leaders in the Muslim world. These programs not only carry great value in terms of official policy, but they also open useful unofficial channels of communication and influence.

The existing U.S. programs of military-to-military exchanges and contacts should be reoriented to reflect new strategic priorities. We should be focusing on greater percentages of rising young officers from military forces in the Islamic world, much as we once altered allocations in such programs according to Cold War priorities by increasing numbers from Latin America, and as we subsequently reflected post–Cold War priorities by increasing the slots allotted to the states of the former Warsaw Pact.

Unfortunately, the Pentagon has been slow to make this shift, evidently due largely to bureaucratic inertia. In 2004, for example, 11,832 students were trained through the International Military Education and Training (IMET) program. Approximately 20 percent (2,351) came from Muslim majority states. These figures become more glaring when broken down. The largest number of students worldwide came from Bolivia (1,807, the equivalent of 77 percent of the total from all Muslim majority states), whereas the largest number of students from the Muslim world come from two states, Sierra Leone (269) and Turkey (267), that reflected priorities other than the "war of ideas" (Turkey as a NATO partner and Sierra Leone due to commitments in the wake of United Nations and regional peacekeeping operations).[46] Clearly, a far more strategic use of the limited slots can be made in terms of allocation, while there is certainly scope to expand the overall number of students brought to the United States.

Equally, it is time to consider an expansion in the structure and funding of the Near East and South Asia (NESA) Center for Strategic Studies, located at Fort Lesley J. McNair in Washington, DC. While highly capable, its size and scope of activities are far more modest than the other DOD-funded regional security centers, primarily due to a difference in funding structures. For example, NESA has 43 faculty and staff, while the George Marshall Center for Security Studies has 247 and the Asia-Pacific Center for Security Studies has 127. It is time to reevaluate this structure and explore whether a comparable shift in size and mission might be appropriate for NESA, along with any additional legislative authorities that would permit it to carry out its mission more effectively.

Bolster high-demand/low-density units to meet current needs. Civil affairs teams are widely recognized as one of the most valuable capabilities the military has in winning local hearts and minds. These units have a multiplier effect in building up local good will and establishing U.S. credibility; many believe that their impact on the ground in places like Iraq will be remembered in individual villages for the next generation or more.[47] Yet for the pure value-added these men and women represent to overall operations, there are simply too few to go around. The units that exist are overstretched, and the fact that they are reservist-based means they are at risk of burning out from repeated call-ups. This problem was already an issue during the

Balkans deployments and has only been magnified by commitments in Iraq and Afghanistan. Simply put, thinking about force transformation must take into account which units are of most value to U.S. strategic goals, what commanders in the field need them to do, and how the relative payback from these units compares with capabilities offered by traditional, large budget acquisitions.

Formalize public diplomacy activities into the budget. The military actually engages in a range of civil military activities that could be described as public diplomacy at the regional and ground level, but they often occur as an afterthought or only during emergencies. For example, the Navy only sends hospital ships to key zones on an ad hoc basis, typically in response to a crisis and when the ship is not committed elsewhere. These types of visits, such as the one during the 2004 tsunami in Southeast Asia, are powerful examples of American good will and demonstrable evidence of the professionalism of the U.S. military. Indeed, many credit the aid that the U.S. military provided on the ground in Indonesia with helping to reverse the downturn in esteem for the United States in the region.[48]

By comparison, when an earthquake slammed Pakistan (not only a hub of extremist groups, but also the only nuclear-armed Muslim state) in 2005, the U.S. Government response was meek at best. Those military assets that were already near the area (mostly a small group of helicopters coming from deployments already to Afghanistan) deployed to the area to help move aid, but the subsequent followthrough was minimal. Overall, the United States committed just $26.4 million in aid, with the potential for additional aid up to a $50 million limit—roughly 3 percent of the amount the Government gave the tsunami-afflicted regions in Southeast Asia. Analysts can debate the relative importance of Pakistan and Indonesia, but treating the opportunity in Pakistan as only 3 percent as important as the one in Indonesia is clearly poor grand strategy. By contrast, a panoply of radical groups sensed the opportunity to prove their own merit and quickly started engaging in a range of aid efforts in Pakistan, seeking to fill the void left by the international community. Affiliate groups of Lashkar-e-Taiba ran a field hospital complete with x-ray machines and operating room, Jammat-e-Islami organized relief convoys and refugee camps, and the al Rasheed Trust (a group whose assets have been frozen in the United States due to its suspected al Qaeda links) has been in the forefront of aid and publicity. At best, the situation was a missed opportunity. At worst, we ceded more ground to radical forces, undermining U.S. national security.

The reality is that high payoff programs are not included in long-term planning and not supported by separate budget items. Such efforts are too important to be viewed as an afterthought or a drag on a unit's regular operational budget. Money spent on creating proof of the professionalism and good intent of U.S. troops on the ground that leave a positive long-term legacy should at least achieve the same amount of investment as the present psychological operations (PSYOP)/advertising campaigns organized by the military (the Joint PSYOP Support Element of the U.S. Special Operations Command has a projected budget of $77.5 million over the next 7 years to spend on creating TV, radio, and print ads to burnish the U.S. image).[49] Exploration should be made of how to recognize such activities as part of counterinsurgency and force protection measures and whether they might be regularized into budgeting (perhaps through the humanitarian operations budget).

Better support public affairs officers. Public affairs officers are often the single point of contact that foreign publics and media have with the U.S. military. During operations, many in the foreign media prefer to deal with them than with diplomatic handlers from other agencies, understandably seeing these officers as a more direct source on what the U.S. military is thinking and doing. We must face the reality that this area is not simply the domain of the State Department. As such, it is absurd that public affairs officers, who are placed in this critical, front-line role in the war for hearts and minds, are not afforded foreign language and cultural awareness in their training programs. Some of the more enterprising have resorted to paying for such coursework themselves. This should be a regular, funded component of their professional development and education.

Our hometown (media) is the world. The link between the military and the press has often veered between cooperation, as in World War II, and contention, as in Vietnam. Recently, the military has set up the embedded reporter program to better manage the inherent problems of press operating in a conflict zone. However, the focus on getting U.S. reporters into such slots and reserving only a small portion for foreign media has been understandable. The merits of expanding access to professional and vetted foreign media should be weighed, hopefully also taking into account the new strategic needs of the United States. In addition, their allocation must be more strategic. Within these programs, a media presence from the countries that matter most in the war on terror has been ad hoc. Having a vetted, professional reporter from Pakistan see firsthand the professionalism of U.S. troops may be more important than having a tabloid journalist from Japan on the scene—and, arguably, even more important than having another reporter from the United States. The distribution across services should also be planned such that gaps will not occur as the focus of operations shifts. For example, during Operation *Iraqi Freedom*, more Muslim world reporters were with Navy units than either Army or Air Force units. These challenges will have to be balanced with security concerns, but an overall strategy is needed.

The Shape of the Global Antiterrorist Environment

An important element in the development of strategy is to identify the components that would comprise a successful completion. That is, understanding the endgame of an idealized policy success can provide a useful guide in what would need to be targeted and achieved to reach such a state of affairs. If the United States were successful in creating a global antiterrorist environment, it would have several key characteristics.

Unified Articulation of Means, Ends, and Goals

The United States has a critical need to articulate an overarching strategy toward terrorism that matches ends, means, and discernable measures. Part and parcel of this is not the issuance of more policy statements, but rather a grand strategy toward the Islamic world that will shape our often disparate policies. In short, a fundamental building block in the global antiterrorist environment would be an American articulation of a positive vision of its goals toward the Islamic world. This is necessary to present a constructive program of what the United States stands for and offers. The side effect of building a cohesive, positive vision is that it will also provide an agenda for allies and friends to support, as well as a programmatic lodestone to contend with other competing visions.

Credibility of U.S. Voice

The American voice will only be effective if it is viewed as sincere. This means that it would be grounded in a dialogue that values and engages the Muslim world, rather than approaching it merely as an audience for better public relations. Underscoring the programming would be an array of outreach activities that create layers of networks of local partners and affiliates in the public and private sectors. These would serve not only as feedback loops, but also to build local coalitions and alliances that will add to our credibility.

At the core of al Qaedaism's support and popularity has been its ability to draw from (and manipulate) the deep sense of frustration felt within the Muslim world over the failing status quo.[50] From authoritarian regimes that fail to deliver effective social services to struggling economies that cannot compete with the forces of globalization, there is a sense in the Muslim world that the region is falling behind.[51] The fundamental challenge for us is that the United States is viewed as an inherent part of this status quo and blamed for the circumstances in the region. While this often is an unfair characterization, it creates a regional reality that must be dealt with, as it undermines America's efforts to speak on behalf of its policies.

In an ideal global antiterrorist environment, the United States would be viewed as opposing the negative aspects of the status quo and supporting the forces that will aid human development and freedom. Our statements would reflect our policy, resonate, and be viewed as credible. The U.S. strategic communications agenda must articulate a vision that acknowledges the underlying anger in the Arab world stemming from frustration at the comparative lack of political, economic, and social opportunity. While this approach will create challenges with any allied autocratic regimes that cling to past practices, an environment in which terrorist groups are undermined and the U.S. voice is credible would be one in which our policies are clearly understood as being on the side of change in the region, not on the side of a failing status quo. We must identify the United States with the positive, supporting prosperity and opposing repression (and not merely through regime overthrow but also through the more difficult challenge of reform).

Consistent but Nuanced U.S. Voice

In an ideal global antiterrorist environment, the U.S. voice would be recognized for its consistency and credibility, and for its depth of understanding, empathy, and nuance in how it engages a diverse world. For example, discussions by U.S. officials of the Muslim educational institutions known as *madrassa*s have, at least as heard from outside, operated under the assumption that all are "schools of hate" that must be shut down or reformed. This approach misses the fact that only an extremely small percentage of the *madrassa*s in places like Pakistan are affiliated with radical groups, while in other states, such as Indonesia, they are mostly government-linked and are in fact sources of moderation, while in Arabic-speaking countries, *madrassa* is simply the ordinary word for a school. As a result, when the United States discusses shutting down *madrassa*s, Muslims view it as striking against moderates in some countries, education in general in others, and rarely as focusing merely on the radicals. Recognition of such regional nuances and differences should be part of any U.S. strategy, as it will add to understanding.

At the same time, the United States must be flexible enough to open dialogues with the diverse set of social groups and actors on the ground. This may even mean seeking to gain allies with whom we differ in world view, just as the Marshall Plan dealt with socialist-leaning unions in Western Europe and Nixon went to China to divide the Communist bloc. The United States ultimately will have to accept that Islamist political groups are among the most powerful and credible groups in the Muslim world.

While we may not see eye to eye with them on many issues, it is time to open dialogues and work on setting a shared understanding of how we can cooperate to improve the lives of the citizens of their countries, as well as the areas in which we cannot. While the concept of U.S. engagement with Islamist groups may be anathema to some policymakers, the United States has already made such compromises with Islamist groups in Iraq—both old-guard Islamist leaders like Ayatollah Sistani as well as new-guard figures like Moqtada al-Sadr—to help steer them and their supporters away from violence, proving that it can be done, and quite successfully.

Isolation and Delegitimization of al Qaedaism

An important lesson from past insurgencies is that the key to winning is not merely to track down every insurgent or terrorist across the globe. Rather, such groups are best defeated by isolating and strangling them in both the physical and ideological realms. In this task, the role of the host community is key, and its full support is necessary, both to reject these groups and reveal their presence. If the host community is supportive, or even neutral and thus tolerant of the extremists, then counterinsurgency efforts will fail.[52] If successful insurgents are like fish in the sea, as Mao suggested, then we win not by draining the sea, but rather by poisoning it so it is no longer hospitable for their radicalism.

A turning point in the global battle of hearts and minds will occur when groups that advocate violence in pursuit of radical aims are not merely condemned for particular incidents by a segment of the more moderate opinion leaders, but when such groups as a whole (and their aims, agenda, and tactics) are viewed as criminals and apostates. This shift must come from within the community. The United States can engage groups and leaders that work toward the goal of isolating the extremists, but the effort will fail if the United States is seen as the genesis of such an agenda. Restoring America's good name will assist such efforts, such that the baggage of widespread anti-Americanism will be made less burdensome for any leader speaking out against radicalism.

The key to this shift will be supporting any communal self-examination that yields the twofold realization within the Muslim *umma* that extremist groups, especially those conducting terrorist attacks against civilians, are operating in contravention of the accepted practices of Islam; and that they are doing so in a way that undermines the well-being of the entire global Muslim community. As such, their activities would not merely be something to explain away (as poor tactics, but proper targeting of an unpopular oppressor), but would appear as a deliberate choice to harm others and to break with Islam. This would entail a full mobilization of opinion leaders against them and a recasting of local and global religious and communal structures to ensure that they do not gain support or infiltrate. The role of conservative clerics and Islamist leaders will be crucial in this. When such a transition happens (and the process appears to be under way among certain communities, such as the Muslim American efforts in the wake of the London bombings), al Qaedaism will wither on the vine.[53] While certain individuals will likely continue terrorist activities, their overall efforts will be akin to what happened with the Red Brigades of Europe or the violent militia/Christian identity groups of the United States: they will be acknowledged as definitive threats that must be dealt with, but not ones that resonate to any strategic level.

Conclusion

The 5 years since the 9/11 attacks have seen an American foreign policy that could in no way be described as meek or ineffective, except in its public diplomacy and strategic communications. From Iraq to Afghanistan, the United States carried out a dazzling array of actions. But it still faces a series of complex and demanding decisions in how it engages Muslim states and communities and communicates its policies toward the Islamic world. A striking feature of our most vexing challenges is that more often than not, they arise in relation to our policies toward those we usually consider our friends and allies—making the challenges more difficult, but also perhaps ultimately more manageable.

With a greater awareness of the challenges ahead, an agenda must be developed in response. There is a glaring need for America to undertake a proactive strategy that is aimed at restoring long-term security through the presentation of American principles in American foreign policy. A key victory will occur when the United States is again seen as living up to its values and, in a region characterized by a failing and stagnant status quo, acting on the side of positive change, whether it is in affording people the opportunity to reach their potential or in ensuring that governance is representative rather than repressive. The tools of public diplomacy and strategic communications can be valuable weapons in the American arsenal. It is not too late to wield them.

Notes

[1] Pew Global Attitudes Survey, "American Character Gets Mixed Reviews: U.S. Image Up Slightly, but Still Negative," June 23, 2005; available at <pewglobal.org/reports/pdf/247.pdf>.

[2] Available at <globalsecurity.org/military/library/policy/dod/rumsfeldd20031016sdmemo.htm>.

[3] The first *National Strategy for Combating Terrorism* was released in February 2003. Mr. Rumsfeld's memo came in October 2003, well after the writing and release, illustrating the sense among senior leadership that the document did not meet strategy needs. A new *National Security Strategy for Combating Terrorism* was released in September 2006, too late to be addressed in this chapter.

[4] See Eliot A. Cohen, "World War IV," *The Wall Street Journal*, November 20, 2001; James Woolsey, "At War for Freedom," *The Guardian*, July 20, 2003.

[5] Samuel Huntington, *Clash of Civilizations and the Remaking of World Order* (New York: Simon and Schuster, 1998).

[6] "What is Public Diplomacy?" available at <publicdiplomacy.org>, July 4, 2003.

[7] Ibid.

[8] A useful discussion of the history and potential of strategic influence operations is Kim Cragin and Scott Gerwehr, *Dissuading Terror: Strategic Influence and the Struggle against Terrorism* (Santa Monica: RAND, 2005).

[9] Joseph S. Nye, Jr., "Propaganda Isn't the Way: Soft Power," *The International Herald Tribune*, January 10, 2003.

[10] The 4th Infantry Division was absent until after the war and thus the United States was unable to bring the war home to core Baathist supporters through an immediate, heavy presence in cities that have since become the focal points of the insurgency.

[11] See, for example, the Zogby International and Pew Forum polls, available at <zogby.com> and <pewtrust.org>.

[12] As an example, see statements made by Fox News host Bill O'Reilly on June 17, 2004: "I don't have any respect by and large for the Iraqi people at all. I have no respect for them. I think that they're a prehistoric group"; "We cannot intervene in the Muslim world ever again. What we can do is bomb the living daylights out of them."

[13] For a further analysis of al Qaeda's health, see the International Institute for Strategic Studies, *The Military Balance 2004–2005* (London: The International Institute for Strategic Studies, 2004).

[14] For further discussion of this dynamic, see Hady Amr, "The Need to Communicate," Brookings Analysis Paper, January 2004.

[15] See Pew Global Attitudes surveys: "Islamic Extremism: Common Concern for Muslim and Western Publics," July 14, 2005, and "U.S. Image Up Slightly, But Still Negative," June 23, 2005; available at <pewglobal.org/>.

[16] Max Boot, "Our Extreme Makeover," *Los Angeles Times*, July 27, 2005.

[17] *The 9/11 Commission Report: Final Report of the National Commission on Terrorist Attacks Upon the United States* (Washington, DC: U.S. Government Printing Office, 2004).

[18] "Bush: Better Human Intelligence Needed," CNN.com, January 18, 2005.

[19] "Arab Ally Snubs Bush Amid 'Unprecedented Hatred' for U.S.," *The Guardian UK*, April 21, 2004; available at <commondreams.org/headlines04/0421-02.htm>.

[20] For example, after the Abu Ghraib scandal, faked videos appeared that showed what were purported to be U.S. Soldiers engaged in murders, rapes, and other atrocities. While the claims should have been easily disproven (for example, the "American" Soldiers in one video that circulated among the Muslim community in Europe were clearly local, amateur actors wearing cast-off uniforms from the Vietnam era), they were now considered credible.

[21] Thomas Regan, "U.S. Image Abroad Will 'Take Years' to Repair; Experts Tell Congress 'Bottom Has Fallen Out' for U.S. Support Abroad," *Christian Science Monitor*, February 9, 2004.

[22] Condoleezza Rice, "The President's Fiscal Year 2006 International Affairs Budget," testimony before Senate Appropriations Subcommittee on State, Foreign Operations, and Related Programs, May 12, 2005.

[23] *The Weekly Standard*, February 9, 2004.

[24] Christopher Ross, "Pillars of Public Diplomacy," *The Harvard Review*, August 21, 2003.

[25] John Sawyer, "Entrenched Distrust Undermines White House Effort to Reach Out," *St. Louis Post Dispatch*, December 10, 2005.

[26] Institute for Global Engagement, March 2006.

[27] Zogby International/Anwar Sadat Chair for Peace and Development at the University of Maryland.

"Arab Attitudes Toward Political and Social Issues, Foreign Policy, and the Media," May 2004; available at <bsos.umd.edu/SADAT/pub/Arab%20Attitudes%20Towards%20Political%20 and%20Social%20Issues,%20Foreign%20Policy%20and%20the%20Media.htm>. According to a poll conducted by Telhami/Zogby, al Jazeera is the first choice for international news for a plurality of viewers in Lebanon (44 percent), Saudi Arabia (44 percent), the United Arab Emirates (46 percent), and a majority of those in Egypt (66 percent), Jordan (62 percent), and Morocco (54 percent). It is the most watched station in each country polled. Al Arabiya is second-ranked first choice in the region: it is the first choice for 19 percent in the United Arab Emirates and under 10 percent in Egypt (5 percent), Jordan (7 percent), Lebanon (7 percent), and Morocco (8 percent).

[28] Shibley Telhami, "Reflections of Hearts and Minds: Media, Opinion, and Identity in the Arab World," The Brookings Institution, April 2005.

[29] See "Revisiting the Arab Street: Research from Within," February, 2005; available at <css-jordan.org>.

[30] Information from "Reporting the Truth: Media Perceptions, Preferences, and Practices among Young UAE Nationals." Public Affairs office of the U.S. Embassy in Abu Dhabi, July 2004; The Arab Advisors Group, September 2004—Saudi Satellite TV and Radio Survey; USA Today/Gallup Polls, "Iraq: Then and Now," April 2004; available at <usatoday.com/news/ world/iraq/2004-04-28-baghdad.htm>.

[31] Office of the Under Secretary of Defense for Acquisition, Technology and Logistics, "Final Report of the Defense Science Board Task Force on Strategic Communication," September 2004, 41–47.

[32] Marine Corps Combat Development Command, "Small Wars/21st Century" (Quantico, VA: U.S. Marine Corps, 2005), 79.

[33] Ibid.

[34] Rice, testimony before Senate Appropriations Subcommittee on State, Foreign Operations, and Related Programs, May 12, 2005.

[35] Author interview with Congressional Fellow, September 24, 2003.

[36] "Final Report of the Defense Science Board Task Force on Strategic Communication," September, 2004, 3.

[37] Hady Amr, "American Public Diplomacy: Some Lessons from Germany," *The Daily Star*, July 15, 2005.

[38] Idea put forward by Stephen Cook, "Hearts, Minds and Hearings," *The New York Times*, July 6, 2004.

[39] John N. Paden and Peter W. Singer, "America Slams the Door (on its Foot): Washington's Destructive New Visa Policies," *Foreign Affairs* 82, no. 3 (May/June 2003).

[40] For example, Pat Robertson, Christian Coalition founder and close associate of the Bush administration, in February 2002 called Islam a "violent religion." Similar remarks were made by Franklin Graham, who called Islam a "very evil and wicked religion." Likewise, Lieutenant General William Boykin was not reprimanded for inflammatory statements in 2004 about Islam that set off a firestorm of attention, comparing his faith with that of a Muslim leader in Somalia: "I knew that my God was bigger than his. I knew that my God was a real God and his was an idol."

[41] Marine Corps Combat Development Command, 69.

[42] Author interview with U.S. Army officer, June 2005, Washington, DC.

[43] Author interview with U.S. Army officer, May 2005, Washington, DC.

[44] "Rumsfeld on Looting in Iraq: 'Stuff Happens'," CNN.com, April 13, 2003.

[45] Author interview with U.S. Navy officer, January 2005, Washington, DC.

[46] These figures are at best only a crude indicator of the way in which attention to the "war of ideas" is reflected in security assistance programming allocations, since there is no easy way of knowing whether the 1,807 Bolivians all participated in a one-hour course in La Paz while smaller numbers of Saudis, Egyptians, or Pakistanis underwent longer and more intensive educational programs in the United States. Nevertheless, it is indisputable that IMET dollar and student allocations have not been dramatically adjusted since 9/11 despite the immensely greater saliency of the Islamic world in the American strategic calculus. Department of State, "Fiscal Year 2006 Congressional Budget Justification for Foreign Operations" (Washington, DC: Department of State, February 2005).

[47] Author interview with U.S. Army officer, May 2005.

[48] See Pew Global Attitudes surveys "Islamic Extremism: Common Concern for Muslim and Western Publics," July 14, 2005, and "U.S. Image Up Slightly, But Still Negative," June 23, 2005; available at <pewglobal.org/>.

[49] "On the PR Battlefield," *Time*, June 13, 2005.

[50] See, for example, Rami G. Khouri, "Lessons from a Journey Across the Arab World," *The Daily Star*, July 20, 2005.

[51] See, for example, the United Nations Development Program Arab Human Development Report series; available at <rbas.undp.org/ahdr.cfm>.

[52] Christopher M. Ford, "Speak No Evil: Targeting a Population's Neutrality to Defeat an Insurgency," *Parameters* 35, no. 2 (Summer 2005), 51–66.

[53] See, for example, "Muslim Groups Target Youths in Anti-Terror Campaign," CNN.com, July 26, 2005; available at <cnn.com/2005/U.S./07/25/muslims.nonviolence/index.html>.

Chapter Nine

Influencing Attitudes, Shaping Behaviors: Implications for U.S. Strategy

Joseph McMillan

It did not take long after the 9/11 attacks for thoughtful Americans to realize that enduring success in any struggle against violent Islamic extremism, or jihadism, would depend in large measure on altering the attitudes of significant portions of the world's Muslim community. It is from that community that al Qaeda and kindred organizations draw their recruits, it is on members of that community that the violent extremist movement depends for financial, material, and rhetorical support, and it is that community's acquiescence in terrorist methods, at least against some targets and for some purposes, that permits such organizations to operate despite concerted efforts to suppress them.

Public Opinion as the Center of Gravity

What has become apparent in the 5 years since 9/11 is that public opinion in the Muslim world is not merely an enabling factor for terrorism but rather the center of gravity toward which the entire jihadist enterprise is directed. As Ayman al-Zawahiri explained to Abu Mus'ab al-Zarqawi in July 2005, "we are in a battle . . . for the hearts and minds of our *umma* [the worldwide community of Muslims]."[1] The centrality of Muslim public opinion to this struggle becomes obvious once we understand the jihadist campaign as a transnational insurgency (albeit one deeply influenced by the phenomenon of globalization) in which violent Islamic extremists are seeking to reconstruct the existing order within (and perhaps beyond) the Muslim world through a combination of violence and political activity, including the propagation of their radical ideology among Muslim populations.[2]

Seen in this light, the messages transmitted to the world's Muslims in jihadist rhetoric are of a piece with the messages transmitted through jihadist terrorist attacks on targets in the West and in countries considered its apostate allies. Difficult as it is to see from our perspective as the victims of terrorism, the acts carried out by violent Islamic extremists are less about us or about affecting our behavior than about generating political support for their cause within the *umma*. Extremists are consciously practicing what

19th-century anarchists called "propaganda by deed"[3] to reinforce their propaganda by word. In the near term, the two weapons, the word and the sword, are aimed at "spreading the sentiment of jihad among the Muslim nation,"[4] and, over time, to establish Islamic governments "as they [always] have been: by pen and gun, by word and bullet, by tongue and teeth."[5]

Clearly, then, affecting the attitudes of the billion-plus Muslims who constitute both the political target and the potential base of support for the jihadist movement must be a central element in any U.S. strategy for the war on terrorism. In this sense, at least, the concept of a "war of ideas" is the right one. This realization, however, leaves a series of difficult issues to be addressed. In particular, having acknowledged that attitudes need to be changed, we must consider carefully just how sweeping a change is necessary. Those who contend that the terrorist threat emanates from the basic nature of Islam as a religion would hold that it is necessary to alter the basic teachings of Islam in some fashion, but is such radical change—with the high costs and long timelines it implies—really necessary to assure the security of the American people from terrorist attacks? Should we be trying to persuade the world's Muslims to embrace globalization, or modernization, or Western-style secular liberalism? Should we be promoting a particular outcome in the *umma*'s internal debates over how Islam should deal with the problems of modernity? Is it essential to alter the way Muslims perceive the United States? Or is it possible to convince them that terrorist methods are illegitimate regardless of what opinions they may hold about America and Americans?

Deciding how fundamental a shift in Muslim attitudes we intend to achieve under the rubric of the war on terrorism must be governed not only by what various theories of the origin of the threat would hold to be optimal but also by what is feasible. Probably the most insightful discussion of what is involved in shifting public attitudes in the context of an insurgency was offered by Sir Julian Paget, a British scholar and practitioner of counterinsurgency. As Paget sets it out, "winning hearts and minds" requires the application of a complex and tightly integrated set of tools embracing not only information operations but effective and fair governance and economic development as well. Paget's five essential elements of a hearts and minds campaign are: demonstrating understanding and respect for the people's feelings and aspirations; fairly addressing genuine grievances and rectifying injustices; building up public confidence in the political system; improving the material conditions under which the people live; and effective public relations and propaganda.[6] The elements identified by Paget as critical to the problem of hearts and minds are the same elements that appear repeatedly throughout the present volume as the key factors affecting how Muslims see the issues of terrorism, radical Islam, and the United States.

While Paget's essential elements would apply to any campaign aimed at winning hearts and minds, it is clear that the more sweeping the change of attitudes that is sought, the more intensive and extensive the political, economic, and informational lines of operation within that campaign must be. Achieving the fundamental change in public attitudes in the Muslim world that some argue is necessary implies an effort of such extraordinary sweep and duration that the Cold War itself would pale in comparison. Indeed, if prevailing in the war on terrorism truly requires a fundamental reorientation of the belief structures of the entire Islamic *umma*, the United States is facing not merely a "long war" but a practically interminable one.

The Credibility Chasm

As will be obvious from the preceding chapters, particularly those by Mark Tessler and Steven Simon, the attitudes of the deepest concern to most Americans contemplating the war on terrorism are remarkably widespread from one end of the Muslim world to the other, and they present a radically different challenge to that which confronted the West during the Cold War. Most notably, our own standing among the population whose hearts and minds are being contested stands in stark contrast to the struggle against communism. Then, the Soviet Union was seen as the oppressor; the United States entered the competition already enjoying a strongly favorable image among the publics of the countries under Soviet control. Today, as the Defense Science Board (DSB) task force on strategic communication pointed out in its 2004 report, it is the United States that is viewed in a negative light. There are no Muslim masses yearning to be free of foreign domination,[7] other than the domination they perceive as being imposed by the United States and Israel.

This lack of credibility among Muslim audiences is a critical deficit in any U.S. effort to reshape Muslim attitudes, even more so now than it would have been in previous decades. The DSB report notes that "fifty years ago, political struggles were about the ability to control and transmit scarce information. Today, political struggles are about the creation and destruction of credibility."[8] In the middle of the 20th century, information was precious; by today's standards, it was hard to obtain, and relatively few organizations could disseminate it widely. The key to successful strategic communication then was controlling the means of transmission. By contrast, in the 21st century, information is abundant—some would say excessively so—and easy to obtain, even in relatively remote places. Anyone with enough money to rent a computer for a few hours at an Internet café has the ability to disseminate any message around the world; for a government to maintain a monopoly over the means of transmitting information is impossible. As a consequence, the premium is no longer on controlling how the message is sent but on establishing and maintaining the messenger's credibility.

Unfortunately, the exponents of radical Islam have established a clear advantage over not only the United States but also the governments of many Muslim states in the battle for credibility among members of the worldwide Islamic community. Radicals of both violent and nonviolent varieties have shown an ability to mobilize and unify a disgruntled community into accepting at least their explanation of the ills afflicting the *umma*, if not their prescription for overcoming those ills. Part of the reason is that the diagnosis they offer, unlike the more thoughtful analysis underpinning the Arab Human Development Reports sponsored by the United Nations, shifts the blame for everything that has gone wrong onto the shoulders of non-Muslims and their "apostate" allies. The central role that the jihadist diagnosis accords to the powerful and strongly disliked United States only adds to its appeal. Moreover, the radical analysis is framed in the emotionally resonant terminology of a religion that is both regarded as unquestionably true and, in many cases, is the key marker by which people distinguish themselves from the oppressive outside world. As a result, not only is the United States disliked, but because its explanations of "what went wrong" and its prescriptions of how to put things right are so out of tune with what most Muslims believe, it is also distrusted.

The United States thus finds itself playing an unending game of public relations catch-up. Any policy errors, inflammatory statements by prominent citizens, or misconduct by U.S. military personnel reinforce hostile preconceived expectations. Unfavorable stories, no matter how baseless or ridiculous, are automatically accepted as true, while favorable stories are dismissed as propaganda. As explained by Steven Simon in chapter three, even the things the United States does that one would expect Muslims to perceive positively—such as intervening against Serbia to stop the killing of Muslim Bosnians and Muslim Kosovars—are discounted as self-serving political stunts—all the more so, as Scott Atran explained in chapter seven, when U.S. officials justify these actions to the American people on the grounds that they are in the U.S. national interest.

Even if U.S. credibility were higher, achieving wholesale shifts in the attitudes of more than a billion people from the diverse range of cultures (almost all of which are alien to Americans) described by Caroline Ziemke would be a daunting task, all the more so depending on how deeply the attitudinal changes are intended to go. As Scott Atran explained, every society has sacred values, criticism of which provokes an intense emotional reaction. Even short of that, however, it is important to keep in mind a point that we know intuitively concerning our own society but sometimes forget when evaluating others: that attitudes and opinions are the product of a confluence of numerous factors, only one of which is information about current events. Moreover, that information is not perceived with perfect fidelity, but is filtered through each person's own perceptual screens. How the screened information affects the recipient's attitudes—and, more to the point, his behavior—depends on a complex of cognitive beliefs about how the world works and normative values about right and wrong. Those values and beliefs depend in turn on the person's upbringing and education, his own personal life experiences, and the norms of the group and society in which he lives—his culture.

Thus, even the most credible information is only one component in the process of attitude formation. For this reason alone, better strategic communication would not be the panacea that many hope it can be for altering the attitudes toward terrorism, radical Islam, and the related constellation of political issues confronting the Muslim world. To assume that better and more credible management of information can have that effect is to assume that the underlying cognitive beliefs and normative values held by most people in the Muslim *umma* are the same as those held by most Americans—in other words, to assume that cultural differences either do not exist or do not matter. Americans, and perhaps Westerners in general, habitually underestimate the significance of such cultural differences. Because of our history, many concepts and principles that matter enormously to people in the Islamic world—such as the power of fate, the paramount importance of devotion to tribe and family, and shame-based concepts of personal honor—no longer matter to most of us in ways that affect our day-to-day lives. As a result, it is fallacious to assume that people from other cultures have the same aspirations for their children that we have for ours, that they would live the same kinds of lives we live if only they could, or—most relevant to the question of shaping attitudes toward the United States and Americans—that they would like us if only they knew us better.[9]

In short, cultural differences, including in the way audiences receive and process information, matter greatly. People who have not been conditioned to perceive the universe as a logical, orderly place will not be impressed with cool, rational Cartesian explanations of world events. To them, conspiratorial, supernatural, or even miraculous explanations may seem more compelling. Messages challenging their normative values—especially their most deeply held sacred values—are apt to provoke not merely incredulity but also anger. Appeals to individual autonomy and freedom, which most Americans would perceive as unquestionably good and true, may be perceived as assaults on the very foundations of society by those whose cultural values teach them that the welfare of the community must come before that of any single person. Similarly, the ideal of freedom of opinion is such a basic component of Western culture that we take for granted that people from other cultures understand and value it as we do. But our commitment to tolerance stems from such premises as Thomas Jefferson's that new moral truths are constantly being discovered,[10] or Justice Oliver Wendell Holmes's that "the best test of truth is the power of the thought to get itself accepted in the competition of the market."[11] The best communications strategy in the world is not going to persuade believing Muslims that the "marketplace of ideas" is a superior means for judging moral truth than the final divine revelation contained in the Koran.

The Challenges of Cross-Cultural Communication

Even in the best of circumstances, communicating strategic messages across cultural boundaries is extraordinarily hard. This is partly just a matter of rhetorical style. Effective public rhetoric in any language is deeply, if subconsciously, shaped by both the cognitive habits of the underlying culture and by the syntax and vocabulary in which its most deeply emotive literature is written. In English, the ideal is a relatively spare style characterized by a largely monosyllabic Anglo-Saxon vocabulary, similar to that of the King James Bible and the Book of Common Prayer, crafted in logically linked sentences in parallel structure. One has only to think of the most memorable political speeches in the English language to perceive these commonalities: Churchill's addresses on the radio and in the House of Commons rallying the British people during the darkest days of World War II, Lincoln's addresses at Gettysburg and his inaugurations, the "ask not . . . ask rather" passage in John F. Kennedy's inaugural speech.

By contrast, the most potent political rhetoric in Arabic is ornate, allusive, and often metaphorical. Arabic style values elegant variation, the restatement of the same thought several times using different words and images (something that in English translation often seems pointlessly repetitive), and the use of hyperbole, which in English translation seems ridiculous. Most Arabic education (as discussed by Kumar Ramakrishna in chapter six) emphasizes memorization rather than deductive logic; as a result, many Arabs are more impressed by a speaker's ability to quote from the canon of classical poetry, especially from the Koran, than to string together a series of persuasive premises and conclusions. Finally, speech in the Arab world, including political speech, tends to be more about making emotional connections—demonstrating empathy with the hopes and fears of the audience—than about conveying objective information or making purely rational arguments.

As a result, American political leaders find it difficult to communicate effectively with Arab audiences. The best possible translation of a speech originally crafted in a spare, logical, Anglo-Saxon rhetorical style will not resonate among people whose rhetoric is exuberant and emotive and whose educational experiences emphasized rote memorization over logical deduction and critical analysis.[12] On the other hand, any American leader who delivered a speech designed to push emotional buttons in the Arabic style would be ridiculed by the audience that is ultimately his first concern: the American electorate. While many Muslims are not Arabs, and thus have different expectations when it comes to political communication, the general point that such messages do not translate well holds true across the board.

Moreover, we must keep in mind that most U.S. official political communication is neither carried out by prominent political leaders nor composed with the rhetorical styles of foreign audiences in mind. Instead, it takes the form of answers to questions from the press at the State Department (working from talking points carefully crafted by career diplomats to eliminate any emotive content, and often delivered in a wooden style intended to keep the press spokesman from showing up his bosses), the Pentagon or a combatant command (which usually receive heavy media coverage only if something has gone wrong, in which case the spokesman is principally concerned with damage limitation and avoiding anything that could be legally construed as an admission of culpability), or the White House (where the objective often seems to be scoring debating points off the reporters, even if that means serious subjects are dealt with in a bantering style). When the welter of unofficial commentary—often considered by people who themselves live in controlled media environments as being more authentic expressions of official U.S. views than what is said by government officials and spokesmen—and partisan jousting is included, it is little wonder that finely tuned efforts at shaping attitudes in foreign cultures go unnoticed or are dismissed as insincere.

An Alternative Approach

Yet the outlook for success in the war of ideas is not as gloomy as the foregoing discussion might imply. Whether success is attainable depends on what we set out to do. We have been discussing the feasibility—or infeasibility—of the kinds of fundamental shifts in attitudes, or even in beliefs and values, implicit in the ideological agenda that has been set forth in current

U.S. strategy for the war on terrorism. If, however, we conceive the immediate objective not as prescribing attitudes but as proscribing behaviors, there is reason for greater hope. In other words, the United States must begin by deconflating Muslim dislike of the United States and disagreement with U.S. policy from support for terrorism, by distinguishing between Muslim acceptance of the radical diagnosis of "what went wrong" and acceptance of the radical prescription for what to do about it. We need to return to the original formulation of the principal objective and strip away the accretions brought on by 5 years of strategic mission creep.

That principal objective is to delegitimize terrorism, putting it "in the same light as slavery, piracy, and genocide,"[13] unacceptable not only to all governments but to all people who consider themselves civilized as well. While clearly it is better for U.S. policy for people to have a favorable opinion of the United States (and obviously, those with such opinions will be unlikely to gravitate toward anti-U.S. terrorist movements), the bottom line is that it matters less that people like us than that they not try to kill us. Within the framework of the war on terrorism, we seek to shape attitudes as a way of affecting behaviors, not as an end in itself.

That is not to say that the so-called war for the soul of Islam does not matter. Muslim public opinion is the center of gravity of the jihadist strategy. Capturing the hearts and minds of the *umma* is the overarching strategic objective for the violent Islamic extremists. But the fact that the United States has a vital interest in ensuring the failure of the extremist ideological campaign does not mean that it is up to the United States to defeat it. The only way Muslims will be able to get on with the vital task of sorting out how Islam will deal with modern realities is for external players to stay out of the open debate. If non-Muslims take sides, the argument becomes one between the indigenous defenders of the faith and the lackeys of infidel powers. The more visibly the United States is involved in the question of what Islam means and what Muslims ought to believe, the more the debate is about us and not about them. The United States Government and others outside the Muslim community can therefore best contribute to this process by providing discrete support and assistance to those combating the jihadist message, not by overtly joining the fray.

Delegitimizing terrorism should be a considerably easier task than shifting more deeply rooted attitudes, beliefs, and values. Public opinion theory generally recognizes that one of the most effective ways of altering an opinion is by persuading the person that the opinion is inconsistent with a more deeply rooted value or belief that he holds. Already a number of Muslim scholars and preachers have begun challenging the extremist analysis of the individual obligation to jihad under present conditions and emphasizing that the Prophet set limits on the means that may be employed even in a just war and the persons who may be targeted.

Moreover, these scholars may find a more receptive audience than is widely assumed. Notwithstanding the view of most jihadists and some Western commentators that true Islam demands violence, the fact is that most Muslims most of the time prefer to live in peace with their neighbors, Muslim and non-Muslim alike. Were it otherwise, it would be impossible for non-Muslims to travel safely anywhere in the Islamic world. While we need to know much more about what ordinary Muslims think, believe, and feel, it is clear from their behavior that not even everyone who cheers when al Qaeda succeeds in striking the United States accepts the case for a universal obligation to "join the caravan" of jihad. And such polling data as we do have indicates that, while the proportion of those who cheer terrorist attacks is troublesome, it is not a majority anywhere.

There is also reason to hope that the classical understanding of the issues involved will reassert itself as responsible Muslim thinkers increasingly express themselves against the extremist interpretations. While it is true that classical mainstream thinking does include important elements that lend themselves to violent interpretation (such as the global dichotomy between believers and unbelievers, the apocalyptic rhetoric of the Koran, and the history of Muhammad himself as a political-military leader, not just a religious teacher), countervailing impulses historically have moderated this violence in practice. One such impulse is that mainstream Sunni Islam gives rulers a monopoly on the legitimate use of force. Another is the traditional respect accorded to *ulama*, those who have devoted themselves to the study of the intricacies of the religious law. Extremists call into question the idea that such extensive study is necessary; they contend that only the Koran and *hadith*—the records of the sayings and practices of Muhammad—are valid sources of the law. The extremists also contend, in an argument reminiscent of that espoused by the early Protestant reformers, that all believers are qualified to interpret the plain language of the scriptures for themselves.

But perhaps the most important of these countervailing tendencies is the premium that Islam traditionally places on harmony within the community of believers. This is an impulse that seems to be deeply felt by most Muslims, and one to which such leaders as King Abdullah of Saudi Arabia have appealed with great success, notably in his recent speech calling for Saudis to stop calling into question each other's credentials as Muslims. This was clearly aimed at *takfir*, the extremist practice of condemning as non-Muslim anyone who disagrees with any of a variety of legal, theological, or liturgical views extolled by radicals.

Furthermore, religion does not exist in isolation. As Caroline Ziemke observes in chapter five, cultural, historic, ethnic, tribal, and class factors also shape behavior. In some cases, these factors may make people more susceptible to the jihadist message. For example, the common concerns felt by many Arabs (fueled by the information revolution) and the fact that so many of the most prominent jihadist leaders are Arabs may well make Arab audiences more receptive to certain elements of the jihadist message. Other Muslim ethnic groups, however, would be less instinctively supportive, while in some cases the Arab-ness of the extremist ideologues may be held against them. In any event, each culture, or "ring of identity," within the Muslim *umma* is shaped by nonreligious factors that tend to make it more or less open to the use of violence. A sound strategy to build a consensus against terrorism obviously needs to ascertain which antiterrorist elements of each culture are most potent and play upon them to undercut the credibility of the jihadist cause.

If our first priority is to stop violent—specifically terrorist—behavior, rather than to change opinions about the United States or to achieve a specific outcome in the reform of Islam or of Muslim governments, anything that influential Muslims say or do that discourages terrorism is a positive contribution. The United States should resist the urge to quibble over the fine points; useful messages do not have to be 100 percent what we would like to hear. Indeed, one could argue that any Muslim opinion leader who echoed the U.S. line completely—on Israeli-Palestinian issues, for example—would soon lose his standing as an opinion leader.

Ideally, Muslim politicians, scholars, and commentators need to explain why terrorism is contrary to properly understood Islam and why the extremist agenda is an inadequate solution to the problems confronting the Muslim people. Even better, they could articulate diagnoses and prescriptions for those problems that might generate mass support for nonviolent alternatives. The visions articulated by these voices need not be congruent with U.S. desiderata to serve the broader purpose of undermining the jihadist vision. A traditional mainstream religious perspective or even a salafi (fundamentalist) perspective that eschews violence probably would be more effective than a highly Westernized secular perspective in drawing the susceptible away from the apocalyptic world view of the jihadists. In fact, growing numbers of salafi intellectuals have begun articulating the view that Osama bin Ladin and his followers constitute a deviant sect, a development whose significance should not be underestimated.[14]

Even those who are only willing to denounce violence as a strategic error can serve a useful purpose. Two years ago, a group of prominent Egyptian radical Islamists bitterly denounced al Qaeda's use of terrorist tactics on the basis not of morality but of expediency. The attacks of 9/11 and others, they argued, had provoked the West into the war with Islam that the Zionists had long been seeking, increased rather than reduced the infidel military presence in the Muslim lands, and brought Islam into disrepute among potential converts. To turn President Bush's oft-quoted axiom around, we should understand that in this particular campaign, at least anyone who is not with the terrorists is with us. It needs to be clear that Muslim governments can be against terrorism without necessarily being pro-United States at the same time.

How the United States Can Help

The main advantages that violent extremists have over Muslim opinion leaders who oppose the use of terror, apart from the benefit of being unambiguously anti-American, lie in the strength of their networks—often built to withstand the opposition of hostile state authorities and their command of the modern means of information dissemination. Perhaps the most important contribution the United States can make to the immediate problem of discrediting terrorism is to enable those who oppose the jihadists to link up effectively with one another and to disseminate their message to the Muslim masses. Those who have the ability to prevail in this war of ideas do not need us to tell them what to say, but they can definitely use help in getting it heard.

To be effective, of course, this assistance cannot have American fingerprints all over it. The United States must learn to be discreet in facilitating the distribution of anti-jihadist ideas, just as it was in the early years of the Cold War when the Central Intelligence Agency helped anticommunist intellectuals in both Eastern and Western Europe combat the tide of Soviet-funded and -guided propaganda. Unlike the Cold War years, we must concurrently be careful not to embrace Muslims who voice opposition to violent extremism. Bringing Lech Walesa to Washington when he was the leader of Solidarity, allowing him to address a joint session of Congress, and having the President award him the Nation's highest civil decoration all burnished Walesa's image among the Polish people for whose hearts and minds he was contending. Doing the same thing with a prominent Muslim opponent of the jihadists would only destroy any credibility he had, and might well be equivalent to signing his death warrant.

While much of this effort should naturally be done through the usual mass media—television, radio, newspapers, and magazines—tailored to the sources of information that are available in each country (as described in chapter three by Christine Fair), we should also be prepared to look beyond those classic outlets. Most obviously, assistance can be given in using the Internet, an increasingly important source of information for young middle-class Muslims in particular. But the impact that the arts and entertainment have on how people perceive the world should also be considered. Grants to writers, filmmakers, and the producers of television dramas can serve to discredit violent extremism more subtly and more effectively than direct argument.

Over the longer term, ensuring the ultimate failure of jihadism as the political alternative of choice in the Muslim world will require addressing that host of problems from which the violent extremists generate support. The United States can make important contributions in many of these areas. Building Muslim states' capacity for governance, in terms of reach into ungoverned spaces and the quality of governance in core areas, will not only deprive terrorists of sanctuary but also alleviate many of the discontents with governments that Mark Tessler, in chapter two, found to be correlated with support for terrorism. Programs to address poverty and other material discontents will serve the same purpose. As Caroline Ziemke discussed in chapter four, poverty and poor living conditions may not directly cause social violence, but the perception of relative deprivation does, as does the feeling of solidarity with the poor held by many who may themselves be fairly prosperous and well educated.

Part of stripping away support for terrorism in the long run is also giving renewed attention to regional flashpoints such as Palestine and Kashmir. These issues are sometimes argued to be merely excuses, not causes, of terrorism. Mark Tessler's findings suggest that they are strongly relevant to Muslims' expressions of support for terrorism, even if it is true that the terrorist attacks that have been carried out against the United States did not aim to solve these conflicts. Ultimately, it does not matter whether one conflict or another can be logically connected in our minds with the terrorist jihad. If we understand that we are dealing with an insurgency being conducted in a globalized environment, it will be apparent that violence between Muslims and non-Muslims anywhere will have a political effect on Muslims everywhere. There was a time when Muslims in Indonesia or Mali would have been relatively indifferent to what was happening to Muslims in the Balkans or the Caucasus; that time is past. The growth of 24-hour satellite television news and the availability of the Internet guarantee heavy coverage of wars. Meanwhile, a growing sense of Islamic solidarity, fueled in part by this reporting, creates a heated political environment that is ripe for exploitation by jihadist ideologues.

The relationship between actual conflict and mass perceptions highlights one of the most important things the United States must do as it seeks to promote the delegitimation of terrorism: to tamp down the level of cultural confrontation between Islam and the West. Fueling a broad inter-civilizational confrontation between Islam and the West is a key goal of the jihadists. Creating a state of permanent hostility would validate the extremist interpretation of the world as permanently divided into two irreconcilable camps between which there can be nothing but hatred and violence. If the radicals can plausibly characterize this confrontation as "Islam in danger," they can play on the widely accepted doctrine that every believer is under a personal obligation to participate in what is known as "defensive jihad," a struggle not to spread the faith to new areas but to protect the *umma* against assault from without.[15] This means that we need not only to be careful of rhetoric that directly heightens the temperature of the confrontation, but also to be sensitive to the way that pronouncements on the universality of American values, the superiority of American ways, and the importance of American power impinge upon the sacred values elucidated by Scott Atran. The problem here is not what we say to Muslims but what we say to each other that is overheard in a world of instant global communications.

Finally, the United States needs to acquire the jihadists' awareness of the way that "propaganda by word" and "propaganda by deed" work with and against each other. Make no mistake: the war on terrorism cannot be won without a robust military component aimed at "finding, fixing, and finishing" terrorist elements. But as we implement that vital component of our strategy, we must remain conscious of the way such kinetic actions affect public attitudes toward us, our partners, the jihadists, and the validity of terrorism as a tactic for change. The poorly planned or ineptly executed use of force—not to mention the commission of actual atrocities—puts us right back on the horns of the dilemma raised by Defense Secretary Donald Rumsfeld: our actions generate new terrorists faster than we can kill the old ones. Moreover, every case of collateral damage, let alone the intentional killing of noncombatants as is alleged to have occurred at Al-Haditha in Iraq, makes it all the more difficult to persuade Muslims who are unhappy about the way U.S. power is asserted that they should renounce the use of violence against noncombatants on their side. This is not to equate intentional terrorist murders with accidental deaths and damage taking place despite the best precautions in the context of legal military operations. It is merely to point out that the people whose hearts and minds are at issue do not necessarily understand the distinctions between these situations.

All Terrorism is Always Wrong

To sum up, altering values is extraordinarily difficult, even in the extended timeframe over which the war on terrorism must be fought. Moreover, a deliberate attempt to alter Muslims' understanding of right and wrong will inevitably provoke a defensive reaction that can only aggravate their sense of being a culture under siege, playing directly into the hands of the insurgents. Instead of calling into question fundamental elements of religion and culture—trying to prescribe what Muslims ought to be—we should focus on proscribing certain things they must not do—namely, carry out, support, or tolerate attacks on noncombatants in pursuit of political or religious goals. We must quietly empower and facilitate the messages, articulated by people inside the Islamic *umma*, that terrorism is evil in itself, regardless of the cause in which it is employed, and the violent Islamic extremists are incorrectly interpreting the Prophet's teachings. Our aim, at least in the immediate context of the war on terrorism, should not be a quantum shift in the ideological center of gravity of the entire Islamic community, but rather a series of small shifts in Muslims' attitudes toward what the faith means for specific practical behaviors.

That does not mean that underlying issues can be ignored. If Islamic history teaches us anything, it is that violent tendencies erupt repeatedly when fundamental problems remain unresolved. But the immediate challenge is to eradicate social support among Muslims for the use of terrorism as an instrument for solving these problems. Hopefully, the essays in this volume will have pointed us in the right direction to achieve that goal.

Notes

[1] Letter, Ayman al-Zawahiri to Abu Mus'ab al-Zarqawi, July 9, 2005, released by the Office of the Director of National Intelligence, October 11, 2005, accessed at <dni.gov/press_releases/letter_in_english.pdf>.

[2] The violent Islamist movement thus meets all the criteria for an insurgency in the definition set forth in Bard O'Neill in *Insurgency and Terrorism: Inside Modern Revolutionary Warfare* (Washington, DC: National Defense University Press, 1990), 13: "a struggle between a nonruling group and the ruling authorities in which the nonruling group consciously uses *political resources* (e.g., organizational expertise, propaganda, and demonstrations) and *violence* to destroy, reformulate, or sustain the basis of legitimacy of one or more aspects of politics. Emphasis in original.

[3] According to Bruce Hoffman, *Inside Terrorism* (New York: Columbia University Press, 1998), 17, the concept was first articulated by the Italian anarchist Carlo Pisacane. Mikhail Bakunin explained it in "Letters to a Frenchman on the Present Crisis" (1870): "We must spread our principles, not with words but with deeds, for this is the most popular, the most potent, and the most irresistible form of propaganda." Prince Pyotr Kropotkin seems to have been the first to use the exact expression *propaganda by deed*, in his pamphlet *Revolutionary Government* (1880).

[4] Draft bylaws for al Qaeda found in the Kandahar house of the late Abu Hafs al-Masri, quoted in Dennis Pluchinsky, "The Global Jihad," presentation at workshop on "Terrorism and Islamic Extremism in the Middle East: Perspectives and Possibilities," co-sponsored by the Center for Contemporary Conflict (Naval Postgraduate School) and Center for Naval Analyses, Alexandria, VA, February 22, 2005. Cited by permission of the author.

[5] "Declaration of Jihad against the Country's Tyrants, Military Series," captured by British police in Manchester, England and distributed by CRA, Inc., in 2002.

[6] Julian Paget, *Counter-Insurgency Operations: Techniques of Guerrilla Warfare* (New York: Walker, 1967), 176–179.

[7] Defense Science Board, *Report of the Defense Science Board Task Force on Strategic Communication* (Washington, DC: Office of the Under Secretary of Defense for Acquisition, Technology, and Logistics, September 2004), 36.

[8] Ibid., 20.

[9] The classic example is the Egyptian father of jihadist ideology, Sayyid Qutb, whose only lesson learned from an extended stay studying in Colorado in the early 1950s was that American society was disgustingly promiscuous and decadent.

[10] "[L]aws and institutions must go hand in hand with the progress of the human mind. As that becomes more developed, more enlightened, as new discoveries are made, new truths discovered and manners and opinions change, with the change of circumstances, institutions

must advance also to keep pace with the times." Thomas Jefferson, letter to George Washington, January 4, 1786.

[11] *Abrams v. United States*, 250 U.S. 616 (1919).

[12] United Nations Development Program, *Arab Human Development Report 2003: Building a Knowledge Society* (New York: United Nations Development Program, 2003), 54.

[13] *National Security Strategy of the United States of America* (Washington, DC: The White House, 2002).

[14] Salafism is the movement within Sunni Islam that calls for stripping away practices and beliefs that salafists consider inconsistent with those of Muhammad's earliest followers. Not all rigorously conservative Sunnis are salafists, and not all salafists support the use of violence to achieve the movement's aims. Quintan Wiktorowicz and John Kaltner, "Killing in the Name of Islam: Al-Qaeda's Justification for September 11," *Middle East Policy* 10 (2003), 76–92, provides an incisive look at the ideological factions within the salafi movement. Salafi antiterrorist Web sites in English include Wahhabi Myth (www.wahhabimyth.com), Salafi Publications (www.salafipublications.com), Center for Victory of Islamic Da'wa (www.troid.org), and Fatwa-Online (www.fatwa-online.com).

[15] Bernard Lewis, in *The Political Language of Islam* (Chicago: University of Chicago Press, 1988), 73, explains that an offensive jihad to spread the faith is an obligation on the Muslim community collectively (individual members may fulfill this obligation by paying taxes to support a professional army, for example), while a jihad to defend the Islamic community is a "personal obligation of every adult male Muslim." Modern jihadists assert that such a defensive jihad does not require a call to arms by a duly constituted political authority, but that does not seem to be the position of the classical jurists.

About the Contributors

Joseph McMillan is Senior Research Fellow in the Institute for National Strategic Studies (INSS) at the National Defense University, specializing in counterterrorism, the Middle East, and South Asia. He joined INSS following 15 years in the Office of the Under Secretary of Defense for Policy, where his positions included Principal Director for Russia, Ukraine, and Eurasia and Principal Director for the Near East and South Asia. Mr. McMillan's recent publications include "Saudi Arabia and Iraq: Oil, Religion, and an Enduring Rivalry" (U.S. Institute of Peace, January 2006), and "Treating Terrorist Groups as Armed Bands: The Strategic Implications" in *Topics in Terrorism: Toward a Transatlantic Consensus on the Nature of the Threat* (Atlantic Council Publications, 2005). He is also the co-author, with Christopher Cavoli, of "Countering Global Terrorism" in *Strategic Challenges: America's Global Security Agenda* (National Defense University Press, forthcoming).

Hady Amr is managing partner of the Amr Group, which promotes economic and social development in the Arab world in such areas as education, technology, youth and civil society, strategic planning, and economic and social analysis. Mr. Amr is a development economist with over 15 years of experience managing projects funded by the World Bank, various United Nations agencies, the Ford Foundation, the U.S. Agency for International Development, and similar institutions. In 2000, he served on the staff setting up the Near East–South Asia for Strategic Studies at National Defense University. Mr. Amr has conducted scores of State Department–sponsored discussion groups in Arab countries on the U.S. foreign policy process. He is the author of *The Need to Communicate: How to Improve U.S. Public Diplomacy with the Islamic World* (Brookings Institution Press, 2004).

Scott Atran is Director of Research, Anthropology, at the *Centre Nationale de la Recherche Scientifique* in Paris, as well as visiting professor of psychology and public policy at the University of Michigan and presidential scholar in sociology at the John Jay School of Criminal Justice, City University of New York. Dr. Atran's research centers on cognitive and linguistic anthropology, environmental decisionmaking, Middle Eastern ethnography and political economy, and cognitive and commitment theories of religion, terrorism, and foreign affairs. He is the author of *In Gods We Trust: The Evolutionary Landscape of Religion* (Oxford University Press, 2004) and (with Douglas Medin) of *The Native Mind: Cognition and Cultural Management of Nature* (Oxford University Press, forthcoming), as well as articles and commentaries in both scientific and public affairs journals.

C. Christine Fair is a senior research associate in the Center for Conflict Analysis and Prevention at the United States Institute of Peace, where she specializes in South Asian political and military affairs. Previously, she was an associate political scientist at the RAND Corporation. Dr. Fair's current research focuses on security competition between India and Pakistan, Pakistan's internal security, analysis of the causes of terrorism, and U.S. strategic relations with India and Pakistan. Her recent publications include "Think Again: Sources of Islamist Terrorism" (with Husain Haqqani), in *Foreign Policy* (January 2006), and "Who Supports Terrorism? Evidence from Fourteen Muslim Countries" (with Bryan Shepherd), in *Studies in Conflict and Terrorism* (January/February 2006).

Kumar Ramakrishna is associate professor and head of studies in the Institute of Defence and Strategic Studies at Nanyang Technological University in Singapore. Dr. Ramakrishna's principal research interests are counterterrorism and the history of strategic thought. He is a member of the executive committee of the Political Science Association of Singapore and of the Singapore Government Parliamentary Committee Resource Panel on Home Affairs and Law. In addition to *Emergency Propaganda: The Winning of Malayan Hearts and Minds, 1948–1958* (Curzon Press, 2002), his recent publications include "The Making of the Jemaah Islamiyah Terrorist," in *Teaching Terror: Knowledge Transfer in the Terrorist World* (Cornell University Press, 2005) and "Countering Radical Islam in Southeast Asia: The Need to Confront the Functional and Ideological 'Enabling Environment,'" in *Terrorism and Violence in Southeast Asia: Transnational Challenges to States and Regional Stability* (Pentagon Press, 2005).

Steven N. Simon is the Hasib J. Sabbagh senior fellow for Middle Eastern studies at the Council on Foreign Relations (CFR). Mr. Simon served the U.S. Government in various national security positions related to Middle Eastern affairs, transnational threats, and terrorism for more than two decades, including 5 years on the National Security Council staff as director for global issues and senior director for transnational threats. He left the White House in 1999 to become deputy director of the International Institute for Strategic Studies in London, then moved on to the RAND Corporation before joining the CFR. Mr. Simon is the coauthor of *The Age of Sacred Terror* (Random House, 2002) and *The Next Attack* (Henry Holt and Company, 2005), as well as a large number of articles and commentaries on the terrorist threat and America's response.

Peter W. Singer is a senior fellow at the Brookings Institution, where he is director of the Project on U.S. Relations with the Islamic World. His current research interests include trends in contemporary warfare, humanitarian operations, peacekeeping, and terrorism. Before joining Brookings,

Dr. Singer served with the Balkans Task Force in the Office of the Secretary of Defense and as a special assistant at the International Peace Academy. He is the author of a number of books and articles, including *Children at War* (University of California Press, 2005), *Corporate Warriors: The Rise of the Privatized Military Industry* (Cornell University Press, 2003), and "The War on Terrorism: The Big Picture," in *Parameters* (Summer 2004).

Mark Tessler is Samuel J. Eldersveld Collegiate Professor of Political Science, Vice Provost for International Affairs, and Director of the International Institute at the University of Michigan. Professor Tessler specializes in comparative politics and Middle Eastern Studies, particularly the nature, determinants, and political implications of popular attitudes and values in the Middle East, and he has presented his research in this area in numerous journal articles. He has also written extensively on the Israeli-Palestinian conflict and is the author of *A History of the Israeli-Palestinian Conflict* (Indiana University Press, 1994). Professor Tessler is a past president of the American Institute for Maghrib Studies and the Association for Israel Studies and was a founding member of the Palestinian-American Research Center.

Caroline F. Ziemke is a military historian and a research staff member at the Institute for Defense Analyses (IDA). She has designed a strategic personality typology to provide policymakers with insight into how states' histories, sources of national identity, and cultures shape their definitions of national interests, how they calculate risks, and how they translate all these into strategies and actions. She is the author of several IDA studies that apply the methodology to terrorism, deterrence, and nonproliferation, including *Strategic Personality and the Effectiveness of Nuclear Deterrence: Deterring Iraq and Iran* (2001), and she is working on a book entitled *Breaking the Mirror: Using Strategic Personality to Understand a World That Isn't Just Like Us,* applying the methodology to the broader arena of political, cultural, and economic interactions.

GPO U.S. GOVERNMENT PRINTING OFFICE : 2006–320-742/00022